Sisters Born, Sisters Found
A Diversity of Voices on Sisterhood

Sisters Born, Sisters Found—the anthology edited by Laura McHale Holland—is what great literature is made of. Stories, essays, poems. Themes of identity, spirituality, sexuality, sanity, insanity. We learn the language of sibling connection while cooking for our dolls, propelling a wheelchair down a hospital corridor, or waiting for our sisters to step off the Greyhound bus. We exchange history/herstory through interpretation of family secrets and we heal with the gift of female intuition. A treasure volume of sisterhood/ womanhood around the world.

— *Teresa LeYung-Ryan, author,* Love Made of Heart: the Mother-Daughter Love Story *and* Talking to My Dead Mom *monologues*

How refreshing to swing around this great, big world of ours following the stories of sisters. Whether factual or imagined, narrative or poetic, the short works in this appealing collection ring true. They're told in all kinds of voices inflected with the music(s) of all kinds of cultures, and yet, they share a mutual esteem for sisterhood in its many manifestations. Not every sister here is admirable—how could they be to ring true?—but their stories accrue, re-calling us to memory, revealing others' lives.

— *Amanda McTigue, author,* Going to Solace

What happens in this exquisite array of the spectrum of sisterhood is discovery of new poets and writers who deserve a louder voice, a chance to talk about women in ways too often usurped by whispering—those myriad details of owning homogametic XX chromosomes that attracts yet deeply, philosophically distances the XY gender. These are songs of linking, love, need, compassion, yearning for some semblance of sameness that makes two women sisters. … For women this is not simply an anthology: this is the definition of sister. For men it is a Diogenes lantern as a guide to understand or appreciate that elusive bond.

— *Grady Harp, poet/author/historian,* War Songs, The Art of Man, *and* Vitruvian Lens

Powerful, intelligent entertaining stories of sisters illustrate the power and freedom in being born female. No sister relationship is casual; all sisters are bonded, not only by their feminine interests, but by their instincts to hold together the world in wise and often surreptitious ways.

— *Kay Mehl Miller, Ph.D, author,* Love Comes At Twilight: A Love Story for Seniors; Living With the Stranger in Me: An Exploration of Aging; *and* Talking It Over: Understanding Sexual Diversity

More than an anthology of sibling stories, Sisters Born, Sisters Found *is a diverse and compelling recollection of self-affirming, private connections— the sharing of insecurities, secret mischiefs, sad moments, partings, even an indestructible Arab-Israeli sistership. Although they share a commonality, each story is refreshingly unto itself.*

— *H.B. Reid, author,* The Adventures of Charles T. Woolley, The Diary of Count Frederigo Alfieri, *and* The Connected

Sisters Born, Sisters Found

A Diversity of Voices on Sisterhood

To: Joan
Happy reading!
Laura

Sisters Born, Sisters Found

A Diversity of Voices on Sisterhood

Edited by

Laura McHale Holland

Laura McHale Holland

Wordforest
Rohnert Park, California

Sisters Born, Sisters Found: A Diversity of Voices on Sisterhood
© 2014 by Laura McHale Holland

ISBN paperback: 978-0-9829365-5-9
ISBN epub: 978-0-9829365-6-6
Library of Congress Control No. 2014916536

Cover and book design by Kathy McHale at McHale Creative
www.mchalecreative.com

To all women throughout the world whose birth families gave them siblings, to those who became sisters through other kinds of bonds, and to all the sisters and brothers who love them.

Contents

Introduction 1

Set One
Scrambled Eggshells – memoir, Jean Wong 4

Flotation Device – memoir, Marie Millard 8

First Meeting – poem, Karen Benke 10

Lentil Soup – memoir, Maria de Lourdes Victoria 11

Pink Moment – poem, Dianalee Velie 16

Outside the Circle – memoir, Ana Manwaring 17

Thieving – poem, Joanna Jones 20

Mythic Sisters – essay, Laura Simms 21

For Jade and Bosa Donuts – poem, Jordan Steele 28

Unlikely Sisters – memoir, Karen Levy 30

The Truth of It – memoir, Dipika Kohli 33

She Proves It – poem, Olivia Boler 36

Set Two
Sister Act – memoir, Vicki Batman 40

Echoes From the Heart – memoir, Mary J. Kohut 44

Sister, I Needed You – poem, Nancy Pogue LaTurner 50

Loons – short story, C. R. Resetarits 52

We Have Today – memoir, Paige Strickland 54

The Twins' Little Kingdom – poem, Nardia Kelly 56

Mud Pies and Escargot – memoir, Sara Catalina Dorame Bard 58

One Sixth – poem, Nancy Cook 62

Greyhound Station – memoir, Olivia Boler 64

Light – poem, Lindsay Ahl 68

The Ceremony—December 1980 – memoir, Skye Blaine 69

Never My Sister – poem, Erica Lann-Clark 74

Set Three

Sisters in Blood: The Papin Sisters – essay, Delphine Cingal 78

Sister Song – poem, Claire Blotter 84

Face to Face – short story, Lisa A. Sturm 85

Behind the Eyes – poem, Wilda Morris 92

Jen-Jen – memoir, Jesse Kimmel-Freeman 93

Mirror – memoir, Mara Buck 96

Just Like Sisters – poem, Brenda Bellinger 98

Mother's Desserters – memoir, Elspeth Benton 100

For Milly's Birthday June 8, 2004, Disclaimer – poem,
  Catharine Bramkamp 104

Soaring into Space – short story, Ella Preuss 106

Dear Rachel – short story, Ruth Stotter 111

Sisters – poem, Janie Emaus 114

Set Four

Mana – memoir, Fabia Oliveira 116

Ripened Apricots – poem, Anne Tammel 120

Sisters in Scribe – memoir, Diane Sismour 122

The Day Mel Tormé Died – short story, Mercilee M. Jenkins 125

After Curfew – poem, Karen Benke 133

The Pretty and the Strong – memoir, Lisa Marie Lopez 134

Her Name is Belinda – memoir, David Lucero 138

Meeting in the Ring – poem, Susan Ford 141

Sisters of an Only Child – memoir, Eva Kende 143

Paper Cranes – poem, Gwynn O'Gara 146

Darkling River – short story, Nancy Pogue LaTurner 148

Asha – poem, Elaine Webster 154

Set Five

From None to Many – memoir, Jan Boddie 158

First Medicine – poem, Gwynn O'Gara 162

Picker Sisters – memoir, Diana M. Amadeo 163

Lucy and Ethel Break In – memoir, Debra Ayers Brown 166

Celebrating Flo's 60th Birthday – poem, Nellie Wong 170

Groovy Sisters – memoir, Nadia Ali 172

Hero – memoir, Pamela Taeuffer 174

Born of a Chill Wind – memoir, P. H. Garrett 179

Light Show – poem, D. A. (Daisy) Hickman 181

A Time of Magic – essay, Patricia Jackson 182

Quilts – poem, Mark Wisniewski 186

Sisterly Tribes of the Modern Age – essay, Erica Brown 189

The Science of Sisterhood – poem, Sue Kreke Rumbaugh 192

Set Six

White Rose – short story, Gaurav Verma 194

Barbie-girl – memoir, Karen DeGroot Carter 199

The Girls From Byron's Corner – memoir, Gloria Beanblossom 203

Come Hike with Me – poem, Wilda Morris 208

Zori Sisters – memoir, Barbara Toboni 209

Sister to Sisterhood – essay, Lynn Millar 212

The Warp and Weft of Sisterhood – memoir, P. H. Garrett 217

Flowers for Leslie – poem, Nellie Wong 219

Twinkies for Breakfast – essay, Elspeth Slayter 221

Devora's Changes – memoir, Marie Judson-Rosier 225

Crossing Over – poem, D. A. (Daisy) Hickman 232

We Always – memoir, Tanya Savko 233

After – poem, Nina Tepedino 236

Set Seven

The Face of the Following Eyes – memoir, John Boe 238

Her Sister's Keeper – short story, Jennie Marima 243

Cranes for Judy – memoir, Ruth Friesen 248

Somewhere Near Jordan – poem, Carson Pynes 252

Idealizing Sisterhood – memoir, Wendy Kennar 253

Pink Ribbons – poem, Monica Nawrocki 255

Barbed Wire – short story, Conda V. Douglas 257

A Unique Gift – memoir, Bernadette Pabon 264

Segovian Riff – poem, Dianalee Velie 268

You Women! You're Such Bitches! – essay, Cath Bore 269

Safe To Dream – memoir, Laura McHale Holland 271

Before I Forget – poem, Ana Manwaring 275

Acknowledgements 276

Pubslush Supporters 277

Author Index 278

Introduction

I embarked upon this anthology project to honor my sisters, Kathy and Mary Ruth, as well as to capture the power of readings I have conducted in recent years at SISTERS Consignment Couture in Sonoma, California. The shop is a cozy place where local authors have shared memoirs, essays, stories and poems by and about sisters of all types. The readings have been heartfelt, memorable and multifaceted, ranging from intense and painful to lighthearted and celebratory.

At first I thought this anthology would be a slim volume consisting primarily of work from friends and acquaintances. Via social media, however, I connected with writers from all over the world who were enthusiastic about this project. So this endeavor grew into something far richer than I had imagined.

I considered several possible ways to organize the varied contents of this collection, but while I did identify each work as a memoir, poem, essay, or short story, I did not create themed sections. (For the purposes of this book, memoir includes personal vignettes in addition to more fully realized memoirs.) Given the size of this book, however, I divided the work into seven sets to suggest places where readers might want to pause. I also strove to create a reading experience that emulates what I experienced when reviewing submissions as they came to my inbox. I never knew where the next writer would take me, what aspect of the sister journey she or he would reveal, or how the work would affect me. However, it took quite a bit of experimentation to approximate a random experience (which was interrupted by myriad emails, conversations, work, etc., and spanned a period of several months) while also making sure there weren't too many, say, poems or essays in a row, or works that would be jarring or otherwise unsatisfactory if they were placed side by side. I believe whether you follow the order I devised or skip around, you will find numerous insights and fresh perspectives on sisterhood.

Editing the stunning array of works accepted for this publication has helped me realize more fully that I am part of a worldwide community of people for whom the sister bond has significant meaning. When I was young, it often felt like my sisters and I were alone in a heartless world. I've succeeded in overcoming that to a great extent, and working on this project has pulled me even further from lingering feelings of isolation. The word "sister" will always bring Kathy and Mary Ruth to my mind, of course, but it will also remind me of the remarkable people I have come to know through this project.

I imagine stories about sisters have circulated since our earliest ancestors gathered around campfires. And sister stories will continue long after all of us walking the earth today have passed on. I hope this microcosm of sisterhood speaks to you, delights you, empowers, vexes and thrills you. I also hope that in the tomorrows that follow, the voices herein speak to people who are yet to be born.

Laura McHale Holland
Sonoma County, California

Set One

. . . .

Scrambled Eggshells – memoir, Jean Wong

Flotation Device – memoir, Marie Millard

First Meeting – poem, Karen Benke

Lentil Soup – memoir, Maria de Lourdes Victoria

Pink Moment – poem, Dianalee Velie

Outside the Circle – memoir, Ana Manwaring

Thieving – poem, Joanna Jones

Mythic Sisters – essay, Laura Simms

For Jade and Bosa Donuts – poem, Jordan Steele

Unlikely Sisters – memoir, Karen Levy

The Truth of It – memoir, Dipika Kohli

She Proves It – poem, Olivia Boler

Scrambled Eggshells

Jean Wong

As soon as Nancy appeared at the door of our eighth-grade classroom, even I, with my home haircut, near-sighted squint and ill-fitting skirt, could see that she stuck out. Her hair was a tangle of kinky, sandy-blonde curls. She grimaced, exposing her big teeth as overly enthusiastic greetings gushed forth. Wearing dated clothes and straw shoes with high heels, she carried a matching purse. No one ever brought a purse to school.

She was like a puppy wagging its tail among crocodiles. Her overtures were met with blank stares and titters. She was quickly relegated to our group of outcasts who suffered not so much from teasing, but the cruelty of being ignored.

The popular girls whirled in a cacophony of sound—casual and animated. They chirped at each other, "Oh, that is so pretty! … You did? … I am SO jealous!" Asian in a mostly white private school, I floundered as my own utterances fell flat, monosyllabic. I yearned to approach one of these dazzling creatures and ask her to teach me how to talk. If only she would take me aside and reveal the formula, I too could own a bright, perky voice.

It was during a dreaded home economics class that I had my first real encounter with Nancy. In this class, girls quickly formed teams while I waited to be picked. Cooking projects involved spilled food, shrieks of laughter, bursts of movement. There was no place to keep my head down, and quietly do my work. I felt exposed.

Nancy and I were paired to make a cake requiring four eggs. I figured I would get the fun part of cracking the eggs, and Nancy could stir. I cracked two eggs and was reaching for my third, when Nancy piped up, "No, you had a turn. I get to do the next one."

Without looking up, I said, "My job is to crack all the eggs." I couldn't believe I was arguing.

"Who said so?"

"I said so." I was horrified that this was continuing.

But when I looked up, a slight smile appeared on her lips. She grabbed for the egg I was holding. It slipped out of my hand and broke in the bowl.

We giggled.

"That's why my mom never lets me crack eggs," she said. "She calls my omelets 'scrambled eggshells.'"

"My mom won't let me in the kitchen. I only get to set the table. My brother gets to do all the fun stuff."

"Why?"

"Cause he's a boy," I said.

"That's insane."

"Yeah, I guess my mom's a little nuts." I couldn't believe I just called my mom nuts! "My brother and Francis always hit me."

"Who's Francis?"

"The boy next door. Once he told me that he and his friends lined up and took turns punching this girl, and he said if I ever told anyone about it, the same thing would happen to me."

I was telling a complete stranger this secret I'd kept for seven years. In the middle of the telling, its power dissolved. I realized it was a story Francis had probably made up.

"My brother would never hit me," Nancy cried indignantly. "He doesn't even know how to hit anyone."

We giggled again. This laughter was a complete surprise to me. It was like tasting the crust of a pizza for the first time, not quite bread nor cake, but chewy, delicious. That was my first experience of Nancy—something unexpected and something different.

◆ ◆ ◆ ◆ ◆

We waited at a bus stop after school. I noticed a bubble gum machine across the street and dashed over to it. I put a penny in the slot, turned the handle, and got one bubble gum ball. Nancy fished two pennies out of her purse and got two. We looked at each other, and rushed towards mischief. Then I managed to find three pennies and got three more gum balls. Nancy ran into a store and got a dime worth of pennies. More pennies began to disappear into the slot. We raced from store to store asking for nickels, dimes and quarters worth of pennies. Bubble gum spilled from the dispenser onto the sidewalk. We rolled on the ground, shrieking with glee, our books scattered, the bus leaving without us.

Could we leave such a mess? Why had the clerks kept giving us more pennies? Nobody had tried to stop two thirteen-year-olds from being utterly ludicrous. What would we say to our moms about coming home so late? What else could we get away with?

. . . . .

When I first visited Nancy's house, I was surprised I'd been invited. You didn't get into my house unless you were family, and even then, you had to go through a series of gates and locks. My house was sealed like a citadel, wooden bars across windows locked tight. Our inner sanctum was as private and guarded as the Forbidden City of China.

Nancy's front door was unlocked. Sunlight swept across the carpet from open windows. In the living room, her mom and dad were sprawled on the couch taking a nap—arms around each other, her dad naked to the waist. I'd never even seen my mom and dad hug.

In her dad's study, books and records lined the shelves. There was nothing but piles of newspapers and magazines in my house. Nancy went through the titles and started talking about Dostoevsky, Mann, Hesse, Tolstoy. She spoke about the authors, casually, like they were her friends. There were books on Judaism. "Jesus was a Jew!" she proclaimed.

She put on a recording by Horowitz. The music coursed through my bloodstream, merry and vital. Possibility bobbed with each beat.

. . . . .

I stumbled out of high school physics, tears streaming from my eyes—*negative charge…terminal velocity…air resistance.* I knew I was going to fail this class. I just didn't have those kinds of smarts. The worst part was that I couldn't even understand the questions the kids asked. I saw Nancy. We headed for the bathroom, our sanctuary.

"I hate physics," I whined. "They're crazy—they're screwing around with a drop of oil. Can you imagine this idiot scientist decides to pour oil around some electrodes, for god's sake!"

Nancy received my torrent. Her eyebrows wiggled as she uttered sounds of sympathy. Encouraged, I started exaggerating and embellishing. Then the best part happened. It began to be fun. Our language turned foul. We snorted. We sputtered. Our voices went up a pitch.

Next came rants about our mothers; hers made her redo all the dishes, mine wouldn't let me quit ballet. We gathered our new arsenal of labels from psychology class and reduced our moms to lunatics—they were obsessive compulsive, dysfunctional, anal.

We spoke about sex and the cute class president who had written a paper on the existence of God. I'd just gone to the library and gotten a stack of books on the "meaning of life." Our moms, sex, philosophy, religion—these subjects would fascinate us for years, and there was the laughter—loud, rambunctious, irrepressible—always the laughter, the hilarity that fueled our intoxication and delight.

The bell rang. We thought it hysterical that we were late. We cracked up, stumbled about, bent over and then caught sight of our goofy, homely faces in the mirror. "Check this scene out!" we screamed. And this became our mantra. For years to come, we peered into mirrors, in bathrooms, department stores, plush hotel lobbies. At birthdays, graduations and every other conceivable situation, arms around each other, we posed. Check this scene out. Check out that we're hurting, ridiculous, high, miserable. Check out that we're alive and going through life together. Check out that we're friends.

* * * * *

Jean Wong is an award-winning author whose work has been produced by the 6th Street Playhouse, Petaluma Readers Theater, and Off The Page. Her book, Sleeping with the Gods, *has been recently published. When writing, Jean sometimes proceeds like a mule; other times a brilliant racehorse speeds. Whatever the process, she's amazed to be alive and telling the tale.*

Flotation Device
Marie Millard

My dad used to say, "Watch for snakes!" when my sisters or I checked the mailbox of our suburban California home. (He was from rural Ohio.) "Watch your intersections," he'd say when we got our driver's licenses. "Root sticking up," he'd announce as we hiked. Dad felt it was his duty to warn us of every possible source of injury.

So how my sister and I ended up floating down the American River in a raft-shaped pool toy, I cannot imagine. But there we were. No life vests, no formal swim lessons, and likely no sunscreen between us, two teenagers swirling and bumping down the rocky, brambly river alongside a hundred strangers in viable vessels from River Rat Rentals.

We laughed at the way our raft threatened to fold up on itself. FOR USE IN POOL ONLY, it yelled at us in black lettering. We felt ridiculous amongst the beer drinking twenty-somethings in their thick yellow rafts with ropes to hold onto should they be thrown out. We could not afford to fall out. Or scrape a rock. Or put too much weight on one finger. I was having a glorious time.

"Hello, ladies."

Water cops! I had no idea there was such a thing. Really, it made sense, with all these people drinking and, well, cruising down the river in pool toys.

"Where are your personal flotation devices?" One of them asked, very official-like, from his expensive kayak.

"We're in it." I don't remember which one of us was smartass enough to say that, but I think this was before I had mastered my big sister's technique, so I'm guessing it was her.

I'm sure water cops are great for saving people, but there's not much they can do to reprimand two teenagers in an inadequate raft. There's no place to get out of the river besides the sand bar by the parking lot where everyone gets out. And the cops didn't have lifejackets to give us or anything, so away we floated, laughing harder than before.

Did we see a metaphor at the time? Not a chance. We were having too much fun, and probably embarrassed about our raft. But isn't that how it is with sisters? You are blessed or stuck with the same parents, giggling and feeling like your boat is a little crazier and more fragile than everyone else's, and yet somehow superior to the others, too, because you are in it, and you have each other.

* * * * *

Marie Millard has contributed fiction and memoir to many anthologies. Her Bible devotional, Seeking First His Kingdom (61 Days of Worry-free Devotions), *is available on Amazon under the name M.L. Millard. It's soon to be joined by* Anaheim Tales, *a* Canterbury Tales-*inspired young adult novella about cheeky teenagers on a charter bus to Disneyland, and* When I Grow Up, *a whimsical children's book for kids to illustrate themselves.*

First Meeting

Karen Benke

The night she came home from the hospital
I taped four pieces of construction paper
side by side, spelled welcome in black crayon
then hung the banner high
against the stars of the front window.
On Dad's chair, I sat waiting
—all the way back on worn leather,
my legs resting over the edge,
my hands in my lap folded neatly.
Here, Mom cradled her down to me, and carefully
I moved the warm blanket back, memorizing
the shape of her head, studying the tiny lines
of her new pink skin. I wanted her
to know me, hear her voice sing my name.
This weight I held was our beginning.
I was told I must always share—my heart
breaking as she gazed back at me.

. . . . .

Karen Benke is the author of Sister *(Conflux Press, 2004) and three* Creative Writing Adventure *books from Roost Books/Shambhala:* Rip the Page! *(2010),* Leap Write In! *(2013), and forthcoming in September 2015:* Uncap That Pen! *A writing coach and a poet with California Poets in the Schools, she lives north of the Golden Gate Bridge with her husband, son, and two literary assistants: a cat named Clive and a dog named Rasco Roon. Visit her at www.karenbenke.com.*

Lentil Soup

Maria de Lourdes Victoria

Nobody knows how to make lentil soup like my sister. Maybe it's the brand of beans she buys, maybe it's the Serrano ham bone she boils in the broth, or maybe it's the pieces of plantain she barters for with her favorite *marchanta* at the market. Whatever it is, all who have tasted her thick, fragrant soup unequivocally agree: of all the lentil soups, hers reigns supreme.

The truth is, my sister doesn't prepare the soup for just anyone. For me she does, because I am her favorite, and because of the history that we share—a history that somehow has left us eternally indebted to each other. And so, every time she learns that I am going to Veracruz to visit my beloved hometown, she rolls up her sleeves and gets busy in her kitchen. There, in a secret ritual that no one else is privy to, she exhorts the powers of the Culinary Goddess and creates her masterpiece. Year after year, she welcomes me thus: with the steaming pot that seals our tacit pact, lentils in exchange for perpetual love. And not just any love, mind you, but real love. *Amor de los buenos.*

There was a time, now long ago, when my sister prepared a different kind of soup. It was a soup made of tree leaves and dirt from the garden. She served it in small, clay bowls—our reward when we were good little girls at the market; when we carried the *morral* without complaint; when we didn't wrinkle our noses at the Don Chemo's smelly fish; or when we graciously accepted the chunk of beef that Doña Petra lowered from a hook and handed over, wrapped in bloody newspapers. Only then, when we didn't make a fuss, we earned a prize, which well could have been a paper doll, or those tiny clay bowls with which my sister served her soup of petals and dirt.

There, under the cool shade of the flamboyant tree, beside the swings, the Chef would set up her kitchen. Her stove was the tree's trunk, curved horizontally by too many hurricanes. An empty crate of mangos was her icebox. A big, flat rock her table. No one was allowed to cook. No one else knew the recipes of her concoctions. If I dared touch the pot, she would quickly swat my hand with the spoon, a dry stick, and send me off to set the table. I wasn't even allowed to decorate the dessert with petals from the *Copa de Oro*. Presentation was key, and it could take all afternoon, but we, her guests—our stuffed animals, my *Bambán* (a black baby doll) and the cat—waited patiently. We didn't dare leave. It was such a privilege to be invited to savor her culinary talents.

On the stairs of the patio of our grandparent's house, she taught me how to make tortillas. We played with sour, leftover *masa* that the Chef would shape into small little balls, kneading and rolling them until they looked like marbles. Patting them between pieces of cut plastic, she would flatten them, careful not to break them apart as she laid them to "cook" on the *comal*—the metal lid of a trash can. I never managed to perfect the technique. All that my awkward hands would yield were grimy little *churros* that looked like African worms from *Bambán's* homeland. The only thing that urged me to improve was the warning from the Chef that women who don't know how to make tortillas were destined to be nuns, live their lives without husbands or children, locked in the Carmelite convent.

In the cookie factory of our uncle Manuel, *El Cubano*, my sister used to make her soup with crumbs. Our uncle would bake delicious biscuits, filled with peanut cream, in enormous ovens. When the trays fell, as they often did, he would give us the remnant pieces to play with. My sister made all sorts of soups, and we ate them until we were stuffed. The pigeons would fly down from the factory's old beams and join the feast. Even today I can still hear their soft cooing when I eat too much.

The Chef improved the quality of her dishes during the summers we spent at uncle Jorge's ranch, *El Coyol*. Her first course was either mangos with worms, or sour grapefruit dropped from a tree. Dessert was always the same: a piece of juicy sugar cane, freshly peeled, which we sucked like a sponge until dry.

More than once the Chef spoiled a dish, like the time of the infamous octopus. She had just turned twelve years old when it was decided that we were old enough to learn to cook properly. I would be her helper. Our task was to walk to the market by ourselves, barter with the merchants, buy the freshest goods, and bring them home to prepare. Our first assigned recipe was octopus in its ink.

At the market, we had no problems. The merchants, who already knew us, indulged us, and even gifted us a head of garlic. We took turns carrying the knapsack all the way home. When we arrived, hot from the sweltering sun, we went straight to the refrigerator and had a drink. We then washed the bag of smelly mollusks. Not an easy job. We had to make sure that not a single, slimy creature slipped down the drain. To clean them, we first had to remove the tooth from the head and then locate the two sacks, one that contained waste and the other that contained the ink. We removed, one by one, the offensive sacks and when we finally finished, we prepared the stew: three cloves of garlic blended with leek, tomato, and a bay leaf. Soon, a delicious fragrance invaded the kitchen. The Chef trembled with emotion. All was going well until we added the octopus. Suddenly the delicious aroma became a nauseating stench. It was then that we realized our fatal error. We had removed the wrong sacks.

When she was sixteen years old the Chef became pregnant, got married, and gave birth to a premature baby. So it was that I lost my childhood companion overnight. After a rushed wedding, she went to live with her husband in an apartment. One afternoon my longing was so great, that in spite of the infernal mid-day heat, I walked over to see her. Deep in my heart, I still hoped that she would come back, even with her baby, to play dolls. As small as he was, I was sure he would fit my *Bambán's* clothing perfectly. Together we would prepare his baby food, in our kitchen under the shade of the flamboyant tree, just like we always had. Together we would lull him to sleep in the swings.

I was certain she could be convinced and remained hopeful until I began to climb up the stairs to her apartment. I heard the baby's shrieks. When I entered, I found her on her knees, franticly cleaning a mess that was dripping down the walls. The baby had a fever. My sister had spent the morning making him his baby food from scratch. Gerber's was outside her newlywed budget. The blender had exploded. She had not allowed the boiled vegetables to cool. The mess had splattered all over the furniture, the appliances, and her tangled hair. Even a renowned chef like my sister did not know how to do everything.

In spite of multiple trips to the city hospital; in spite of pilgrimages on knees to the Basilica of Guadalupe; and in spite of prayers, many prayers, the baby put his little wings back on and returned to heaven. My sister's innocence went with him. All that remained behind was an empty sister who, shortly thereafter, moved to a *finca* far, far away, in a place forgotten by God. One of our mother's uncles had taken pity on them and had offered her husband a job.

Every good chef understands that for a dish to turn out perfect, one must be patient. The recipe never comes out exactly right the first time around. Sometimes, one must bake and throw out twenty cakes before that spongy and golden perfection, worthy of being decorated, is brought forth. This was something my sister knew well. Something she learned back then, at the sea, when she used to make cakes with sand. It takes many tries and often one must beat the egg whites a little longer, or soften the butter a little more, or sift the flour with more persistence. And because she understood, she didn't lose hope. She intuitively knew that, sooner or later, her womb would bake perfection worthy of the bitumen that would cover the bitter cracks of her heart.

And they came, her daughters, one right after the other, in cinnamon and vanilla flavors. They came ready to eat her baby food with hearty gusto. The Chef's inspiration returned. She quickly ran to the market to demand again the best vegetables, the juiciest fruit of the season, filleted meat, and the freshest fish. She boiled, baked, and cooked, solidifying her love with each dish. And in a fevered tango of pots and pans, my sister fed her flesh-and-bone dolls, watching with relief over every kilogram of weight gained that made them grow and rooted them firmly to life.

One sad day, my sister's husband left her. He wanted to take the girls but they did not sway; they stayed with their mother. They understood that only she could soften their pains, sweeten their tears, and ripen their memories. Life had suddenly changed the menu. ... There were difficult moments when my sister thought she would have to serve petal soup to her daughters. Too many moments, she would say, in which she had to dilute the beans. Fortunately, it was not the first time she had to improvise. She bargained with the merchants and learned to make stews out of bones and vegetable peels and broths with shells. She learned that life is like a cactus salad. The fruit's delicious pulp is right underneath its spines. My sister endured the pain and earned the fruits of her labor: the respect and love of her daughters. A much better prize than paper dolls, or little clay bowls.

Today, in a warm kitchen recently decorated by my sister, our grandchildren sit around her table. The Chef serves them a steaming plate of lentils they devour by the spoonful, fighting over the plantains. And with this sacred ceremony, my sister and I once again seal our pact: lentils in exchange for perpetual love, and not just any love but real love, *Amor de los Buenos.*

* * * * *

Maria de Lourdes Victoria is an international, award-winning, bilingual author. She writes novels, short stories and bilingual children's books. Her second novel, Beyond Justice (Más Allá de la Justicia), *took third place for the prestigious Planeta Book Award, 2010. Her first novel,* The Children of the Sea (Los Hijos del Mar) *was a finalist for the Mariposa Book Award, 2006. Her short stories have been published in numerous literary journals. More information may be found at www.mariadelourdesvictoria.com.*

Pink Moment

Dianalee Velie

And so for the morning we practice being
eight years old again, two sisters pedaling
bicycles, yours powder blue with white daisies,
mine innocent pink with creamy roses.

We fill our wicker baskets with adult treasures
of triple crème cheese, fresh mangoes and syrah
wine from the Ojai Valley, unlike the trinkets
from our past, Queen Anne's Lace, mica rocks
and the peanut butter and jelly sandwiches
we toted up Maple Avenue into the "woods,"
a patch of greenery in an industrial suburb,
where we played until the sun began to set
and Mom called us home for dinner.

Tonight we toast our bond with Pink Moment Martinis,
adult pink lemonade blended to reflect the rosy cast
of the Topa Topa Mountains at sunset,
soft, smooth mountains, that during the day seem
to roll in undulating waves of green-velvet sphagnum moss.
Remembering our mother, we vow to continue our spa reunions,
to be coddled, wrapped, massaged and rejuvenated,
until the day Mom finally calls us home.

* * * * *

Dianalee Velie is a graduate of Sarah Lawrence College and has a master of arts in writing from Manhattanville College. She has taught poetry, memoir, and short story at a number of East Coast universities and colleges, as well as in private workshops throughout the United States, Canada, and Europe. Her award-winning poetry and short stories have been published in hundreds of literary journals. She is the author of four books of poetry and the short story collection Soul Proprietorship: Women in Search of Their Souls.

Outside the Circle

Ana Manwaring

Your sister is dead. Burning tears seep from your eyes as you drive your car or grill halibut on your patio. In moments of clarity, you realize that it's grief. But why do you grieve? Dallis was a mean girl, your nemesis. Your Moriarity whose sole purpose in your life was to bust your chops. Even in your dreams she shows up, a black cancerous blob come to shut you down. Her tapered fingers with deathly purple manicure reach across the dimensions and choke you. You wonder if you're going crazy. You don't recognize your cat.

A control freak, she liked you when it served her. You did it her way or no way—it was always her way. Your mother encouraged it, keeping you outside the circle of mother and daughter. For your mother, the sun rose and set on Dallis—you could never compare.

You could have celebrated Dallis's life at the Art and Garden Center. You might have wondered at the hundreds of people who attended and said such nice things. You might have joked that most of them came for the open bar. But you weren't invited. So you pound furiously at your keyboard and question your existence. Have you always felt so angry, so disenfranchised? Be honest.

Look into the glass your mother always held in front of you. That's the gold standard, the image of Dallis Jean the Jovial Jelly Bean Queen, staring back at you.

"Why can't you be more like your sister?" your mother accuses.

"A bitch?"

"I don't know why you say things like that."

You want to quip, "You taught her." What is it they say, that cliché? The apple doesn't fall far from the tree. You remember them, mother and daughter in your sister's bedroom after school, apple-cheeked and giggling, at your expense. The Beatles trill "oooooooo!" softly in the background. Just loud enough for you to hear.

You look up from your book. "Turn it up," you call.

"Buy your own record, ugly," Dallis replies.

You ask your mother to drive you to the record store.

"Your sister bought it. We don't need two."

It was your favorite record, and Dallis didn't buy it. Mom did. But you knew better than to expect equity.

Your job was to take the blame. If your sister clinked the lid closing the cookie crock, she'd say, "Mo-o-om! She's stealing cookies." You knew to disappear. It was safer than trying to fight for the truth.

But often you did argue. You fought, pitched tantrums, your anger too big to contain, like an explosion of inflammable gas, burning bright and hot.

In the early years of your parent's marriage, you sisters went together to piano lessons at that Victorian on Fifth. Your fumbling fingers never found the keys. The teacher dropped you. It was the same with ballet. You were relieved. You wanted to take ice skating lessons, but until you lost weight, you weren't allowed.

"Little Lotta, too fat to ice skate!"

Dallis took the lessons, wore the cute skating costume. You sat and watched each week until she fell on the hard ice and quit. You also watched the synchronized swimming. How you longed to don the frilly cap and jazz dance around the pool in line with the girls wearing matching suits; to dive into the pool on cue and twirl, flip, flutter, all in perfect time. Weren't you the one they called a born fish? You could hold your breath for three lengths in the pool.

But the banishment wasn't all ancient history. You weep now for the sister you thought she had become until she stopped speaking to you. She'd done that before, frozen you out, many times. Then she'd drop back into your life as if in the middle of a conversation with her gossip and her opinions and her desires. That was her thing if you fell out of her favor: the silent treatment to your face and gossip and lies behind your back. The childish "stupid, ugly and fat" matured to "incompetent, dishonest and greedy." You heard the whispers, the lies that poured out, poisoning your mother's family against you. Yet you always believed you and Dallis would reconcile. Even at her deathbed, holding her purpled claws, you thought surely you and your sister would reunite.

At the church memorial her children move away from you; your cousin turns her back on you; no one offers you condolences. Don't they know you grieve, too? Your guilt confronts you. Did you try hard enough? Did you do enough? Did you turn your back, play her game? You practiced forgiveness and your anger dulled; your grief became a yellowed bruise. You rejoiced when your sister's cancer went into remission. But your notes and birthday wishes couldn't tame the monster eating her bones.

During the service, you imagine your father waiting at Heaven's gate. Will he greet her with anticipation and joy? Or reprimand? The mean part of you hopes she's chastised, hopes she won't get away with it—how she's treated you. You want to stamp your foot and yell, "Da-a-d, Dallis died without loving me." And see your father stand for you. This time, sending her to her room; cutting off her money; failing to raise her above you. But the game's over. You can never win the love she didn't feel for you, and it comes to you that your grief is for something that never existed. You mourn sister, not Dallis.

Dallis is dead, enemy to the last. You'll never know why she pushed you out, but your world has shifted and you no longer care.

* * * * *

Petaluma Post *columnist Ana Manwaring teaches creative writing and memoir through Napa Valley College—Upper Valley Campus and privately in Sonoma County. In addition to writing poetry, Ana crafts fiction, both literary and thriller genres, and performs her work in bookstores, coffee houses, on public radio, at book festivals, in senior centers, community centers, libraries and classrooms. To learn more about Ana, please visit www.anamanwaring.com.*

Thieving

Joanna Jones

My sister steals.
She steals food from the pan, food from my plate, takes
finger-quick nips of chicken and peas and
hisses when she gets caught in the steam, then
smirks and licks her lips.
She steals clothes.
Steals them and wears them proud, wears them hard, like
they're hers to ruin and rip and stain,
to sweat in and shrug on and have peeled off her, then leave puddled and
dazed on her bedroom floor.
I want them back badly, and I take them too, but
she has a way of moulding the world, and now my clothes fit her form.
I knew when she took my boyfriend's t-shirt
that he wasn't mine anymore.
I only ever took one thing from her, surely the worst of all:
a pair of battered ballet shoes,
sweat-yellowed and frayed and bent, with tide-line blood stains on
    wooden blocks and
two soles arching up like lovers. She broke them in
with blistered skin, with crippled toes that she hid on hot summers and
bones that ground sweet and slow.
And when she came home, she laid them to rest,
nestled together like Russian dolls in a tissue papered shoebox.
I took them
and I tried to put them back, but
somehow the shoes wouldn't go.
That's what we do: we take and we tear 'til it's just us girls,
scrapping for bones.

· · · · ·

Joanna Jones works backstage as a theatre technician and is currently studying international politics at Aberystwyth University in Wales. She has had work displayed in the Aval Ballan gallery and published in Popshot *magazine, and has been nominated for the 2014 Forward Literary Prize (Single Poem category).*

Mythic Sisters

Laura Simms

When I was growing up, my grandmother's sister lived on our street in Brooklyn, but I never knew that. I only knew I was named after my great aunt Lea. My Hebrew name given at birth was Lea. I wasn't told that a red brick apartment building I passed often, a structure with no charm or light, was her home. In nightmares I saw its elevator descend to sub-basements; I dreaded the door opening and awoke in terror of impending danger.

When I was seven Lea's daughter came to live with us. No one mentioned she was family. Decades later, I still have scant information about my grandmother and her sister. I only know that Lea (renamed Libby in North America) and my grandmother Mahlia (renamed Molly) came from northern Romania in 1900. In 1909 they received a telegram that stated, "Everyone killed in a pogrom. Do not return." In the 1950s Lea had a lobotomy. That is why her daughter came to live with my family. I imagine Lea was alone in that red brick building.

Lea's story is a tale of shame, silence, and displacement. The removal of a sister is mythic. I have reflected on the power of mythic and literary sisters like Scheherazade and Dunyazad in literature; Leah and Rachel in the Bible, as interpreted by feminist scholars; and the sisters of Egyptian mythology, Isis and Nepthys. In these stories, sisters are the agents of change, restoration of spirit, and renewal of wisdom. They resuscitate that which is dead of life or heart. In most retellings, only one sister is emphasized or mentioned.

Connecting the fragments of my great aunt Lea's tale is a personal restoration. Acknowledging secrecy in my family brings forth that which was lost.

> *"Ah, Sister!" says Isis to Nepthys*
> *"This is our brother.*
> *Come let us lift up his head.*
> *Come, let us rejoin his bones.*
> *Come let us reassemble his limbs.*
> *Come, let us put an end to all his woe,*
> *that so far as we can help, he will weary no more."*

With Isis and Nepthys, we bask in the radiance of their magical chants. Their voices, in chorus, do what no one else can do. The two sisters, described as dark and light, travel between day and night, death and life, and physical and spiritual existence.

When I was a child, my family lived in a white farmhouse in the center of our block. We had a wraparound porch and two gardens: one manicured in the front and one messy in the back. The back was the place of my endless enactments. I played all the parts in fairytales and episodes of Robin Hood. But the area under my bedroom window, where the sun never shone and nothing ever grew, was my magic territory. There I engaged in a secret game with a neighbor's orthodox Jewish daughter. She was my hidden sister in purpose and play. We buried broken toys, socks, and rejected earrings. We created funerals like priestesses: digging and singing, conjuring up the tales that were never told. We were voicing the memory of the millions who had died in the Holocaust and were never mentioned in our houses.

Meanwhile, inside my home, the Swedish blonde cook, the African American cleaning woman and my mother comprised a wild women trio. Together, they prepared and served meals. All this rich sistering went on. Yet it transpired without mention of my grandmother's sister who lived behind closed doors. For a child, this unspoken narrative was palpable. Hence, my game of funerals and eulogies.

"Sorting through the meaning of sisterhood in our lives requires attending to all three modes: that of the literal sister(s), the surrogate sisters, and the sister within, the archetype." – Christine Downing (Psyche's Sister)

My grandmother died at a young age, which marked my mother with sorrow. And my father's absence for five years during World War II, the subsequent death of my mother's father, the horrific news of concentration camps, and displaced persons streaming into the neighborhood stunted my mother's potential for ongoing happiness. Born into this sadness, I sensed having a sister could bring me the comfort and intimacy my life lacked. When I was six my mother said I would have a sister. Overcome with happiness, she announced, "I am pregnant!" Then she vanished with no explanation. When she returned weeks later, she didn't mention my sister. Years afterward, she said my father had forced her to have an abortion "for economic reasons." A different kind of lobotomy.

When I was twelve, my mother had a stroke. Her sorrow became manifest. She spent afternoons with a neighbor named Esther, whose parents were also from Romania. I was never privy to their conversations, which took place in Yiddish or Romanian.

The story of Scheherazade and Dunyazad frames the stories in 1001 Nights. *As the daughters of King Shahryar's Vizier, they were the only young women protected fromthe ruler's murderous plot against women. Enraged and humiliated by his wife's betrayal (she was found in the arms of a slave) the King murdered his wife and her lover. Then, each evening after dinner and a wedding, he took a new bride to bed and had her beheaded in the morning. Thus, he sidestepped his pain—until Scheherazade offered to marry the King.*

Long after my mother and father were deceased I returned to my old neighborhood. As I approached Esther's home, I visualized my mother, her cane against a chair, sitting with her close friend Esther in the kitchen. I knocked on the door. Marilyn, Esther's daughter, answered. "Funny you should come today. My mother just came back from the hospital. She had a stroke. She asked about you yesterday," she said. Inside I saw Esther in a nightgown at the kitchen table, her cane propped beside her chair. I felt drowned with emotion as memories broke loose.

At eleven years old, unable to understand the stories spun by my mother and her close friend, I would sit on a step in Esther's backyard, listening to voodoo music and watching Haitian musicians and dancers rehearse with a young Alvin Ailey. My mother's secrets were not as immediate or alluring as the mystery unfolding in the yard. I was drawn in by rehearsals meant to heal Esther's daughter, whose husband had died in a car accident the day they were married. It was my first inkling of a kind of truth, bathed in mystery, different from unspoken secrets. It was a way of healing.

At first The King refused to marry Scheherazade.
But he finally agreed. The wedding night ritual took place while her father, the vizier, waited with sword in hand behind the door. Before

*sleep, however, Scheherazade made a request. She explained that
each night she told a story to her sister, whose joy was to hear a tale
before she went to sleep. Could she not invite her sister to the bed-
room and tell one last story?*

*The King was unaware of how Scheherazade's stories could move in
irresistible fragments between sisters—and through him. He did not
know his cruel heart would be transformed.*

When I visited Esther, her voice was weak. She said to me, "I want to
tell you something about your mother, but I am too tired. Can you come
back soon?" I promised to return and left thrilled that some of my moth-
er's secrets might be revealed. When I called a few days later, Marilyn
told me her mother had died. The door to that world remained closed.
If I'd had a sister, like Isis' sister Nepthys, we might have sung Esther's
voice back to life from the land of the dead. Or I might have listened, like
Dunyazad, to my mother's tales and been myself transformed.

*When Osiris, brother and husband of Isis, was killed
in a devious plan, the sisters turned themselves into birds. They
flew to Byblos where the King's body was hidden in a pillar. They
retrieved the corpse, then hid the dead King among the rushes. But
Set, the jealous brother of Osiris, found him. He cut the body into
fourteen pieces and scattered it over Egypt. Isis with the help of
her sister found the pieces of his body. Only the phallus was gone,
swallowed by a fish. They formed a phallus with barley and grass.
Isis made love to the body and became pregnant. In unison the two
sisters sang Osiris back to life into the other world so a path for all of
us would exist after death between worlds.*

My longed for sister and I would have plumbed whispered dreams
and messages and found my great aunt's story. We would have pieced
together her history even after she was dead. We would have sung: "Sister,
dark sister, you were disappeared. But secrets may be heard in mysterious
words. They can be retrieved like the dark sister's incantations." In this
re-dreaming, silent desecration is transformed into a flowering stream of
stories.

*"[L]istening and watching ... in all the descriptions we are given
of the world, the silences, the absences, the nameless, the unspoken,*

the encoded, there we will find the true knowledge of women." –
Adrienne Rich (On Lies, Secrets and Silence)

I used to be repelled by the story of Leah and Rachel, two sisters set against each other by deception. In this tale, my namesake, Leah, was cast as a "weak eyed" substitute bride. Rachel's only virtue seemed to be her beauty. However, after I first heard the tale, feminist Jewish scholars gathered lost fragments of their story and gave voice to what had been politically erased. They revealed the sisters were priestesses, devoted to the goddess of their homeland, who nurtured family, earth and spirit. Like Scheherazade and her sister, Leah and Rachel knew ancient chants and stories.

Leah means "cow" or "gentle eyes." Rachel translates as "ewe." Their relationship is one of deepest connection and regeneration, of tears and milk. Their incantations honor sustenance and renewal. Even in the biblical retelling, they birthed a nation. Now we know how they did it. Words shared among sisters serve fertility. As biblical scholar Savina Teubal explained, this sharing also "provides safe delivery." The secret is the power that words wield in unison. The fertility is physical, psychological and psychic.

Retelling sister stories, and my own true tales, reveals the significance of the fragments left by my grandmother and her sister. The silence I ignored for a long time, comes into the light. It redeems their legacy. Daughters of a Grand Rabbi, they were sent alone into forced marriages. They were wrenched from homeland and family, and not permitted to grieve. My mother inherited the taboo against revealing truths. In telling these stories, I claim the lost sisters of my family and the revelations they bring.

> *Scheherazade had courage, compassion, skill and intelligence. After each night's story, King Shahryar, enthralled, was compelled to know what would happen next. Hence, Scheherazade survived. At first he attributed his emotions to characters in the stories. But as his own imagination—the re-creator of each incident and character—deepened with intelligence, he looked into the mirror of his own actions and was heartbroken to see the despot he had become. Scheherazade didn't blame or instruct the King. She facilitated his transformation*

through a bond with her sister. The sisters tricked him into knowing his innate tenderness. Within the space between sisters, he became a true ruler.

In most texts of *1001 Nights*, the role of Dunyazad is barely mentioned. But when the full story is told—and heard—it is the key to healing. Translated from the Persian, Scheherazade means "Liberator of the City." Dunyazad means "World Freer." Through the sisters' dual presence, the storyteller was saved, and all young women were released from a hideous doom. Lifting the veil on the role of sisters is essential repair. The listening was the conduit that enabled the story to enrapture the King and open his heart. Dunyazad is as vital to the outcome as Scheherazade. The connection of sisters is the provocation for enduring change.

It is the empowered listener, and the space between, that enable the work of *1001 Nights* to take place. When we listen today, we become Dunyazad, the vehicle of liberation. This dynamic between teller and listener is more powerful than the content of the text. It is the territory where change manifests and renewal takes place. The living word made sound, from voice to ear through the body of the King, is the journey of "safe delivery." The delusion that understanding and learned abstract ideas are more true than experience is proven inadequate. Bringing together a living, compassionate teller and a receptive listener is a renewal of sisterhood. It is a restoration of heart intelligence. We need remembrance of this space between in our world today.

The King's transformation took place at night. Just as Osiris, protected by two sisters, came through the dark passage, King Shahryar returned to his senses. The Bible, when reconnected with history, restores the missing links of female presence. Sisters bring peace back into a conflicted world. Devoting ourselves to authentic communication, telling and hearing in person, takes us across a fabricated boundary. We, like the Arabian sisters, are moved back into communion, imagination, and soul. The single rigid story model is undone. Bias and entitlement are alleviated through the secret sacred weapon: the reciprocity of the spoken story.

We return to participation in the world rather than a learned disconnection that breeds violence and dogma. The sisters take charge of the space between. In essence, they connect the dots. What is very moving is that Scheherazade understood that it is not only women who suffer from disconnect. The King had to be cured for a genuine return to wholeness and continuity of the world.

It is time to recognize the pulsating space between us when telling and listening to stories. The rarely honored story of Scheherazade and Dunyazad needs to be reinstated. Scheherazade and her sister invited us into the treasure house of healing from disconnection and secrecy, as did Leah and Rachel, and Isis and Nepthys. We need to incorporate this realization of sister in the way we respond to the earth and to each other. It is a family relationship unlike any other. It engenders palpable interdependence. Sharing of sister voices is a ritual that provides safe passage through the dangerous territory of enraged monsters and Kings, returning us into the light of compassion and transformation.

* * * * *

Laura Simms, an award-winning storyteller, author, recording artist, teacher, and humanitarian, has performed one-woman shows throughout the world. Described by The New York Times *as "a major force in the revival of storytelling in America," she works on projects promoting peacemaking, creativity, and community dialogue. Laura has established storytelling projects in post-Katrina New Orleans and in Haiti. She is a contributing editor for* Parabola Magazine *and has five books published including her most recent,* Our Secret Territory: The Essence of Storytelling. *Laura's website is www.laurasimms.com.*

For Jade and Bosa Donuts

Jordan Steele

To my sister
not by blood but by shared insecurity
and dress size
I wish I knew who first told you
your eyes were not bright enough
to blink staccato Morse code love notes to the moon
so I could reverse time and bottle up his words
before they clawed their way to you,
tie them to a skipping stone and
watch them skid across the Pacific before
sinking to the depths where they have no clout
for hagfish have far more confidence than they should.

You of fresh baked terra cotta skin
and a laugh composed of Louis' trumpet solos
can't you see you were built with pride
to teach the world to dance again,
to shout from sagging apartment buildings
for the rest of us to pick up our paintbrushes
and splatter the sidewalks with Sam Cooke soul
so everyone walking through town will see
that we are here and we are more beautiful
than downpours in the desert
or the streaks of spilled milk in our galaxy.
You of midnight doughnut runs
and secondhand mandolins
can't you see,
without your lighthouse eyes we are lost
in triangles of doubt and shame
and sore slumping shoulders,
deaf to our own climbing crescendo symphonies.

Sister
not by blood but by shared revelation
and maple long johns
I wish I knew who first told you

your voice was not loud enough for the sun
to hear you sing so I could chase him outside
with an old corn broom and
sweep away the singed and curling traces of
everything still binding you to fear
just like you did for me.

* * * * *

Jordan Steele was born, raised, and currently resides in Phoenix, Arizona—a true rarity in a state of transplants. She holds a BA in English from Northern Arizona University and works with vulnerable youth populations, teaching basic life skills and teen pregnancy prevention. Jordan writes poetry mostly for herself, but plans to write fiction as a means to empower the youth she now serves.

Unlikely Sisters

Karen Levy

We were like two schoolgirls, giggling in front of the bathroom mirror in the restaurant where we were sharing a Mediterranean feast. The fact that I had recently turned forty-five, and that in a month Eman would join me in celebrating the same number of summers, made no difference. It was just one more fact we had in common like the daughters we were raising, now both watching their mothers revel in an unlikely friendship that had begun thirty-five years ago.

While the mirror reflected two distinct images, the Muslim woman with the long sleeves and the pink head covering exhibited as wide a grin as the curly haired, bare shouldered Israeli who had last seen her friend when she was ten. I complimented Eman on the skirt she was wearing, its delicate lace softening the severity of its modest floor-length cut. She reached out and gently touched my daughter's cheek, telling her that she looked just like me when I was that age.

Back at the table, nothing extraordinary took place during the meal. Eman was attentive to her child's needs, as I was to mine. Her daughter enjoyed the fries more than her vegetables, as did mine. We made the kind of small talk expected under such circumstances. We commented on the dishes before us, the warm weather we didn't mind and the love we shared for Israel, the country for which my heart still yearned, despite the U.S. citizenship I had now held for years. The truly personal questions would have to wait for another time, another visit.

Later, during the brief car ride to the same home in which Eman had lived since my last visit to her village in Northern Israel, Arab music blared from the radio as she pulled over to point out various landmarks while I snapped photos to help me remember until my return. As her car climbed the last slope before her house, I saw the rebuilt medical facility where my mother had worked as a nurse in the 1970s, and where I had occasionally accompanied her like any child going to work with a parent. It was here that I had first met Eman, whose mother had been responsible for keeping the nurses' station clean and making strong sweet tea she offered in amber-colored glasses.

Now seventy-six, Eman's mother greeted me with a kiss on each cheek, inviting me back into the home where I had come to play as a child, where I sat on pillows around a low table and ate homemade pita bread warm from the oven. Despite the joy we shared in each other's company and the disregard for whatever made us different, those childhood visits came to an abrupt end when, in 1976, Arab residents burned down the medical facility where my mother was employed. Israeli nurses who had tended to the children of those very same protesters were trapped under a table inside the burning building. My mother was not at work that day, nor did she return once calm was restored. It was the last time I saw Eman for decades.

Yet despite distance, strife, and the passage of thirty-five years, I could not forget the little girl who had been as welcome in my home as I had been in hers. I recalled the wonder in her eyes as she gazed at the Mediterranean for the first time during a visit to my home. She had been equally delighted with the bubble bath my mother had drawn for her later that afternoon. We fell asleep that night, sunburned skin against cool sheets, giggling together despite Eman's limited Hebrew and my complete lack of Arabic. We did not need words to convey how happy we were to be together, oblivious as only children can be to the world in which we lived and the wars that had kept our people apart. When my mother returned her to her village the following day, Eman raged, demanding that her own mother provide what she had not known she lacked until my mother showed her what lay beyond the only world she had ever seen.

I had no idea whether our friendship had left as lasting an impression on Eman as it had on me, but finally, I set out to find her even though all I had was her first name and a description of where her house had stood in comparison to the nurses' station. With the help of Google I came across an Arab artist who lives in the same village (now a city) as Eman and who took the time to help a stranger with a mission to find a childhood friend. When after weeks of searching he found her, he didn't have to explain much before she knew he was talking about me. And when I called the number he provided, all I said was hello, and Eman knew the voice on the other end of the line was her old friend.

And here I was again, sitting in Eman's living room enjoying coffee prepared in the *finjan*, a small pot similar to the one in which I too make the aromatic drink for special guests. We exchanged gifts prepared for the occasion, Eman laughing at the Barbie I had brought across the world to replace the one I had given her when we were ten. On the phone before my family and I headed to Israel, Eman had complained that she had yet to forgive her mother for giving the doll away years ago. When it was time to leave we snapped several photos and promised to write before my family and I made our way back down the hill, leaving one of the many Arab cities nestled in Israel's Galilee.

So where do our loyalties lie? I am an Israeli-American, a former member of the Israeli Defense Force and as anxious about the fate of my native country as I was when I lived there. Eman is a Muslim woman living in Israel, a woman whose neighbors were among those who had torched the nurses' station yelling "Death to Jews" on that sad day in 1976. But, as Eman emphasized during our first phone call, we are both children of Israel, and I know in my heart that it's not so easy to hate someone with whom you've giggled in front of a bathroom mirror. We are unlikely sisters.

* * * * *

Karen Levy is an Israeli-American writer. She spent her childhood traveling between her native land and the United States. Following her military service, Levy earned a BA in comparative literature from UC Davis, and an MA in English/creative writing from California State University Sacramento. Her work focuses on themes of divided loyalty and the search for home. Her memoir, My Father's Gardens *(Homebound Publications 2013) is nominated for the 2014 Pushcart Prize.*

The Truth of It

Dipika Kohli

Seattle lay at the tip of a long diagonal from my parents' state, which is all the way on the East Coast in North Carolina. I'd needed to put distance between my family and me. Jealous of friends whose parents came to visit—taking them out for posh meals in Belltown, sharing and connecting—I saw that being Punjabi-American meant being mostly quiet about the things that really mattered. Which is why it was so hard to deal with, when the thing that happened did.

In Seattle, I was looking for real connection, perhaps something to make up for a sister I didn't have with whom I could confide, a sister I could comfort, and be comforted by. I'd imagined that my little brother could do that, since we had the same experiences together in our early years. But, of course, he's a guy.

In the gleaming city in the Northwest, there seemed to be plenty of chances to meet people, especially smart women. I got it into my head that I could invent some composite of personalities who might "be there" for me—in a way that my brother couldn't—when things got hard, or lonely, or too quiet and gray. Could I make friends with lots of women, and somehow, in so doing, manage to create a feeling, at least, of having someone close by who was female and kind of knew me?

As we age, we see it more clearly: people have their own stuff going on, all the time. So it wasn't personal, when no one seemed to care too much about how it had felt to lose my baby-in-the-making. First pregnancy. A puncturing diagnosis. A heartwrenching, gut-choking choice.

"It's like carpooling," said one friend, a photographer with an artist's eye. "You know people for as long as they're traveling the same vector with you, but when your paths veer, that's it. You say goodbye. Maybe you'll see them again, maybe you won't." Driving up I-5 from Portland, she at the wheel and me riding shotgun, we kept our gazes forward-facing, through a giant windshield, rain patters just starting. We were quiet for a long time. I didn't know she would be one of those who'd fade into the background, like we missed the connection to a new road and a farther-on exit, when I'd tell her through trembling quivers that I'd lost my pregnancy, after all. *It's like carpooling. Maybe you'll see them again, maybe you won't.*

Getting pregnant the summer of 2005 was supposed to be a highlight, wasn't it? But that thing happened. The diverging, and pulling away. "I'm kind of busy this week," came the responses to invites for coffee or lunch. Old girlfriends didn't want to hear how I was so tired all the time, or felt like having to pee, or what a flutter in the abdomen, just there, just new, could trigger in the heart. Pregnancy and the newborn became topics relegated to Internet forums, where we all participated knowing how contrived it was, what with oversaturated JPEGs and impossibly smart captions.

Having just turned thirty-one, I was thinking that this was it, the next phase, the thing to talk to about with girlfriends I'd been getting to know over nights out, what with listening to their stories about dating, about teenage crushes, about the books we liked, and the places we were discovering. Wasn't this the most fantastic place of all, the one that we'd most want to share in? But, no. It was, "Oh, congratulations, but I've got other plans." Had I been wrong about the sense of connectedness with these women, also my age, also in the city, seeking and searching? A twinge of failure hit me, there.

Then, I got the diagnosis.

My baby had a defect.

A stubborn, extra chromosome. Down Syndrome.

*   *   *   *   *

My mother, a woman I don't talk to, had told my relatives not to call me, because I was "depressed." People who did reach out said, "Just try again." They didn't know the whole story. Which is exactly why I was so relieved to find I did, in fact, have one true friend. Paige, a medical doctor, sensed it. She brought a single-stem, white flower over to my apartment one afternoon, minutes after I'd picked up her call and said, "Will you come over?" We often went for spontaneous walks around the neighborhood, but that day, we stayed put.

I buzzed her up and opened the door. Her eyes looked to me as though they already knew, even as she extended the offering. "You just sounded so sad on the phone." We stood in the doorway and I blurted the whole thing—feelings of already pulling away from the little being in my abdomen, but wanting to cling to her, too—collapsing, holding my belly, feeling the little scoot of the newly forming bones. Five months along. Paige knew what that looked like, as in scientifically, and told me, straight up. She held my wrists the way she'd held the stem and let me speak. She was there, to hear me, when the deep fright, loneliness, and the biggest ache my heart has ever known swallowed me whole in overwhelm.

Even though Paige is in another state now, and I'm in Asia, and we don't talk or message each other, I'm still very grateful to her. She was there for me, in a way no one could dare to be, right then. At that darkening-sky moment in our shared carpool of life, she was summer light. I'll never forget how much that mattered, how much strength she imparted to me to trust myself to do the thing I didn't *want* to do, but knew I would. I learned just how vulnerable a doctor could be when she wasn't in a pressed white coat in a hospital, wasn't on stage, wasn't even trying to be, but was totally honest and open. For all my life I will remember the shape, color and scent of that very essence of how it felt just then to have, for an afternoon's instant, one very real, very true friend.

* * * * *

Dipika Kohli is the author of The Dive, *a true story about fetal loss and its multiplicity of complications. Find Dipika at @dipikakohli or at Kismuth Books.*

She Proves It

Olivia Boler

Second grade, John Hancock Grammar School
San Francisco North Beach, 1978
I'm the new kid in a Cantonese/English bilingual class
Half-and-half in a sea of Asian faces
Wondering where I fit

Dodge ball at recess, two days in
A girl bounces on her toes beside me
As we gleefully avoid the pelting red rubber
What's your name? I'm Susan. Do you want to be my friend?
So it begins, and that is that

Inseparable are we. Obnoxious even.
An exclusive club for two
I convince her we can share our lunches
Sip from the same straw
Despite what her mother says about germs
Because we are like sisters

We certainly fight like sisters
You don't know what you've done!
I'll never speak to you again!
Oh, the drama
But the next day, all is forgotten
Maybe even forgiven

We are inseparable, unless Mrs. Yim
Separates us for talking/arguing too much
Rarely happens

We are the good girls. Susan,
The smartest in our class
I make "tremendous strides" in
Math, excel in reading and writing

Third grade comes and everything changes
I'm swept away, transferred to

A magnet school across the City
80-minute ride roundtrip on the
Yellow bus, a crucible of childish mayhem
Every day, long and lonely

The new kid again, mixing in a sea of rainbow faces but
The girls who dazzle me hold their friendship out like a carrot
Toy with my mind, my heart
We like you, we just don't want to play with you
Your breath smells
Your shoes are ugly
You like Michael Jackson? Gross.
We listen to Rush.
You're teacher's pet
Go away
Why don't you just die?

Susan is sanctuary
We meet at the Rec Center on weekends
Swim like mermaids and devour chow mein
Sleepovers at my roomy apartment

At hers, I'm welcome
To watch TV and play in the living room or
On the bunk beds she shares with her little brother
In the bedroom they share with their parents
Divided by a curtain

Her mother, a Chinatown seamstress,
Sews me a set of Chinese jacks
Made of cloth scraps stuffed with
Uncooked rice

Susan, my sister from another mister
She proves those mean girls wrong
She proves that I am worthy
Worthy of love
Worthy of friendship
She proves it
Even if I don't always believe it

Years pass, our friendship holds
Through it all: middle and high schools,
Grad school and med school, jobs and relationships
Marriage and children and cross-country moves

Susan wonders, *When I first spoke to you, was it*
In Cantonese or English?

* * * * *

Olivia Boler is the author of two novels, Year of the Smoke Girl *and* The Flower
Bowl Spell. *She earned a master's degree in creative writing from UC Davis. Her
stories have appeared in the Asian American Women Artists Association anthol-
ogy* Cheers to Muses, *the literary journals* MARY *and* The Lyon Review, *among
others. She lives in San Francisco with her family. To find out about her latest
work, visit http://oliviaboler.com.*

Set Two

. . . .

Sister Act – memoir, Vicki Batman

Echoes From the Heart – memoir, Mary J. Kohut

Sister, I Needed You – poem, Nancy Pogue LaTurner

Loons – short story, C. R. Resetarits

We Have Today – memoir, Paige Strickland

The Twins' Little Kingdom – poem, Nardia Kelly

Mud Pies and Escargot – memoir,
Sara Catalina Dorame Bard

One Sixth – poem, Nancy Cook

Greyhound Station – memoir, Olivia Boler

Light – poem, Lindsay Ahl

The Ceremony—December 1980 – memoir, Skye Blaine

Never My Sister – poem, Erica Lann-Clark

Sister Act

Vicki Batman

Every Christmas Eve, my family drove to Grandmother's house for the yearly celebration. No ifs, ands, or buts. The entire clan made the journey. I never minded. For me, this event truly launched the gift-giving season. And being like every other small child enraptured with receiving presents, I eagerly anticipated the occasion.

Laughter and love filled Grandmother's red brick home as did good cooking, like smoked turkey and fixings. Desserts, too numerous to count, included her special tomato cake and mincemeat pie. Every baby was handed around the room until cranky and screaming for mom. Aunts and uncles found moments to see how school fared with nieces and nephews. My cousins, sisters, and I gathered in our own spot for "killer" Uno. All had a grand time.

After dinner cleanup, presents were passed around. The bows were removed and the paper ripped as we tore into the gifts. Grandmother received the most; some of which were interesting—a silly knickknack for her book shelves, knee-hi nylons, a serviceable sweater, yarn for knitting, kitchen tools, denture products, a school craft project.

Afterward, the relatives would visit a bit longer. Then, my family would load up in "Big Blue," our Ford station wagon, and drive home to wait oh-so-anxiously for Christmas morning to arrive. And it did in a *big* way.

My love for the season grew while I grew. As my sisters and I sang along with the holiday hits playing on the turntable, which featured the well-loved classics of Bing Crosby, Frank Sinatra and, my all-time favorite, Nat King Cole, we wrapped presents for Mom, decorated the family tree with the handmade sequined ornaments, and baked sugar cookies. We helped Dad untangle miles of blue and green Christmas lights to hang on the house and set the six-foot cardboard Santa just so, next to the front door, which was adorned with a plastic wreath of fir, poinsettia, and a red, satiny bow.

Our family treasures decorated the living room. A glittery silver-and-red reindeer and Santa display went on top of the buffet. Four stuffed mice in candy cane-striped clothing sat on the piano. A music box from our long-time neighbor was placed on the coffee table. And for the finale, a Styrofoam angel topped the tip of the white-flocked tree. Nothing looked better.

Back then, our family had no cable network. In fact, it was unheard of. So we relied on mass-broadcast stations for our viewing pleasure. We popped bowls of popcorn and spread a generous supply of napkins in front of us each evening to watch television specials like *How the Grinch Stole Christmas, Merry Christmas, Charlie Brown,* and *Miracle on 34th Street.*

One program in particular captured our hearts, a musical about snow and love and doing something extra special for someone at Christmastime. The elaborate sets, costumes, and music by Irving Berlin thrilled us. We'd felt Christmas had truly arrived after viewing this extravaganza — *White Christmas.*

Around the time I'd turned fourteen, my parents splurged on a color television for the family room. The small, black-and-white set in their bedroom was transferred to my room with the admonition we could watch it only on special occasions. Since my sisters and I were major rule followers, the TV sat on Mom's closed sewing machine cabinet at the foot of my bed, rarely viewed.

That year, after our annual holiday visit to Grandmother's, we urged Dad to hurry through touring neighborhood light displays. We just had to get home quickly so we could watch our favorite movie. The minute the garage door opened, my three sisters and I hit the bathroom and raced through brushing our teeth. We slung on our new Christmas nightgowns and piled on my bed in front of the tiny television. Right after the news ended, the movie came on—yipee!— and we were instantly entranced. We bounced, danced, and sang our way through the show. However, one song in particular stayed with us—*Sisters*—especially because we were four sisters. That song became our song.

The actresses looked gorgeous. They wore sparkly dresses with full skirts fluffed out by net petticoats. Tight bodices curved their figures into doll-like forms. Impossible high heels shod their feet. They waltzed around with enormous dyed-to-match feathered fans and danced steps we felt for certain a body couldn't do.

Their song spoke about the tight relationship sisters had. How devoted they were to one another. How they cared for each other, sharing things like clothing. No one could split them up, not even a guy, which seemed funny to me. Even though my sissies were awesome, we wanted to be, and to have, a sister like the movie portrayed.

The following year, we brought my eighty-something grandmother home on Christmas Eve to spend Christmas day with my family. We thought it great fun when she'd pulled her little five-foot body onto my bed to watch the movie, too. But sleep got the better of her and we snickered at her snoring. We sang "our song" quietly, and occasionally, smothered our giggles so not to wake her.

As I sat on my double bed with my grandmother and sisters, I took in the scene. For at that moment, an incredible thought smacked my head — my holidays were perfect. Life was perfect. I had everything.

As only time could do, it tick-tocked by. Sisters went away to college or moved elsewhere to work. Grandmother passed to the great reward and the cousins scattered, celebrating the holidays with their expanding families. Nevertheless, a tradition had been firmly rooted in my parents' home. To celebrate, we came from our respective lives and gathered at their house to watch our movie on Christmas Eve.

One day, I married my handsome husband, and eventually gave birth to two boys. Technology had evolved and *White Christmas* was converted to VHS, and then DVD. No longer did I have to wait for Christmas Eve to watch my favorite holiday film. I could watch it any time I desired.

But I didn't. It wouldn't have been the same.

Neither did my sisters. We saved it for Christmas Eve.

To this day, I plop my family on the couch with treats and drinks, and we turn on *White Christmas*. I sing all the tunes. When the signature song ends, contentment swells inside me. I fight back tears. My holidays are perfect. Life is perfect. I have everything.

Funny, my men refuse to sing with me. Maybe some things are best shared with sisters.

* * * * *

Like some of her characters, award-winning author Vicki Batman has worked a variety of jobs including lifeguard, amusement park ride attendant; hardware store, department store, book store, antique store clerk; administrative assistant in an international real estate firm; and a general "do anything gal" at a wealth management firm—the list is endless. She has completed four manuscripts, written essays, and sold short fiction to the True *magazines, Noble Romance Publishing,* Long and Short Reviews, *MuseItUp Publishing, and The Wild Rose Press.*

Echoes From the Heart

Mary J. Kohut

My first recollection of life was in the Tennessee Children's Home in Nashville. I remember my little sister, but the home wouldn't admit she was my sister; they said she was just a little girl I became attached to. I must have been two-and-a-half or three years old at this time.

I recall the day my sister left the home, and remember crying and running after the car that took her away. I also remember missing her very much. I would save one of my cookies from each meal for her. I kept them in my locker. One day, the lady who took her away brought her back to visit me. I excused myself, ran upstairs to my locker for the cookies, and gave them to my sister. I cried again when she left.

Shortly after this, a lady and man came to the home and wanted to adopt me. They were allowed to take me for a one-day trial. They took me for a ride and treated me to a big ice cream cone. They hugged me a lot. I felt good about them. Soon they returned and took me home with them. They lived on a farm in Blunt Springs outside of Birmingham, Alabama. I was happy with them. The lady—I called her Mom Susie—took me to town and bought me my very first pair of patent leather shoes. You know, the kind with straps that had to be buttoned with a hook. I loved those shoes so much. I would wipe them off every night and sleep with them.

I got where I could talk with Mom Susie a lot. I told her about my little sister and how much I missed her. She promised she would try to get me another sister soon. This made me very happy. The man—I called him Uncle Lewis—wasn't home much. He traveled a lot for work. They weren't married, but I didn't know that then. He was good to Mom Susie, and he always brought me a little gift whenever he came home from one of his trips.

Finally, the day came for us to see about getting me a sister. Back to Nashville Mom Susie and I went. Uncle Lewis didn't come along. We stayed in Nashville with Mom Susie's brother, his wife, and their two children, Sam Jr. and Mary Lou. I really liked Uncle Sam and Aunt Myrtle, and Junior and Mary Lou. Uncle Sam would take us fishing. Many weekends we spent the night in a tent, and we would wake up to fresh fish and corn bread cooking over an outside fire. When I think of childhood fun times, it has to be when I stayed with Uncle Sam and his family. It seemed like we stayed a very long time with them, but I didn't mind. The day finally came when Mom Susie said she had found a sister for me at St. Mary's Orphanage. I didn't sleep a wink that night.

I was up bright and early with anticipation. After breakfast, Mom Susie and I were on our way to St. Mary's. I had expected to see a younger child, but Margaret was about my size and age. We were left alone to play and get acquainted while Mom Susie and Mother Superior talked in another room. After a while, Mom Susie and I returned to Uncle Sam's. She said she had to promise to bring up Margaret and me as Catholics, and after I got baptized, we could have Margaret on a trial basis. I was soon baptized. Mom Susie had started calling me Jeanette from the day she took me from the home, so she had me baptized Mary Jeanette Ballentine. (I was born Alberta Wanda Riggs.) Shortly after my baptism, we took Margaret back to Blunt Springs. Needless to say, I was happy. Margaret and I became good friends and playmates.

I don't know whatever happened to Uncle Lewis, but I can't remember seeing him again. I do know Mom Susie changed. She became anxious and worried about not having enough food and money to keep up the farm. It was hard for her to keep good hired hands, too. I was often hungry.

Mom Susie would sometimes lock Margaret and me in the closet when she went shopping. One day, she left us in a bus station. We were there all day. Evening came, and we told the guard what had happened, and a lady from Welfare came and took us overnight. The next day Mom Susie came to get us.

One day, she pushed me out of the passenger side of the car on a highway. The scar over my right eye is from that incident. I believe now she wanted to kill me for insurance money.

Another day, I can't remember why, she became angry with Margaret and picked up a lard can and hit Margaret on the head. All I could see was blood all over Margaret. I tried to make her stop hitting Margaret, and she turned on me, hitting me. My forehead and leg began bleeding profusely. Later, she knew Margaret needed a doctor, so she drove us to a hospital in Birmingham. She told the doctor a cookie jar had fallen on Margaret's head when she was trying to get a cookie, and several pieces of the pottery had struck me and cut me, too.

The next morning, the county sheriff came to our house and took Margaret and me away. We both spent a couple of days in another hospital, and later stayed with a lady from the Child's Welfare Department. It seemed like a long time before there was some sort of court date, and Margaret and I were separated after that.

I wasn't told where Margaret went, but I went to a Catholic orphanage outside of Birmingham. I later learned that Margaret went back to St. Mary's in Nashville. I also learned the authorities from the State of Tennessee had been looking for us. Mom Susie wasn't supposed to have left Tennessee with us, and never did officially adopt either of us.

Somehow, Mom Susie found out where I was and tried to get me back. She would visit me, but I was never left alone with her. I remained at the Birmingham orphanage from fourth through seventh grades. During the first half of eighth grade, right after Thanksgiving and without any warning, Mrs. Elrod from the Tennessee Children's Home came in the middle of the night and took me back to Nashville, where I was left at St. Mary's Orphanage.

I was sad to leave my friends in Birmingham, but eager to see if Margaret was still at St. Mary's. After asking around and talking with Mother Superior, I learned Margaret was no longer there, but I wasn't told where she had gone. When I think about my early childhood, it seems I would just begin to know the other children when I would be moved to another home. Some of the children at St. Mary's had been together for a long time. I longed for the relationships they had and wanted most of all to have a "best friend."

I graduated from eighth grade at St. Mary's, and good students were able to attend St. Cecilia's Academy in Nashville. We would stay at St. Cecilia's during the week, but had to return to St. Mary's for the weekend. The other St. Mary's graduates were sent to St. Louis, Missouri, to a vocational school. I had a feeling that's where Margaret might have gone. I wrote to her there, but never received an answer.

Anyway, I really liked the academy. I met some fine girls and had fun, too. I helped in the lunchroom and helped clean classrooms and the gym, but had plenty of time for recreation. On weekends, we would help in the kitchen and watch and play games with the younger children. During the summer months, we helped with the activities at the Girls' Summer Camp. I enjoyed that. We were like "big sisters" there.

Then, just like before, halfway through my sophomore year at the academy, Mrs. Elrod came in the night and took me away. I stayed one night in the Tennessee Children's Home, but after breakfast, we left by train for Chicago, Illinois. The date was December 7, 1941. I heard over the radio that President Roosevelt declared war with Japan! I left only with the clothes I wore, leaving many treasured pictures and mementos behind.

At St. Ann's on the north side of Chicago, I remained a ward of the State of Tennessee until I was eighteen years old. St. Ann's received some board money from Tennessee for me. St. Ann's was a novitiate, where young girls could study to become nuns. It had high concrete walls and was secured with a police guard. Since I'd left everything, including my address book, back in Nashville, I lost all contact with my friends there. I did write to Mrs. Elrod from time to time, and she would write me back, which surprised me. I didn't want to lose contact with her; after all, she was the only one left of my past. In time, she was to tell me about my little sister.

I wasn't quite eighteen when I graduated, and we had to be eighteen before we could get a job, because we couldn't get a Social Security card back in those days before we turned eighteen, and we needed that card to become employed. Since I didn't stay on to become a nun, Mother Superior placed me with a family to be a nurse for their little girl. I received room and board, and I believe, $10 a week for spending. Mrs. Elrod sent me a complete outfit as a graduation gift, too: a pretty two-piece, green-and-white check outfit, slip, stockings, my first pair of dress shoes, and a purse with $100 in it. I couldn't get over that. That $100 started my first savings account.

The family was so sweet to me. Both parents worked, and their little girl was just as cute as could be. We got along just great. When I turned eighteen, they started me with my first life insurance policy and paid on it until I left them for an office job about six months later. I lived for a while at the YMCA near where I worked in downtown Chicago.

I got a job at the Burlington Railroad office as a typist-clerk. There, I met Ellen, who lived in Downers Grove, Illinois. She and I became great friends. We found out that Western Electric in Cicero was doing defense work during World War II and was hiring, so we both went there and got better paying jobs. Ellen wanted factory work, and I got a typist job, where I used my first electric typewriter. They were so large and heavy back in those days. Later, I transferred to a stenographer's job. More pay and more work, too! But I liked it and stayed there until I got married and was expecting my first baby.

When I started "showing" at about three-and-a-half months, I told my boss and prepared to leave Western Electric. There was no such thing as maternity leave or benefits back then. While I had a little time on my hands, I decided to write Mrs. Elrod to let her know how I was doing, etc., and asked her to please tell me the truth about "that little girl" at the Tennessee Children's Home. The answer I received (and I still have that letter) stated that "that little girl" was indeed my sister! Well, I was so taken with this truth, I couldn't hold back the tears of joy. I had to tell my husband, Joe, all about it, and we talked about maybe going down to Tennessee to see if we could find my family. But first I had to have my baby and save some money for the trip.

Our Kenny was born on January 4, 1948. A tiny little lad. I was so proud of him. Finally, I had something I could really call "my own." When Joe had his vacation that summer, we decided to venture out to see if we could locate some or all of my family.

When we arrived in Nashville, we decided to begin our search at the courthouse. The lady there listened, with interest, as I told her about our plan to locate my family. I noticed she was looking at me with great interest as I spoke. She asked me if I knew whether we were at the Tennessee Children's Home in Nashville as young children. I answered yes. She said I looked like someone she knows, and she may know my sister and the person who adopted her. I was speechless. She excused herself and went to check her records. She was excited on her return and said, "Yes, I do know your sister!" She then phoned the lady she knew as my sister's adopted aunt.

Aunt "T," as she was called, was excited to hear I had finally called. "Hurry on out. I'll prepare Bobbie for your visit," she said. By this time tears were rolling down my cheeks and the lady at the courthouse had moist eyes, too, as she wrote down the directions to Aunt T's. Aunt T and my sister were sitting outside on the porch as we drove up. When I got out of the car, my sister ran toward me. Needless to say, our embrace was tearful and lengthy. We hugged and kissed and hugged some more. I introduced Joe and Kenny. Aunt T immediately took Kenny, warmed his bottle, changed his diaper, and laid him in a crib in a nearby room, where he fell fast asleep.

As we talked, I learned that Bobbie's adopted mother had died. Her adopted dad didn't want to care for her, so Aunt T and Uncle Jake raised Bobbie along with their daughter. It was Aunt T, along with Bobbie's adopted mother, who had brought Bobbie to the home to see me. Aunt T also said she and Uncle Jake had decided to adopt me after that visit, but when she returned to the home, she was told I was no longer there. I've often wondered how different my life would have been if that adoption had taken place, but mostly I am happy to give thanks to the dear Lord for reuniting my sister and me once again.

• • • • •

Mary J. Kohut's Echoes From the Heart *is adapted from a memoir Mary gave to her children before her death at the age of 73 in 1999. After growing up as an orphan, and then locating her sister Bobbie, Mary learned that her mother had been married twice. In addition to having three full siblings, Mary had several half siblings, most of whom she was able to meet as an adult. A proud wife and homemaker, Mary had six children, twelve grandchildren and five great grandchildren.*

Sister, I Needed You

Nancy Pogue LaTurner

In childhood

To come to my bedroom
where I lay, spread-eagled
in a fit of pique
over yet another clash with Mother.
You would hover upside down,
crazy-faced,
until I broke
from pout to smile, giggle, laugh.

In teen times

When my cuteness fled,
displaced by gargoyle gawky,
you could show me
confidence and
how to fluff limp hair,
gloss chapped lips and
teach me to walk with a sky string
to hold my head up high.

Far away

On another continent, lonely,
I longed for your cheery letters,
twenty years worth, until, at last,
I returned to make my home
with your thoughtful advice
about shelf paper,
Roman shades, and
color schemes.

In later years

As my hair turned white,
gravity tugging on wrinkles
and sags, vague pains in odd places,

you would take my sleepless midnight calls,
rub my shoulders,
brew some tea
when all else failed,
be there at the end.

I needed you, dear Sister, all my life —
but you're my invention;
how I wish you'd been born.

* * * * *

Nancy Pogue LaTurner cherishes life-long membership in the sisterhood of writers. Her stories and essays have been published in The Albuquerque Almanac *as well as in several anthologies*—Wisdom Has a Voice, Writers' Shack Anthology, *and all four volumes of* Seasons of Our Lives. *She is also the author of* Voluntary Nomads: A Mother's Memories of Foreign Service Family Life. *Besides writing, Nancy loves hiking in the mountains and kayaking in calm waters.*

Loons

C. R. Resetarits

"Hear?"

Addie throws the question over her shoulder. Gertrude stands ready with a basket for gathering berries.

"No," Gertrude replies.

"*Chanson des voyageurs.* Song of souls sold for passage back to France. Some nights, you see them in their glowing *chasse-galeries*—flying canoes, falling through the sky back to earth."

"I like old stories."

"Old? Phooey. Way of the north woods."

"Have you more ... ways?"

"*Non.* Indians do, of course. Never point at a shooting star, they say, because if you ever hide, another shooting star will point at you in turn and give you away."

"Ah."

"Phooey. A Frenchman need never hide. Point away. And then make the sign of the cross. *Mon Dieu! ...* What is that?" Addie points to a man crawling at the edge of the woods.

"Your brother, Michel. He's become an accomplished botanist."

"Ah, *bon.* I feared a *loup-garou*, a wolf-man. They try to befriend lone travellers. *Tres mal.*"

Gertrude nods. "I wish we could stay longer."

"But, soon. When you and Michel come to settle with the baby. ... Of course, you'll get married with your people."

"What?"

"Oh, he told us all last night, after you turned green and we sent you to bed. ... Ah, but child, why cry now? The milk is spilt."

Gertrude collapses among the herbs and strawberries, like an unstrung marionette. Addie sits silently next to the sobbing girl and takes her hand. "But it's all settled now. *Mais, c'est la vie.*"

Overhead, loons call.

"But of course you know about loons?" Addie points skyward.

Gertrude looks up, lips trembling.

"Only if you're caught crying when loons call, it's a sign of good fortune. Propitious."

Gertrude laughs and buries her face in the folds of Addie's skirts.

* * * * *

C. R. Resetarits has had short fiction published recently in New York (Transportation), NANO, *and* Post Road. *New short-shorts will be out soon in* Vagabonds: Anthology of the Mad Ones 3, No. 1 (*Weasel Press, 2014) and* The Newer York Book IV. *Her essay on Hawthorne, gender, and genre appeared in* Literary Imagination, *and her poetry collection* Brood *will be available this winter from Mongrel Empire Press.*

We Have Today

Paige Strickland

"Paige, this is Tammy." I'd waited twenty-six years to hear those words. After searching for ten months, I finally found my birth mother's oldest daughter, and now I had something I'd wished for all my life: Sisters! I found an older sister and a younger sister. My older sister was Tammy, and we connected first.

I grew up as an adoptee in a small family. I had one brother who was six years younger, and no cousins my age. It seemed every girlfriend I had had a sister or two, and I always admired how my friends and their sisters looked so much alike, traded clothes, and shared girl-talk. My brother was a great guy, but our relationship could never be like that.

The night that long-anticipated phone call came, I was both prepared and not. Once I'd learned that I had a birth family, and they could be found, I set out on a mission to unearth every detail I could that might lead me to blood relatives. I became passionately driven to get at the truth of that other dimension of my life, and my sisters were out there someplace. I hoped like mad they were as curious and open to me as I was about finding them.

The search for my birth sisters took me all over the town where we were born. Like an old-time detective, I tracked my birth-people through old phone books and criss-cross directories in libraries, and via microfiche records in courthouses, person by person. This was before the Internet and all the social media sites we have today. I was equally driven to seek out my birth father's family, but for the time being, all signs pointed toward my birth mother's people.

At the end of my search, I'd sent a letter to a man in California I believed to be a former husband of my birth mother. (She was no longer living.) He was the only person on earth who would know about her kids. I'd given him all of my contact information, and waited.

When that call came, a glass-block wall opened up. I knew something/someone was on the other side, but I hadn't been able to see or hear anything of substance before that night. Tammy and I talked for three hours and shared our life stories about family, kids, states we'd lived in, schools we attended, dogs and cats, TV, books, everything. Tammy put me in contact with our other sister, Kelli, and we exchanged photos. Our eyes matched. We'd all grown up differently, but our eyes made us part of one another.

Later, I made contact with my birth father's daughters. More sisters! I have five half-sisters in all, but we don't think about the "half" part so much. When we first met in person we caught each other staring at the other's hair, profile and hands. We glanced back and forth at our children's similarities, the freckles, noses, ears and cheeks.

I did not grow up with my sisters. We didn't get to fight over nail polish, Barbies, or who took someone's favorite shirt. We weren't able to debate over who was hotter: David Cassidy or Donny Osmond. We didn't have teachers who fondly remembered one sibling and had too high of expectations for the other. We did not share a mother or grandmother who might look at one girl and accidently call her by the other's name. We've known one another for decades now, but still cannot dash into the Hallmark store and buy a mushy birthday card reflecting on growing up together.

That's OK, though. We have today, and even if we live far apart, or our work and kids' schedules steal our time, we do have each other. Our kids have cousins. We don't blame anyone for a past we'll never share. We embrace the present and treasure our chances to cheer at kids' games and graduations, dance at weddings, rejoice at births, mourn when we need to mourn, work when we need to work, and laugh every chance we get.

. . . . .

Paige Adams Strickland, a teacher and writer from Cincinnati, Ohio, is married with two daughters. Her first book, Akin to the Truth: A Memoir of Adoption and Identity, *is about growing up in the 1960s through 1980s (Baby-Scoop Era) and searching for her first identity. It is also the story of her adoptive family and, in particular, her father's struggles to figure out his place in the world while Paige strives to find hers. After hours, she enjoys family and friends, pets, reading, Zumba fitness, gardening, and baseball.*

The Twins' Little Kingdom

Nardia Kelly

A kookaburra's laugh patters the periwinkle
sky like rain (though no cloud darkens the
brow of the horizon) and he is startled
from his self-appointed post at the top of the looming

gum, a bone white tower overlooking
the small, valley kingdom. Streaming from the top
of the tiny fold in the hill come the two girls, their hair
in waves like flags carried by noble messengers—

they giggle at the indignant squawks of the sentries as if
some joke has been shared. Other voices waft down
but forget their way among the trees. A pledge is made
to the velvet beds of clover and the court of magpies and

mudlarks; to live in glamour, just like the spring day,
bright and chuckling like the clear creek. They leap
above it, swinging limbs in a dance that echoes the flight
of the visiting lorikeets, while the ground soaks up warmth

from a blanket of patchwork light. The ebbing, clear water
slides over moss-green rock silkily, and toes splashing
in the creek bed knock each other as fingers pluck teasingly
at the grass, and secrets bubble between them and breeze

away—the afternoon is lazy and content with this. Leaves float
on the trickling current that they whisper to. The mynas swoop
down and observe their rituals of friendship, and the girls swoop up
and whoop with mischief together. The pair thread daisies

through their hair, and weave through saplings, following the lines
of a story in which they play as the heroes together. This
is their private world, in the charm of the eucalyptus air,
their memories shared secretly with the thick, sticky trees,

whose rough skin guards the dreams of life in trials of smoke.
Their loyalty remains mirrored in water, rippling from the touch
of the smallest insect's twiggy limbs, reflecting the clear
sky and each other's smiles and the shriek of cockatoos.

* * * * *

Nardia Kelly grew up in a shire in Victoria, Australia, creating stories with her twin sister and pretending their acre-wide property was a few hundred miles wide instead. This is her first publication, besides winning a poetry competition in 2004. She's currently working toward a bachelor of design degree, learning to write for interactive media, and can be contacted on Twitter at @indigodecay.

Mud Pies and Escargot

Sara Catalina Dorame Bard

Unbelievable! I was at the prime of my life, six years old, and I was dying. This was it. I careened through the house, banging and crashing along. Tears sketched jagged lines down my muddied face as I made my way to the kitchen. My mom turned toward the commotion. She stared at me, suspicion clouding her eyes.

"What's all this about Sara? What have you done now?" she asked, reaching out to me.

I shook my head and answered in a muffled voice, "Mmph wahmnt mme," which translated to: "It wasn't me."

"What in the world is in your mouth?" She leaned close to inspect.

I flailed my arms and attempted to yell out, "Mmphails!" which translated to: "Snails!"

I started to wail. Snot and tears covered my face as snail froth bubbled out of my mouth and nose. I let loose a rabid foam-filled gurgle. The snails were straining in between my tongue and teeth, pulsing against the back of my throat, writhing around, trying to find an escape and desperately emitting froth with every passing second.

My mom winced and recoiled slightly as my sister ran up behind me. I stiffened. I could feel her hot breath on my neck. Only moments before I had broken away from her evil grasp. She must have known she'd be busted now. It was only a matter of time. After the evacuation of the snails, she'd get hers.

"Sonia, what's going on? What's in Sara's mouth?"

We both turned to look at my sister; Mom with her curious eyes and me with my blowfish mouth. This was her chance to come clean.

"I don't know," Sonia said, widening her chocolate-colored eyes.

"I think she's trying to tell me she has snails in her mouth." My mom motioned to me.

I nodded my head and prayed the snails wouldn't tumble down my throat.

"I wouldn't know." Sonia answered calmly.

"Mmeyerrrr!" which translated to: "Liar!"

"Well, I'll be a dirty bird! Why in the world would you put snails in your mouth?" My mom looked slightly exasperated with me even though I was the one with the mouthful of snails.

"Because she's crazy, Mom," Sonia said.

I groaned and rolled my eyes. Oh, I'd show her crazy.

"Sara thought it'd be funny and put a bunch of snails in her mouth," Sonia told my mom without batting an eyelash.

"Hmmmm." Mom leaned toward me. I could see in her eyes she knew my sister was full of it, but the truth would never be told if I ended up choking to death on a bunch of snails.

Through crossed eyes, I watched my mom as she poked her finger in between my puckered lips. She hooked her pointer around a snail and pulled it out of my mouth with a "come-hither" motion. It made a wet "pop" as it flew out. After a few minutes of poking, pulling and popping, every last mollusk was out of my mouth.

The three of us stared down at the mound of writhing and fizzing snails on the linoleum floor. Most were dead, chomped to their demise by me. Black guts torn loose from their army green bodies.

Mom was the first to move, crossing her arms over her chest. "Explain."

I ran my tongue over my teeth, feeling the grittiness of shells and tasting the remnants of tiny bodies. I wiped the drool and snail bubbles from my mouth and took a deep breath.

"Sonia opened a stupid restaurant," I began. Then I recounted what had ensued.

"Be my first customer," Sonia commanded proudly as she showed me her sign: SONIA'S RESTAURANT. It wasn't flashy, but sometimes the best eateries aren't.

Could be fun, I thought, and smiled at her as I reached for the menu.

I read her entrées aloud. "Salad Greens." I knew those would be the weeds I'd spied her yanking earlier. "Mud Pies" was obvious enough, but the last entrée I didn't recognize: "S-cargo?" None of the options sounded good to me, but since we were pretending, I figured anything I chose couldn't be that bad. Besides, wasn't I being the dutiful sister by supporting Sonia's new endeavor?

"I'll have the Salad Greens please."

"We're all out."

"Hmmm, okay then, I'll have the Mud Pie."

"We're all out of that too."

"Fine. Then I'll have the S-cargo. Whatever that is."

I should have sensed danger as a Cheshire-cat grin spread over my sister's face.

"Oh, good choice. You'll love it."

"I don't even know what it is." I laughed.

She sniggered and said, "Something really special." Then she turned on her heel to retrieve my meal.

She hurried back, carrying a bowl covered with a towel, to better hide the "big reveal" she told me. She stood beside me as she uncovered the bowl. The bowl was full of living snails. I swallowed. I was relieved this was just pretend and I didn't really have to eat a bowl of creepy-crawly snails. A lone snail had suctioned itself to the side of the bowl and was trying to inch away. I nudged it back, causing it to pull its antennas back into its tiny head.

"Ew, gross," I said as I wiped the slime on my pants. "No thanks. I think I'll eat somewhere else."

"Too late!" My sister sang out to me, "You ordered S-cargo so you're going to eat S-cargo." Suddenly, she yanked me to the ground in a sumo hold and sat on top of me, pinning my arms to my side with her legs.

I squirmed under her hold and screamed, "Sooooooonnnnnnniiiiiiiaaaaaaa get off of me!" I hoped our mom, or even some stranger off the street, would come to my rescue. "I don't want to play with you anymore!" I gritted my teeth as she loomed above me, holding the bowl of snails near my face.

"Eat one," she demanded.

"No!" I bit down on the inside of my lips to keep them closed tight.

"Just one, come on. I want to see it," she pleaded with me, then pinched my nose.

I held my breath for as long as I could. When I finally opened up to inhale a full mouth of air, she seized the opportunity to slip the snails from the bowl into my mouth. My cheeks pouched out as the snails fought to find room. I could taste the dirt from the garden and feel the ooze of the frantic snails sliding down my throat. I was afraid to spit them out in case I ended up swallowing them instead. I was sure they would live in my stomach forever.

Sonia giggled and continued to sit on me until I started frothing from my mouth. She stared at me like she thought I was going to die. I also thought I was going to die. Maybe she thought the snails had given me rabies. Whatever it was, something threw her off and I felt her knees loosen from my arms. I took my chance and heaved her body off of me with a strength that was new to me. She toppled backward as I jumped up. She cried out to me, but I was already off and running to the house to find Mom.

SONIA'S RESTAURANT would be closed for good. I'd not only see that she never worked in this town again, but I'd look forward to the moment when it would be my turn to "cook" for her.

• • • • •

Sara Catalina Dorame Bard works for an Internet startup in Berkeley, California. In her free time, she writes fiction and personal essays. This is her first personal essay to be published. After many years of intense therapy, Sara is finally able to enjoy leafy greens and escargot, though she still steers clear of mud pies. She lives with her husband and cat in Northern California.

One Sixth

Nancy Cook

I am one
of six. Sisters.
Nine years, two months between
oldest and youngest.

I am one
of six, fourth
from the top, third from the bottom,
oldest of the youngest —

that's how we
describe things.

We live two in
Cleveland, one in Arlington, one
in Cincinnati, one in Atlanta,

and one west
of the Mississippi.
We're orphans, our parents dead twenty-
eight and thirty-seven summers.

Every year
we congregate
in our hometown after Christmas.
We spend an afternoon

without children,
spouses banned, just
a few bottles of wine and everyone's
best baking. We laugh,

we tease,
we story tell, we
recollect our mutual past, the same,
but mostly different

in the ego-
centric plot
of memory. We never speak of
pay raises, promotions,

kids' grades,
trophies, jackpots, golf
handicaps, pounds lost – anything
that might suggest a betterness.

We laugh, we tease,
we downplay and self-
deprecate. But last year, someone
dared to ask whom

our parents
treasured most.
All agreed our mother had no
favorites and all agreed

our father did.
Six names mentioned.
And after much animated con-
versation, the consensus

was still too far away
to be discerned. We would not
be reconciled. So now it seems we
six are guaranteed

to never know
who won.

* * * * *

Nancy Cook and her five sisters grew up in Ohio. Nancy now lives in St. Paul. Her most recent work has appeared in Adventum, Eleventh Muse, Halcyon Magazine, *and* St Petersburg Review. *Among other thing, she runs the Witness Project, a series of community workshops that enable the development and dissemination of stories of, by, and for populations underserved by the justice system.*

Greyhound Station

Olivia Boler

A steady, chugging rumble fills the air, turning it slightly warmer and murkier. The Greyhound bus from Vacaville has arrived in the San Francisco terminal, and we are there to greet it, my parents and I. It pulls into its slanted, oversized parking spot as it does every other Friday evening when we come to greet my sisters.

The loud, honking gasp of the air brakes startles me, as always—you'd think I'd know better. Whatever fear I might feel is almost immediately pushed aside, though, by a new flavor of adrenaline—anticipation. We watch for them: two smiling girls, one blonde, slender, and tall; the other brunette, younger, with round apple cheeks, and rabbity teeth marked by a front-tooth gap I envy. Kathy and Sarah. Both have blue eyes like our dad's and their mom's. My own mother, my father's second wife, and I have brown eyes and black hair. These are the only obvious outward signs of my Chinese ancestry.

I pay little attention to the other travelers who make their way down the steps of the bus, just as soon as the driver pulls the lever, opening the door. I only have eyes for my sisters, ten and seven years older than I, and so amazing, so full of love and fun. I'm pretty sure they possess a magic that makes the world more beautiful and full. Whenever they're around, colors shine brighter, scents are sweeter, and food tastes more delicious.

Most of the time, I'm the sole occupant of one of the two bedrooms in our North Beach apartment. I slumber in my own unglamorous, non-canopied twin bed covered in a thin white-and-blue comforter (not my favorite colors; I prefer pink). I play alone with my collection of toys and board games. I read my books to myself or coerce one of my parents to read to me. Occasionally, my mother arranges for a friend to join me for what these days is labeled a "playdate," but in the 1970s and '80s is simply called "coming over to play."

Ostensibly, I'm an only child. Yet across the room, in the opposite corner, stands a set of bunk beds, the mattresses covered in matching brown- and yellow-striped chenille bedspreads. I sometimes pretend the bottom bunk is the interior of *I Dream of Jeannie*'s bottle, plumping it up with pillows and stuffed animals.

For two nights every other week, my sisters dive under the bunks' covers, Kathy on top, Sarah on the bottom. They whisper and sing and giggle in the dark, and I get to join in. We all fall asleep without my usual nightlight. Instead of fearing the gloom, I thrill in it, emboldened by their presence. They protect me from the Wild Things that haunt my bedroom windows when I dream. Their invisible shield covers every part of my being. I grow warm with a dizzying joy.

They are here!

My sisters tumble off the bus, launching themselves toward us. They love to hug and kiss. Touchy-feely. They embrace our father and my mother. Finally, it's my turn to get caught up in their arms and laughter. They carry small, soft-sided suitcases that zip up and have large flower patterns—blue and green on one, orange and yellow on the other. They talk and talk and talk—over each other, to my dad or mom or me, to strangers, to each other, finishing each other's sentences, breaking off now and then to argue some crucial point, whether it's what they ate for lunch or where they went the day before last, it doesn't matter. Their voices are music filling up the usual silences.

We walk through the Greyhound bus station, past the no-frills plastic seats in the terminal waiting areas and the large, molded contraptions bolted to the concrete floor that mimic living-room armchairs. Small black-and-white TV sets grow out of the arms, playing off-air snow. If you insert coins, you can watch a channel. We girls find these fascinating and sometimes—on Sunday afternoons when we do all of this in reverse—we sit in these chairs and watch the snow.

Sundays are always a small heartache, a rupture as my parents and I wave goodbye to my sisters, watching as they board the bus back to Vacaville and their mother. The two of them crowd together by a window seat and wave, blow kisses, stick their thumbs in their ears and waggle their hands while crossing their eyes, enthusiastically mashing their noses into pig snouts against the glass.

But before then, the whole delicious weekend awaits us. Picnics on the grass at Aquatic Park followed by sticky-sweet sundaes at Ghirardelli Square. Romping at Children's Playground in Golden Gate Park with per- haps a ride on the grand old carousel. Dinners at diners like Copper Penny, the Hippopotamus, or Zim's. Maybe we'll get dim sum in Chinatown, my mother ordering all of the dishes in fluent Cantonese or Mandarin, depending on the restaurant.

Definitely, we'll watch Saturday morning cartoons (and when we're older, stay up late for *Benny Hill* and *Saturday Night Live*). We'll play tag and hide-and-go-seek in the apartment, tearing through the small space, shrieking with delight, and our father will roar at us to cut it out, goddammit! He'll send each of us to stand in a corner of the living room for five minutes as punishment. Instead of being cowed and anxious, as I am when this happens while I'm disciplined on my own, I'll feel a part of something, a good something that is innocuous, secure, and safe.

Other times, I'll watch in fascination, like a spectator at a prizefight, whenever my sisters argue, calling each other liar! Occasionally they'll accuse me of being a spoiled brat, a stinging accusation that I mostly believe. But their anger is always short-lived, and soon I am once again cuddled up in their arms, a living doll.

We'll sing along to my parents' few "cool" records—The Beatles and Peter, Paul, and Mary. We'll pretend we are the von Trapp family in *The Sound of Music*. I, of course, get to be adorable little Gretl, while Kathy and Sarah quarrel over who is most fit to play sexy sixteen-going-on-seventeen Liesl. If I'm very lucky and they're feeling indulgent, they'll humor me for a while with my "babyish" games of dress-up and Barbies.

We are half-sisters, but I claim them as whole. Every day of my young life, I look forward to those trips to the Greyhound bus station, seeing beyond its utilitarian blandness, its grime, its coldness. It is a place that delivers joy, happiness, and love. It provides the people who alleviate the loneliness I sometimes feel as an only child. It casts in shadow, at least temporarily, the uncertainty of my parents' slowly disintegrating marriage.

Eventually, my sisters stop riding the bus, first Kathy, then Sarah. They move away from Vacaville, go off to college. They start careers, have families of their own. We get in our cars to visit them, or they drive to us. Still, I think of those Friday evenings at the Greyhound station, the humble, under-appreciated portal that, every other weekend of my childhood, gives me the gift of my sisters.

· · · · ·

66

Olivia Boler is the author of two novels, Year of the Smoke Girl *and* The Flower Bowl Spell. *She earned a master's degree in creative writing from UC Davis. Her stories have appeared in the Asian American Women Artists Association anthology* Cheers to Muses, *the literary journals* MARY *and* The Lyon Review, *among others. She lives in San Francisco with her family. To find out about her latest work, visit http://oliviaboler.com.*

Light

Lindsay Ahl

I made you mad only twice: once when
   I questioned the possibility that that couple left the aisle

just because you were black, and once when
   I didn't believe your tan was darker than it had been.

I was out of it, raised in the desert where these things
   didn't matter. I know now you were probably right.

We could enter joy with just a box
   of yellow raisons and a shared cigarette.

We were always in touch, fifteen years, maybe, when
   one night I call and you are sitting on your kitchen floor,

telling me your boyfriend is a drug addict, you work
   in a factory and you no longer ever want to speak to me.

As though my stupid meaningless job was better, as though
   my boyfriend didn't slam his hands through doors

and get stoned every night, as though we weren't invincible sisters
   smoking cloves and listening to music. You should know
     it's always

you and me, me and you, in Chicago in your gold car blasting
   Prince, *I Wanna Be Your Lover*, our music so loud it's the brightest

vibration heaven has ever seen, we're traveling through clouds, and we travel
   without mass, like light, and we'll never stop.

. . . . .

Lindsay Ahl's chapbook, The Abyssians, *was a finalist for the 2013 National Poetry Chapbook Award. She has a novel,* Desire, *out with Coffee House Press. She was a Fletcher Fellow at Bread Loaf for Fiction in 2004. She publishes Shadowgraph (www.shadowgraphmagazine.com), an arts and culture journal.*

The Ceremony–December 1980

Skye Blaine

I plodded down the hallway toward Thomas's hospital room. I dreaded going back to face his piteous crying, and my inability to ease his spasming Achilles tendon. Then I spotted a halo of blond curls coming toward me, and I recognized my closest friend—a sister, really—Susan. I dashed forward and we wrapped our arms around each other. I clung to her for a moment, soaked up her courage, wisdom, and understanding. She could make me laugh, take me away.

Although I had sighed when I stood at the hospital door and watched my ex-husband, Ray, head for home, deeper feelings collided—I resented he could leave, but was vastly relieved he had. I had spent the past nine hours vigilant to every nuance of his mood. When he had bellowed at Thom's main nurse, "Fuck! Can't you stop this misery?" I placated everyone so Thom had the best chance for a positive outcome. But the nurses scurried down the hall and out of sight, I'm sure to complain about us behind our backs. Thomas and I took the rap; except for the jobs licensed staff must do—medications and changing intravenous fluids—they left Thomas's care to me. I mopped his face, held the urinal and the small, harvest gold throw-up pan. I crooned songs to him. My knees shook with exhaustion and fear—and even deeper, unexpressed, unmollifiable rage. Knowing Susan had answered my SOS—as friend, confidant, support—felt like balm spread on festering sores.

She pulled away to get a good look at me. "How is he? You seem wiped."

"It's bad," I said, took her hand and walked toward his room. My feet slogged along the floor. "He tolerated the anesthetic, but he's been in agony since before he even fully woke up." I stopped and sighed, wondered where I would find the strength to take more air in. I tried to straighten my shoulders. "I'm not blowing this out of proportion, either. I hate for you to even experience this. Listen—you can hear him from here."

She paused, cocked her head. "Oh my. Poor kid. Poor you." She dropped my hand and looped her arm through mine, drawing me closer. "I'm here for you, remember?"

I leaned into her.

We sat with Thomas until nightfall. Finally, from morphine and exhaustion, he dozed. After leaving my number at the nursing desk, Susan and I trudged toward the Ronald McDonald House. We didn't talk on the way. Clouds rolled in, obscuring the stars I longed to see. My child's shrieks echoed in my head. I knew he would wake in the night, and guilt plagued me that he would have to endure wracking pain with only brief interventions from the impersonal nurses. I would be talking with my good friend, snuggle in a warm bed, and maybe sleep the whole night through. Nonetheless, I had to have this break.

I opened the door to the room and staggered inside, grateful for the dirt-cheap, clean accommodations. That didn't change how I felt about the framed clown that sneered above the bed. His picture hung in every room, and he gave me the creeps.

To save money, we had packed sandwiches to eat for dinner. When I snapped open Thomas's Star Wars lunch pail, the musty smell squelched any appetite I might have had. The limp tuna sandwich stuck to my fingers, but I forced myself to chew and swallow a few bites. I was grateful to be away from the bustle of the hospital, the stink of Pine Sol, the regular alarms and beeps from the medical equipment. We ate without talking, somber and shell-shocked.

I had brought precious objects from home—anything to try and change the atmosphere and steady me—a small polished worry stone, prayer beads, and a sage-and-lemon balm stick, so I could waft cleansing smoke through my room. At the last minute, I had added a tiny carved box to my suitcase. The contents of this box plagued me. I had turned my bedside table into a makeshift altar and placed these items on it for safe-keeping. Reaching over to touch my prayer beads, to run my fingers over their buttery, olive wood surface, I picked up the box instead.

"What's in there?" Susan asked.

I closed my eyes for a moment. This was embarrassing. "My wedding ring from my marriage with Ray," I said.

"Really!" She leaned over and smoothed her finger on the box's carved surface. "Why are you holding on to it?" she asked. "And why did you bring it here?"

I opened the box. "I can't just throw it away—doesn't feel right, or honoring. My son's about to walk on his own for the first time in his life. Five years late." I rubbed at the nagging, chronic pain in my low back, the result of carrying him. "It's past time I'm my own person, too." I unfolded the forest green velvet, and touched the ring. "I loved this man; this ring symbolized our caring and commitment, even if it didn't last."

She tilted her head and frowned at me, mystified. "I've seen Ray act downright mean to you. Hanging on to his ring is beyond strange."

"Yeah, you're right." I had been clinging to misery.

"It seems really important you finish with this."

"But how?"

Susan pondered my question, and we were silent for a while. She had gained strength and faith in herself the hard way, through the loss of her children, and the courage she'd mustered to get through it. She always had valuable insight to share.

"A water ceremony?" she suggested. Curious, I stared at her. Her gaze held a wicked quality I've come to recognize and love.

"Come on," she said. "We'll tidy the bathroom first, and burn the sage to purify the space. Then we'll sit on the floor and create your ceremony."

I nodded, slowly. I glanced up and grimaced at the clown, then stood on the bed and turned the painting so it faced the wall. That clown would not be privy to my ceremony.

The bathroom already looked clean, but it needed to be my clean. I found Comet, a rough scrubby, and even rubber gloves under the sink. Susan and I worked on every surface, inside and out. I vented my frustration at Ray on that toilet bowl, scrubbed until I had emptied the day's rage out of me. Then I lit the stick; the sage and lemon scent dissipated the acrid stench of both the cleanser and my bitterness. We settled ourselves on the tile, on either side of the sparkling toilet.

I opened the little box and fingered the pounded silver band. My chest went tight. I could still hear the tap-tap-tap of his jeweler's ball-peen hammer. My sense of dread still felt fresh in the surface marks. "It feels awful to flush something he made."

"Could you give it away, or sell it?"

"Not in good conscience; passing along unhappiness feels like really bad juju." I turned the ring and peered at it closely in the light. I could see a shadow of myself in its surface. He was still hammering on me today.

"What have you learned from Ray?"

"I saw his potential. I learned a hard lesson—you'd better love your mate exactly the way he is, with no expectation of change."

She pursed her lips. "What did he take from you?"

I turned the ring slowly. "The confidence that I know how to pick a loving partner."

We sat for a while … it was so quiet, I could hear the loud tick of my Little Ben alarm clock in the other room.

"What did he give you?"

"He gave too much," I said. "He gave himself away, and then hated himself—and me—because nothing was left." I held the ring and offered prayers for Ray, that he would find his own way, and peace would enter his spirit.

"You ready?" she asked.

I nodded, dropped the ring into the bowl, and watched it settle to the bottom. Then I pulled down the handle. The water swirled and flushed. Susan and I both rocked forward and stared into the bowl. The ring had not budged. I flushed again. The ring sat stubbornly on the bottom, its hammered surface reflecting the round ceiling light above.

I pressed my fist against my mouth to stifle a nervous giggle. I whispered, "Now what do I do?"

Susan met my gaze, her eyes wide. Then a titter burbled out of her. Soon we were both laughing uncontrollably, hysterically. Tears poured down our cheeks. I gasped for air. I wasn't laughing at the ceremony; we both understood the seriousness. The anxiety of the day had simply erupted. That kind of pressure requires venting.

It took ten minutes for us to regain control. My sides ached, and the muscles between my mouth and my ears were rigid from laughing. I unrolled some toilet paper and mopped my eyes.

She peered through the water at the ring again. "I hope it's not an omen."

"Omen?"

"Omen of how present he will be in your life. Like he won't go away."

"He isn't supposed to go away; he's Thom's dad." I said. "But I am afraid of his temper."

"What's underneath?" she asked. "Even deeper down."

I closed my eyes. Resistance still clogged my heart. "I have a responsibility to set boundaries, for both Thomas and me."

"Yes, you do."

I pushed up my sleeve, plunged my hand into the bowl, and grabbed the ring. It felt different now, not so sacred after its sojourn in the toilet. Admitting my weakness, hearing it spoken out loud, had girded me. "This sucker has to go," I said. "Now." I wrapped it neatly in toilet paper, set it lightly on the water's surface, and flushed again. I held my breath. The water swirled, whirled, and down it went—ring, paper, and all.

* * * * *

Skye Blaine writes memoir, essays, and fiction, developing themes of aging, disability, awakening, and the human predicament. She earned an MFA in creative writing from Antioch University. Her memoir manuscript, Blood Bond, *won first prize in the 2005 Pacific Northwest Writers Association literary contest. She read her personal essays on KRML 1410 Radio in Carmel, Calif. Other essays have been published in* In Context *(now* Yes!)*,* Catalyst, The Register-Guard, *and the* Eugene Weekly.

Never My Sister

Erica Lann-Clark

She was only my cousin
never my sister
our mothers were sisters
I was the younger one
She the older
just like our mothers

cousins, not sisters
still we slept in one bedroom
in that Brooklyn
apartment we shared
where many trees grew
not just one

but each of us were
the only one
our mothers ever had

long gone now, mothers
and we the old
between us have
fifteen grandchildren
our great revenge
on the killers
who made us like sisters

each the other's
doorway to the past
where we started
our long, lucky lives

* * * * *

Erica Lann-Clark has been a featured teller at numerous storytelling festivals, including the Exchange Place at the National Storytelling Festival, and entertained audiences across the United States and in Canada, Thailand and Singapore. She is the Associate Director of Storytelling for Stagebridge, a senior theater company based in Oakland, and hosts a storytelling radio show on KKUP Cupertino. Her work has been published in anthologies of prose and poetry. Her plays have been produced in New York, Ashland, Santa Cruz, Los Angeles and San Francisco.

Set Three

. . . .

Sisters in Blood: The Papin Sisters – essay,
Delphine Cingal

Sister Song – poem, Claire Blotter

Face to Face – short story, Lisa A. Sturm

Behind the Eyes – poem, Wilda Morris

Jen-Jen – memoir, Jesse Kimmel Freeman

Mirror – memoir, Mara Buck

Just Like Sisters – poem, Brenda Bellinger

Mother's Desserters – memoir, Elspeth Benton

For Milly's Birthday June 8, Disclaimer – poem,
Catharine Bramkamp

Soaring into Space – short story, Ella Preuss

Dear Rachel – short story, Ruth Stotter

Sisters – poem, Janie Emaus

Sisters in Blood: The Papin Sisters
Delphine Cingal

A bloody eye on the stairs!

Those words were my first encounter with the Papin sisters, and I was about nine years old. Somehow, one of my classmates had found out about these two sordid murderesses from a far away past and had told me. For me, especially as a child, it was too gruesome for words and, I must admit, I long suspected my friend of having told me a tall tale.

Alas, she had not! The only mistake she'd made in relating the true-life tale was that the eye hadn't been wrenched out with a spoon as she'd told me, but with bare hands. The hands of two sisters who had probably gone mad.

For most people across the Atlantic Ocean, Le Mans is mostly known for its twenty-four-hour car race. It's also a very peaceful city, with a particularly attractive historical city center, especially in the vicinity of the cathedral.

The double murder took place on February 2, 1933. That evening, René Lancelin, a solicitor and insurance broker, came home to find the door to his home on rue Bruyère locked and bolted from the inside. The light in the room of his two maids was on. His wife, Léonie Lancelin, née Rinjard, and his twenty-year-old daughter, Geneviève, were supposed to have joined him for dinner at a friend's house. Lancelin called the police. The commissaire arrived with two police officers and a clerk. It should be noted that the two police officers' names were Ragot (Gossip) and Verité (Truth). Truth is what everyone would be looking for; gossip is what they would find.

What the police found after breaking a back door was unimaginable: first, an eye on the stairs, then the corpses of the lady of the house and her daughter, both killed and slashed like rabbits in 1900 French cookbooks. Both women had been knocked unconscious, bled to death, had had their eyes wrenched out while they were still alive, and had their thighs and legs lacerated.

The maids, Christine and Léa Papin, were both found in bed after having cleaned themselves and changed into housecoats. In answer to police questioning, both sisters asserted they had had to defend themselves against their mistresses.

Ever since that day, that case has raised the constant question of the sanity and the humanity of the accused. Journalists were obviously the first to write about the case, but many artists have also raised the same interrogations.

In 1934, Jean Cocteau wrote a spoken song for Marianne Oswald called *Anna la Bonne* (Anna the Maid) about a servant (called Annabel Lee, in reference to Poe's poem) who poisons her mistress. One year after the Papin murders, however, everyone got the true meaning of the song. In 1947, Jean Genet used the song in his play, *Les Bonnes*, which was clearly influenced by the Papin case, even if Genet himself always denied it. Nikos Papatakis adapted Genet's play for the screen in 1963. Both Jean-Paul Sartre (in *The Wall*) and Simone de Beauvoir (in *The Coming of Age* and *Memoirs of a Dutiful Daughter*) wrote about the two murderesses. The surrealists were also fascinated by the case and described the two sisters as victims of class struggle. But more interestingly here, Jacques Lacan, who had just completed his Ph.D on paranoid psychosis, became engrossed in the Papin case also. Ruth Rendell's *Judgement in Stone* and Claude Chabrol's adaptation of the novel, *La Cérémonie*, also echo this case. Jean-Pierre Denis, in 2000, tried to be more faithful to the original case when he directed *Les Blessures Assassines*. It is, however, interesting to note that the fascination for this French case crossed the Channel when Nancy Meckler directed *Sister My Sister* in 1994.

To aid in understanding the case, I will outline the facts. Christine (1905-1937) and Léa Papin (1911-2001) were the daughters of an ill-assorted couple who separated when the mother found out the father had been molesting their eldest daughter, Emilia. When Emilia left home to become a nun, her two younger sisters became very close. They had no one else in the world to care for them. The mother, who lacked motherly instincts, placed her two daughters in various homes, generally as maids, and took away most of their earnings.

Christine was finally hired as cook in the Lancelin household in 1926; Léa became a maid with the same family two months later when the Lancelins hired her on Christine's recommendation. They were both rather well paid for the time, and René Lancelin even provided them with insurance should any accident befall them. For the first time, they were working together and, from then on, Christine took her role as a mother substitute very seriously. After a while, both sisters refused to turn their salary over to their mother and ceased to be in contact with their family altogether.

In 1931, both sisters went to see the mayor of the city, apparently in a certain state of stress and confusion, accusing the Lancelins of persecuting and sequestering them. They also accused the mayor of taking the Lancelins' side in the affair. The mayor advised the family to dismiss their maids, which they didn't do because the Papin sisters were "perfect maids." This expression tends to indicate that something is too good to be true (as Agatha Christie's Miss Marple later pointed out in "The Case of the Perfect Maid" published in *Miss Marple's Final Cases and Two Other Stories*).

On the day of the murders, the sisters had just had their iron repaired, and Christine was taking care of a pile of linen that needed ironing when a fuse blew, and the house ended up in darkness. When the mistresses came home, Christine told them the ironing was not finished because of that, causing a fight. Léa joined her sister, and both Mrs. and Miss Lancelin had their eyes purposefully removed in the process. Then they were knocked out with a hammer and a tin pot and lacerated with knives by the two maids, who then proceeded to expose their victims' genitalia. Incidentally, before taking pictures of the crime scene, the police lowered both women's skirts to protect their decency, which didn't respect influential forensic scientist Edmond Locard's guidelines at all.

The only explanation the two sisters gave is that Mrs. Lancelin had become violent, as she had apparently already been on one occasion when she had dragged Lea to the floor, forcing the maid to pick up a piece of paper. At first, the sisters insisted the fight had been so violent that the murders were really self-defense. Later on, however, after Léa had been put in a different prison cell to separate the sisters, Christine recanted and admitted she had attacked the two women, asking Léa to help. For every statement Christine made, Léa only confirmed her sister's successive versions of the murders.

During the one-day trial, the defense lawyers (Germaine Brière, the first woman criminal lawyer in France, for Christine, and Pierre Chautemps for Léa) tried in vain to convince the jury that both women were mad. However, they were both found guilty as charged. Three psychiatrists had declared them sane, but one, Doctor Logre, had asserted neither sister was guilty but that the culprit was … (suspense in the court-room!) the duo, Christine and Léa put together.

Christine was sentenced to death. However the guillotine was often considered as something women should not have to go through, and Christine's sentence was commuted by President Albert Lebrun to life imprisonment. Yet her mental state very quickly degraded, and she was put in a lunatic asylum in Rennes where she died, having only once set her eyes on Léa again. She had apparently not recognized her sister then. Christine stopped eating altogether and died in 1937.

Léa was sentenced to ten years penal servitude without the possibility of returning to Le Mans for twenty years. She was released in 1943 and lived in Nantes with her mother afterward. She even found a job as a maid but under a pseudonym.

The trial centered on two things: one being class struggle, the other the unfeminine violence and the so-called unnatural behavior (meaning homosexuality) of the two perpetrators. They might have been homosexual … or not. Somehow, as was also the case with Juliet Hulme and Pauline Parker in New Zealand in 1954, a very close and obsessive feminine bond is often depicted as homosexuality, especially by men, and always to increase the revulsion felt toward murderesses.

As indicated in her 1982 memoir, *La force de l'âge*, Simone de Beauvoir obviously saw the class element in the murder, the two sisters being or believing they were the avenging arm of the working class against an unfair and inherently violent system. But De Beauvoir also described the element of love between the two, which led the younger sister, Léa, to embrace Christine's mad ravings and paranoid constructions. According to Sartre and De Beauvoir, the trial was unfair. French law prevents mad people from being tried in court: if declared irresponsible by doctors, they are sent to a psychiatric institution until they are cured, if possible. Like Paul Gorguloff, who had murdered President Doumer the year before and had asked to be executed, the two sisters were the scapegoats society needed and therefore decided to prosecute, with the complicity of doctors who declared the accused fit to stand trial.

Such a gruesome murder started the imaginations working. Some people said the two sisters had been engaged in an incestuous and homosexual relationship and that the murder had come about because Mrs. and Miss Lancelin had caught them in flagrante delicto. Homosexuality stopped being a crime in France only in 1982, and the World Health Organization stopped considering it as a crime in 1991. This is, for instance, Paulette Houdyer's theory when she explains in her 1988 book, *L'affaire Papin, Le diable dans la peau*, that the two victims had had their eyes wrenched out for something they had seen, meaning they had caught their murderesses in bed.

This is very unlikely since, as Frédéric Chauvaud, one of the most prominent specialists of the history of criminality and its punishment in France, pointed out in his 2010 book, *L'effroyable crime des sœurs Papin*, the family followed a very strict routine, and the two women had arrived home at their usual time. So it does not seem likely that the two sisters killed to protect an incestuous homosexual relationship. The motive, should there be one, is to be found elsewhere. However, Christine and Léa's behavior in prison was slightly promiscuous (at least for 1933) and, when Léa was taken to another cell, Christine, in a mad fit of rage, yelled, "give me my husband back!"

Whether or not the Papin sisters were engaged in a homosexual and incestuous relationship, there was an indestructible bond between them. They were sisters, alone in the world, with quite dreadful parents, and working as domestics, which does not tend to favor a healthy and carefree work environment. They were probably everything to each other—mother, father, child, and spouse—but, whatever that bond was, it was of the contra mundum type. Lacan summarized it in his 1993 *La Revue du Minotaure* article, "Motif du crime paranoïaque: le double crime des sœurs Papin," as a relationship of three elements: Christine, Léa, and the couple they formed. He insisted that this relationship created madness. Lacan defined this psychoid paranoia as a "délire à deux," a paranoid delusion created by the relationship between two people, which could be translated as dual delusion.

Jean-Paul Lauzel stated in *L'information psychiatrique, À propos des sœurs Papin* that the Papin case is one of our modern myths. Indeed, it might have become a real myth, influencing so many famous writers and directors because the two sisters said very little about what their relationship was, what sisterhood really meant to them. This allowed every one of us to project our own fantasies of what a sick sibling relationship can mean.

It was, in fact, the same for the close friendship bond between Hulme and Parker: being minors, they were not allowed to testify nor speak in court. Their lawyers did all the talking, as did their accusers. Only much later was Juliet Hulme able to deny the homosexual relationship between the two girls, admitting only to an obsessive relationship based on fantasy, books, dreams, and a friendship close to sisterhood where one would kill for the other even if it was a complete mistake. Juliet thought she was saving Pauline's life, since her friend was threatening to commit suicide should the two be apart one day. That "délire à deux" ended up with the horrible murder of Pauline's mother and the twisted explanations of the public who was not allowed to hear the perpetrators' voices. (Peter Jackson's 1994 movie, *Heavenly Creatures*, was made before Juliet Hulme—now writer Anne Perry—came forward and finally chose to explain her story.)

As far as Christine and Léa were concerned, they chose to remain silent until their deaths, almost seventy years apart. I shall therefore leave Léa the final words, those dreadful words uttered to the police upon arrest, and which left space for all the theories, all the fantasies and all the works of fiction: "I am deaf and mute."

* * * * *

Delphine Cingal is a specialist of British and American detective fiction. Her Sorbonne PhD dissertation was about British detective fiction author P. D. James. Cingal also has a Master in American law from the Sorbonne. She is a founder of the international detective fiction festival in Neuilly-Plaisance. In 2009, the French Ministry of Culture awarded her the title of Chevalier des Arts et des Lettres (Knight of Arts and Literature) for her work for the festival and her scholarly research. She teaches at Paris 2-Pantheon-Assas University.

Sister Song

Claire Blotter

A sister is your sister is
your second face under skin
a flip book a half cousin
of your spirit- different sometimes
difficult but echoing some deep
rooted seed in bone marrow sister
grows and sleeps and weeps
with you   sister in these
girls growing side by side
remembering or in total
denial sister hand and
sister face close as
twin beds across a thin
aisle sharing a pillow or
a dream or a drink
of water mysterious
sisterhood   paradoxical
joining of two separate
selves into
harmony

* * * * *

Claire Blotter writes and performs poetry with body percussion and movement. Her work has been published in Barnwood, Gargoyle, California Quarterly *and* Kindegarde: Avant-garde Poems, Plays and Stories for Children, *among other publications. Her third chapbook,* Moment in the Moment House, *from Finishing Line Press, is dedicated to her creative sisters, whom she loves dearly. She has taught poetry writing and performance at Bay Area universities and through the California Poets in the Schools program.*

Face to Face

Lisa A. Sturm

Tessa surrendered her sneakers, since shoelaces were not allowed. Then Delores, a middle-aged nurse with coffee-colored skin, brought her into a small room at the back of the nursing station. There, Delores told her to remove all her clothing. Tessa stood shivering on the green linoleum, feeling more like a criminal being admitted to jail than a patient being hospitalized for depression. Delores went about her business in a methodical fashion. When instructed, Tessa raised her arms up over her head without discomfort. It was the spreading of her legs and the small flashlight in the health-care worker's hand that gave her pause.

"Some kids bring drugs, diet pills, small weapons; ain't much I haven't seen. I just have to check for that and then we're all done and I'll take you to your room," Delores promised.

Tessa tried not to flinch when she felt the tongue depressor part her labia and the heat of the light confirm where Delores's eyes must certainly be focused.

After examining and shaking each article of clothing carefully, Delores returned everything to Tessa except for Charlie's sweatshirt. "If you want to wear this, then we'll have to remove the string around the neck. It's your choice. We could just check it in, and then it'll be returned when you leave," Delores said.

Tessa touched the arm of the sweatshirt hanging from Delores's arm. "Cut the string. I need it."

With the string cut and removed, Tessa tugged Charlie's crew sweatshirt over her head and crossed her arms, hugging herself. Delores led her through the unit, pointing out the marker board that listed the day's schedule and meal times, as well as the names of the nurses, aides, and social worker on duty that day.

"We expect you to go to groups. You don't have to talk if you don't want to, but we want you there."

"Will there be individual therapy?"

"The social worker will see you tomorrow, and the doctor will be in either tomorrow or Friday."

"What does the doctor—?"

"Medication, everyone goes on medication," Delores said. "If you're in the hospital, you pretty much have shown that you need it." She noted Tessa's wrinkled brow and added, "It doesn't mean you'll always need it, but sometimes it helps for a while. You'll see."

Tessa took in her new surroundings as they walked. The lighting was harsh and fluorescent; the floors, a scuffed-up celery color. The cinder-block walls and dented Sheetrock displayed scattered murals of trees and flowers. The furniture was all heavy oak and bolted to the floor so that it couldn't be thrown in anger.

"This is your room here. Your roommate is …" She glanced down at her clipboard. "Jasmine. We try to divide people up according to age, so you'll be more comfortable." Delores' finger glided across a white sheet of paper. "Oh, look at this; you two have the same birthday! You're both eighteen, huh; don't often see that. The cupboard and drawer on the right are yours."

Delores observed Tessa, who walked in empty-handed. "I'm sure someone will bring you some things tomorrow. Goals group is at eight, so try and get some sleep." She closed the door and left Tessa in the semidarkness.

A red light glowed in the corner of the room, next to the ceiling, and a dull fluorescence filtered through the frosted window next to her roommate's bed. Tessa lay down on the thin mattress and tried to keep the wool of the blanket from scratching her skin. The sheets were stiff and smelled of soap, and the whole place gave off the scent of industrial pine cleaner, which made her gag. She got up, dashed to the bathroom, and lifted the toilet seat. Crouching over the bowl expecting to vomit, she instinctively went to move her hair away, but then realized there was nothing to move—she had cut off her beauty. A small amount of bile rose from her stomach, but nothing more.

Once in bed, Tessa tried to face the window, but the light jarred her. It was then that the tears began to fall, and her body shook with emotion. She was grateful her roommate was a sound sleeper, for she couldn't control the sobs that escaped her throat. At some point, her body gave in to exhaustion and she drifted off to sleep, only to be awakened three hours later by one of the aides knocking on the door.

Tessa looked at her watch and saw that it was seven-thirty. Her roommate stirred and then buried herself beneath her blanket. Ten minutes later, the aide was back, this time opening the door and speaking to them directly: "Jasmine and Tessa, rise and shine. Group is in twenty minutes, so if you want to shower, now is the time."

Tessa sat up and for the first time made eye contact with her roommate, who was staring at her critically.

"When did you get here?"

"Last night; you were already asleep. I'm Tessa."

"Jasmine. Did they make you come here?"

"Not really. I mean, I guess they thought I'd hurt myself."

"You told 'em that?" Jasmine shook her head. "Big mistake; never tell 'em how you feel. Never tell 'em the truth either. I learned that the hard way."

"So how did you get here then?"

Jasmine pushed aside her blanket and sat up, displaying stiff white bandages on both her wrists. "I guess if I was gonna do it, I should have made sure no one found me. That way, I'd be someplace in heaven or hell instead of locked up in this place."

"We're locked up?"

At this her roommate chuckled. "Uh-huh! What you think? Only way to get out is to have the doctor release you because you're all stable or whatever it is they want you to be." She grabbed a brush and stroked it through what looked like chemically straightened black hair, smoothing it away from mocha skin and into a ponytail. "If you want a shower, you best take it now; otherwise, them nurses be back and tellin' you it's too late."

"What about you?"

"Me? Takes me two minutes. I'm used to a houseful a kids. Wake me when you out."

The water in the shower was mercifully warm, and the water pressure strong as it beat against Tessa's tired shoulders and back. The shampoo smelled harsh and institutional; the soap was no better. Toweling off with a thin, scarf-sized towel, she surveyed her dirty clothes now in a heap on the lime-green tiles. She had no choice but to put them back on.

"I'm out," she called, rubbing what was left of her hair with the towel. Without any calming hair product, her head would soon look like a blond Q-tip.

Jasmine surveyed the situation. "My hair stuff is in my drawer if you want to borrow something until your own comes. Just don't use my comb or brush. Try some pomade." With that, she shut the heavy bathroom door.

Ten minutes later, Tessa followed Jasmine into a compact meeting room. Unhappy young adults of every color and stripe filed in after them. The unit was full, so aides had divided the patients and formed a group for those under twenty-five. Some shuffled in wearing fuzzy slippers, pajama bottoms, and sweatshirts, their hair pressed up against their heads, with lines from their pillows still etched on their faces. Others had taken the time to apply heavy eye makeup and slide into tight-fitting jeans.

Each person announced an individual goal for the day. Then they all moved to the common room for breakfast. Tessa trailed after Jasmine, feeling like a lost child. She didn't want to be so needy, but she hadn't yet figured out how to navigate the hospital routine, and she was frightened. Several patients in the unit seemed to seethe with anger. She imagined they had been hospitalized not because they were a danger to themselves, but rather a danger to others. She sensed Jasmine would know how to handle herself with such people, so she followed her lead.

Jasmine tolerated her new roommate. She allowed Tessa to shadow her through the day, sitting next to her at meals and groups. She even convinced Tessa to take the medication that the doctor prescribed. "If you don't take it, they'll label you resistant to treatment and just keep you here longer. You might as well just down it and get the hell out of here." Jasmine's eyes looked defeated, as if she had learned to accept so many truths like this.

• • • • •

At the end of the day, Tessa and Jasmine settled onto their beds, with the overhead light fixture buzzing down on them.

Tessa considered her roommate now. "What made you do it?"

"Why you askin'?"

"I want to know—if you want to tell me, that is. Maybe I could understand and make sense of things, or … I don't know; I don't even know what I'm saying."

Jasmine gazed upward. "Only thing I've learned from all the shit in this world is that there ain't no way to understand it." She paused for a moment, then said, "I usually don't talk too much. … But if you want to talk about what happened to you … I could listen."

In that moment, there was nothing Tessa wanted more. Thoughts of the events that brought her there had been playing over and over in her mind, and this perseveration had done nothing to help her make peace with the past. She sat cross-legged on her bed and faced her roommate. "Okay, so I was at college at Columbia University."

"So you're smart."

"More like a hard worker, but anyway—"

"No, you're smart." Jasmine offered. "Go ahead."

"So I met this really amazing guy who is a senior, and he's already taking graduate classes, and he's just beautiful; I mean, a beautiful person in every way, not just physically, and for some reason, he liked me and things were going really well … except for last week, when I threw up on his parents' dining room table, but other than that …"

Jasmine smiled. "But there's an ex-girlfriend."

"Yes! How did you know that?"

"Someone like that always has an ex."

"Yeah, I guess so, and she of course wanted him back. I mean, why not? Right? So she decided to dig into my life and find something. But what she found was stuff that I didn't even know about!"

Jasmine nodded, listening.

Tessa continued, "I always knew I was adopted, Jasmine, but she found out who my birth parents were! I don't know how exactly she did it. My boyfriend, Charlie, thinks it was her dad's assistant who researched it, but anyway … she also discovered that I have a twin sister. It turns out that my mother was this fifteen-year-old black girl who was raped by this white dude, and my twin sister is also black!"

As soon as Tessa spit the words into the air, she wanted to suck them back in. She hadn't thought beforehand about how they might be received by an African-American.

Jasmine blinked and pulled her lips taut as she considered what Tessa had said.

"Oh, that didn't come out right," Tessa said. "It's just that I'm not who I thought I was, and my father was a rapist! It wasn't that my mother … I don't care … it's just—"

Jasmine lifted her right palm up, like a crossing guard stopping traffic. "You don't have to explain to me. It is what it is. If I thought I was all lily-white and then found out my mother was black, I might be upset too. The world ain't fair and our society favors whites. Even some blacks don't wanna be black—least not a dark shade a black. The lighter the better; the finer your features, the more attractive you are. People will tell you they proud to be African-American, and I'm proud too, but thinkin' you're not black and then wakin' up one day to find out you are? That's one heavy thing to sort through. The rapist thing, though, I'd forget about. Where I come from, lots a people do lots of bad things. It could be he was on drugs or somehow out of his mind. It doesn't mean anything about you."

"Really? You wouldn't think your father is this animal, so there must be some piece of you that is horribly violent? Or that someday you'll be punished for his terrible behavior?"

Jasmine sat up straight, her eyes determined. "The sins of the father? That's what you're stuck on? In my church, we don't play it that way. I never met my father, and he was no one to be proud of, still … I ain't gonna spend my time thinkin' 'bout it. It's a waste and won't get you anywhere."

Jasmine's words soothed Tessa and helped her begin to see things differently. Tessa felt oddly close to her. "Thank you for saying that."

Jasmine sniffed in deeply. There was a pause. "Hey, so … when's your birthday?"

"July 14, 1994—same as yours. Don't you remember? Oh, maybe you were sleeping. The nurse told me when I first came in. Yeah, we were born on the same day … that's kinda cool."

"Hmm … so …" Jasmine tugged off a small piece of skin, leaving behind a crimson dot of blood blooming on her thumb. Her eyes darted around the room. "Do you know anything about your twin?"

"All I know is that she's darker than I am and probably went to some local family, maybe even around here. It's one more mystery."

Jasmine rose to her feet and stepped toward the door. She reached for the handle. But then she paused, seemingly lost in thought for several moments before pacing back to her bed, where she stood frozen, her eyes dazed.

"Hey," Tessa reached out and touched her arm. "You all right?"

Jasmine twisted her hands together, and then her eyes caught Tessa's. "So … if you came face-to-face with your sister, how would you feel? I mean … would you want to know her?"

. . . . .

Lisa A. Sturm is a psychotherapist in private practice, and writing is one way she processes all the emotions of her work. Her short stories and creative nonfiction have been published, or are forthcoming, in Moment Magazine, Tulane Review, Willow Review, Serving House Journal, Mom Egg Review, The New Jersey Jewish News, *and* The Jewish Standard. *She received a* Willow Review Spring 2014 *Award and a 2013 Writer's Relief Peter K. Hixson Award. "Thicker than Water" is an excerpt from her first novel,* Life on the Other Side.

Behind the Eyes

Wilda Morris

We think we know
the stories of our sisters,
nurtured in the same nest,
nibbling the same scraps.

First hatchling is born
to untried parents
who learn by doing.

Another season
and the same parents
are not the same,

and each fledgling,
somehow unique,
calls forth a different response.

Look closely,
there are secrets
hidden behind the eyes
of each sister,
something you never knew.

* * * * *

Wilda Morris has three sisters by birth and two by marriage, and several found sisters. Workshop Chair for Poets & Patrons of Chicago and Past President of the Illinois State Poetry Society, Wilda has led poetry workshops for children and for adults in three states. Wilda's book, Szechwan Shrimp and Fortune Cookies: Poems from a Chinese Restaurant, *was published by Rockford Writers' Guild Press. Wilda Morris's Poetry Challenge, at http://wildamorris.blogspot.com/, provides monthly contests for poets.*

Jen-Jen

Jesse Kimmel-Freeman

It's hard to believe I am about to be twenty-nine, six years older than you were when you died. The memories still flood my mind: days on the beach, concerts, and singing in your Bronco—Tonka, as you called her—at the top of our lungs. How did we turn from those moments to that one Sunday? At times thoughts of that day eclipse the rest: your smile, your laugh, the little beauty mark under your right eye.

I returned home after volunteering at the Jewish Home for the Aging. The air was stifling, but not from the weather. It was only March. Mom looked over at me, her face blank as though the world had slipped from her grasp. Tigger, our brother, stood in the hall doorway, his body half hidden in shadow. He turned and pulled me into a crushing hug.

"Jennifer's dead. She killed herself." His words dropped like rocks in my mind. I didn't understand. You were such a life force; your zeal surpassed anyone I knew. The thought that you would intentionally leave this world? Impossible. I shook my head in silent protest, as though I could simply push it away and it wouldn't be true. Tigger's tears fell on my head.

I pushed him away. "That's not funny." My voice shook.

He embraced me again. I could see Mom through a space between his arms. Her face said it all. You were gone.

I felt the world stop and speed up simultaneously. What happened next? I'm not sure. Only sixteen years old, I wasn't allowed at your apartment to help tend to your things. I didn't get to see you until the viewing. But so much bombarded our family in those moments. Mom was convinced you were murdered. The pieces could fit together to prove her right, but no one in law enforcement wanted to hear the pleas of a grief-stricken mother. Would you blame them? You know how Mom used to get. We were broken. You were gone. It didn't matter how; you were simply gone. And you took a part of each of us with you.

You were my best friend, my guiding star, my rescuer. And yet, in your moment of need, I wasn't there for you. No one was. You called that day. I was too busy talking to the latest flavor-of-the-week to pass the phone to Mom. I clicked over and told you I was talking to Josh and I'd have Mom call you back. I never did. I simply forgot. It wasn't that you weren't important enough; I was just too lost in my own world to remember something as simple as a call. You called Tigger, too, and he never called you back. The guilt from that also killed a part of us.

Oh, and the viewing. I made sure they put you in your white dress. The one you loved so much; the one you wanted to be married in. But since your neck was marked with the bruises from Kona's leash—the leash you apparently used to hang yourself—they cut a piece of the garment to cover your skin. I wish I could say you looked like yourself, angelic and asleep, but it wasn't you. It was just flesh the undertakers had tried to make look like you. You know, they put pink lipstick on you ... pink! Mom had a fit and wiped at it, then went to get someone to change it. I was asked to "keep you company," but I knew you weren't there. Your hands were shriveled; your shell was already withering away.

Afterward, the pain festered. Suicide. My young mind just couldn't understand it. And Mom lashed out, throwing blame like a spear at the hearts of those who were hurting as much as she was.

Sorrow and anger waged a silent war through my heart. I was furious the world had the gall to move on without you. I just couldn't understand.

I wish you had made a different choice. We could've taken on the world together, gone to college together. Maybe that would've made you happier. But playing that what-if game doesn't change the fact that you're gone. So here is my farewell to you, Jen-Jen. You were a building block of my childhood. You are the reason I became a writer. You may have only been here for twenty-three years, but in that time you touched the very soul of the world and made your mark on the people who knew you.

I lost you, my big sister, in 2002. There isn't a day that goes by that I don't feel guilt over your death. It doesn't matter that I had nothing to do with it, that I was just a teen, or that I couldn't have done anything to stop it. That is one of the curses of surviving a loved one's suicide. I am left with the guilt and the lingering what-ifs. I am left wishing everyone would take a moment for those in their lives who are suffering—you know, say hello, smile, offer a candy bar, show the generosity you always possessed. One small gesture could make all the difference. You were my world even if you didn't realize it. And you'll forever live in my heart. Goodbye, Jen-Jen.

* * * * *

Jesse Kimmel-Freeman was born and raised in the sun-kissed world of Southern California. Jesse has written six novels, four short stories, four illustrated children's books, been part of several anthologies and is working on the next pieces to her series. When she isn't hard at work writing, she enjoys spending time with her wonderful children, loving husband, and furry family. They have many adventures and several misadventures, but it all makes for a good story in the end. You can email her at jesse.kimmelfreeman@gmail.com.

Mirror

Mara Buck

Throughout my teenage years, on the marble-topped table in our living room, there rested a hand-tinted photograph of an angelic child. A golden-haired toddler with knowing aqua eyes clothed in a pinafore of the same shade. A shy smile flitted on rosy lips. A Breck advertisement imprisoned within the perfection of the moment.

When my friends came to visit, they were drawn to the photo and would comment, "Who is that beautiful child?"

I would shake my head sadly, my eyes downcast. "Ah. That's my sister, Marilyn. She was hit by a truck just after that picture was taken. Mother insists on still keeping it there. So very sad. The family doesn't speak of her."

I never had a sister. I was annoyed that my mother displayed that early romanticized picture of me, mocking the real me, the active me, the intelligent me, not the perfect toddler who became the adolescent (and then the adult) disappointment.

In later years, on one of those evenings of tea and conversation, while we were discussing the family history of which aunt had married which uncle (interspersed with comments on my own unfortunate shortcomings), my mother said with uncharacteristic abruptness, "Perhaps if your sister had lived, you would have been happier, less lonely, a nicer person."

I rolled my eyes, afraid Mother's mind had finally gone. "Mom, no. I never had a sister. That was only a nasty trick I played on my friends when they asked about that photo on the marble-top table when we were in the old house. Remember?"

"No, honey. You did have a twin. She never lived, was never really born. But twins ran in your dad's family and I was carrying twins. That's why I had to have a cesarean. You were a big healthy baby and you lived." She pursed her lips as only mothers can. "I thought I told you all this before." My mother reached for an Oreo and shook her head. I was still being difficult.

"No, you didn't. I never knew. A twin?" I wanted to hear so much more, but my mother had already left the room and I heard the can opener in the kitchen. Cat food time. A pressing duty of more consequence than focusing on old wounds. That was that. No further information deemed necessary. Such has always been the way of thrifty Yankees.

Today, decades later, I discover that idealized photograph buried in the bottom drawer of the desk I inherited from my mother, the glass cracked, the frame tarnished, and I'm invaded with longing, like whisps from a dream, stunned by how much I miss the me that could have been, the twin unborn, the sister that almost was.

* * * * *

Mara Buck writes and paints in the Maine woods. Her work has won awards or been short-listed by the Faulkner Society, the Hackney Awards, Carpe Articulum, Maravillosa, and has been published in Drunken Boat, Huffington Post, Carpe Articulum, Living Waters, Corner Club, Orion, Pithead Chapel, Caper, Clarke's, Poems For Haiti, The Lake, Apocrypha, *and others. Current projects include a novel and a collection of strange stories of Maine.*

Just Like Sisters

Brenda Bellinger

Growing up together
we wore the same clothes
and undressed, in the mirror
looked almost like twins
especially when we were young

We faced all of the "firsts"
from training bras
to slow dances on the gym floor
avoiding deliberate hands
of boys with clumsy feet

We shared laughter, sweat,
our loss of innocence,
the swelling joy of pregnancy
then nurtured the little ones
embracing their tears and sniffles

Side by side
puffed up with pride
we watched the children grow
never realizing
we took each other for granted

Softening with age
we carried ourselves
across the threshold of fifty
and thought we'd outrun the bear
until a malignancy was revealed

You chose the knife over the beam
and left behind a flat, routine scar
that looks like a ragged smile
concealed by a cold silicone form
as if you could be replaced

. . . . .

Brenda Bellinger writes from a never-quite-empty nest on an old chicken farm in Sonoma County, California. Her story First Smile *won the nonfiction award at the 2009 Mendocino Coast Writers Conference. Brenda's writing has appeared in various anthologies as well as in* Thema, Poets & Writers *online and the* California Writers Club Literary Review. *She has been working on a young adult novel and is currently negotiating with her characters over revisions.*

Mother's Desserters

Elspeth Benton

Walking home from junior high and high school in Madison, Wisconsin, in the mid-1940s, I never remembered that, on many Wednesdays, our living room would be filled by seven or eight ladies, who'd just shared a delicious homemade dessert (hence the name they'd given themselves, the Desserters). One of them would be reading Jane Austen, Charles Dickens, or Anthony Trollope aloud to the others, who were all mending or knitting.

"Oh, darn," I'd think as I stepped inside. I couldn't just go to the icebox and make a peanut butter sandwich. Instead, I'd have to go greet Mother's friends. And the kitchen would be full of their dessert plates and forks and cups; there'd be crumbs and watery bits of whipped cream in the sink.

Still, it wasn't so bad. Every single one of them was delighted to see me, for no reason I could fathom. They hardly knew me, after all. Yet there was no mistaking their pleasure when I arrived. As Mother had instructed me, I went around the group, shook hands, greeted each woman by name, smiled, and answered questions. "Do you have much homework tonight?" "What are you studying now?" "How are you?"

How was I? I was a million miles from them. I was saving for a slinky new sweater. I had a crush on Dave Matson. My girlfriend and I had schottished all the way home after learning the dance step that morning in gym class. My geography teacher was impossible. I couldn't understand gerunds in Latin. I was desperate for my period to begin and my breasts to sprout. What would I wear to school tomorrow? These ladies, with their smooth pink cheeks and eager eyes, what were they to me? Every one of them was at least fifty years old! However, through the years, I came to know about most of them and, most importantly, about who they were to me.

Alice Bown, wife of the Chairman of the University Medical School, had a funny, chortling laugh and no chin. She was a Bryn Mawr graduate and dear friend of my mother's—Mother had come to the United States from Scotland on a scholarship from Bryn Mawr. Alice opened her home to Mother and me during the war for a few weeks until we found an apartment, and at other times, as well. Her husband, Carl, did the autopsy on my father when he died, at 76, of unknown causes. Alice's and her husband's finances weren't as strong as one might imagine; they moved into a tiny, second-floor apartment after he retired. I remember visiting them in the apartment; we laughed a lot, and Alice kept saying to Carl that I was a "pretty nice girl!"

When I came home with my first baby for a short visit in 1955, I still didn't get how these women loved and supported each other, or that I, too, would be their age someday. And though I doted in private on my little one and thought she was the most perfect creature ever, I was grappling with the fact that she'd been "accidental"; her arrival had knocked out my husband's and my plans for him to get his degree while I taught school. I entered the living room, holding my adorable, healthy little daughter in my arms, and, once again, experienced the delight of my mother's women friends. "Isn't she sweet!" they cooed. "May I hold her?" "Does she sleep through the night?"

"What are they so excited about," I wondered. "A baby's a baby, and this one came before I felt ready for her." I hadn't yet figured out that almost all the world rejoices in a baby. A few months earlier, each of these women had gone to the trouble of sending me a baby gift by mail from Wisconsin to New Jersey. They all knew my little one had come before we'd planned, but their excitement and love was uppermost—and contagious. I still didn't know how John and I and baby Helen were going to make it, but I felt stronger when I returned to New Jersey.

Twenty years later, Carl and Alice moved to a large, new retirement home at the same time as Mother. Alice went into dementia in her last years. The retirement home had strict rules, and dementia wasn't allowed. Incontinence was another no-no. Mother secretly looked after her, trying to keep up appearances so Alice and her husband wouldn't have to move again.

Nancy Olsen, another Desserter, was the wife of a dean at the university. He was a decade or two older than she, and adored her, Mother told me. Nancy had a gentle voice and sweet smile. She would have loved to have a child of her own. When I married, she gave me six royal porcelain china cups and saucers, each a different pattern. Later, when both she and Mother were widowed and I would return to Madison from California on visits, Mother told me how they took turns driving each other grocery shopping, and phoning in the morning to check on each other. One day, Nancy didn't answer. Mother walked the couple of blocks to Nancy's home, and found her, dead, in her kitchen.

Jean Reilly was probably the youngest in the group. I knew her by sight only, as the mother of a younger girl I went to school with. I remember her coming in with groceries on one of my last visits home. Like Mother, she was widowed, aging, becoming more frail, living alone in the comfortable home where she'd raised her family. The winter months had become dangerous for these women. One could slip and fall so easily on the icy sidewalks, just putting out the trash.

Katherine O'Neil, with premature snow-white hair, was the only Desserter who wore lipstick. She and her much-older husband had one child, a girl a year older than I. Katherine had two black Scottie dogs, and I often met her walking them around our neighborhood. When I was in third grade, I went into her backyard and helped myself to a dozen or more spring daffodils, taking them home to Mother as a "birthday gift." As punishment, my parents made me dig dandelions out of our front yard at five cents a basket, until I'd earned twenty-five cents for a flat of pansies to give Mrs. O'Neil. Katherine was warmly regretful about my punishment, insisting it wasn't necessary.

Once each year, over perhaps three decades, the Desserters traveled to Door County in Northern Wisconsin, where they spent a week sans husbands, went into ecstasies over the spring wildflowers, laughed and shared with one another. At home they were the Desserters, fixing fancy desserts for each other, enjoying books together, and catching up on their mending. But on these annual expeditions, they called themselves the "Wild Women."

Now I understand and appreciate how my mother, who tended to be reserved in her Scottish way, received validation—she was, after all, an immigrant—as well as identity and support from these dear friends. Perhaps the group's biggest gift to me is that, all my adult life, wherever I've lived, I've started support groups with women friends—reading

French, sharing confidences, or learning about parenting. When I'm sick, they bring me food. We laugh and cry and share together. The immigrant in me perks up and blossoms in the light of these connections. Dear ladies of the past, and dear friends of today, I bless and honor you!

· · · · ·

Elspeth Benton, author of the mystery Crucial Time, *has been associated with early childhood education for thirty years. She taught parenting classes through Pasadena City College, and directed a co-op preschool and two childcare centers in Southern California. She also lived three years in France as literature and culinary school student and wife of a medievalist. More recently, she's studied creative writing, appeared in musicals, edited books, and joined Redwood Writers. She lives in Santa Rosa with her cat, Cosette, near her children, grandchildren, and great-grandchildren. http://elspethbenton.com.*

For Milly's Birthday June 8, 2004
Disclaimer

Catharine Bramkamp

I apologize
the enclosed gift in no way obligates us
to embark on
            one of those awful
                        guilt riddled
                                    life-long
gift exchanges that so quickly deteriorate into,
            Oh hell, it's your birthday again?

This is a one-off gesture:
you mentioned
            you needed a purse.
Though we had time for wine
and discussions of how to avoid
            the holiday season
            those donuts
and strategies on convincing
your husband it was
his idea.

We never did
formulate
            the perfect transparent
            exit strategy
and we forgot to shop.

but don't worry
I had this
and thought of you

From now on:
            tasteless cards
            hour phone conversations
            never enough time.

* * * * *

Catharine Bramkamp is the co-producer of Newbie Writers Podcast, which focuses on newer writers and their concerns. She is a writing coach and author of a dozen books including the Real Estate Diva Mysteries *series,* Future Girls *(Eternal Press) and the poetry chapbook* Ammonia Sunrise *(Finishing Line Press). She holds two degrees in English, and is an adjunct professor for two universities. A California native, she divides her time between the Wine Country and the Gold Country. Learn more about Catharine at http://www.newbiewriters.com.*

Soaring into Space

Ella Preuss

Tidying her brothers' room—where Blanca spends only one night a week—because "everyone has to help around the house." Doing all the dishes at ages eight, nine, ten while her little brothers dash about, shout with glee, leave messes for her to pick up. Keeping silent out of fear when her father's wife yells at her. "See what a waste of space you are!" the woman screams, each word driving a nail into Blanca's tender flesh. That is what being a half-sister means to Blanca.

She wishes her father would tell his wife not to give her so many chores (or at least ask the eldest brother—only a few years younger than Blanca—to help her out). But her father cowers like a beaten dog at his wife's every display of ill temper.

Blanca loves her brothers. She just wants to play, too, and be part of the family. But she is pushed to the sidelines, where she watches her brothers race outside with other children, climb trees, jump from branches high above and become spider monkeys swinging from limb to limb.

She sees happy families on the telly and craves their warm love, knowing she can't have it. She reads about it in her books, and understands the difference between fiction and reality very early on. Only princesses get a fairy godmother, and that she is not. In her father's house, Blanca is given love cut in half like the cakes she wants a little bit more of but is too shy to ask for. And this half-love comes in a small box, dressed up and labeled "True Love," shoved down her throat.

Two days out of seven become her least favorite days of the week. Her mother notices the change in her daughter the second she steps into her house. It's as if Blanca is leaving a bag full of bricks out the door, the weight that was pressing onto her shoulders forgotten for a while. At least until it's time to go back to her father's place.

She often goes to birthday parties with her brothers, her father, and his wife (never ever does Blanca call her stepmother, for a mother should care about you, and that, this woman never does). To everyone, Blanca is introduced as "their half-sister." Those words twist, change shape and cut deep into her muscles. But her skin always heals. Does she not laugh with them like a regular sister? Clean their messes? Coax them into eating their morning oatmeal? Watch films with them? Read them books they cannot yet read on their own? She knows "half-sister" is just a term, but to her it seems to have been conjured up by the evilest of witches, designed to torture.

Finally, when Blanca is old enough, and her brothers don't need her to chase them around and spoon-feed them anymore, she resists when her father comes to pick her up for another stay at his home. She begs her mother, her stoic expression never betraying her real fears, "Please don't send me to Papa's anymore. Cleaning up his house is a tiresome thing." Not even with all the powers in the world would I be able to keep that woman happy, she thinks.

"What!" whispers her mother in indignation. "You were not Cinderella last time I checked. Let your father come. He will hear my piece." Blanca's mother's outrage has never been so extreme.

At her mother's screams, Blanca's father, the beaten dog, wiggles, whines and backs away. The only words that come out of his mouth are excuses and meaningless apologies that Blanca's mother's yells drown into nothingness. Such is her mother's force and the strength behind her screams that her father's backed into a corner, uttering words meant to explain his wife's and his own behavior toward the child.

Witnessing this, Blanca realizes her father's wife is no other than his puppeteer. This comprehension peals a veil from her eyes and, squinting at first because this new world is too bright, she finally sees the strings attached to her father's limbs, going all the way out of her house and, undoubtedly, into his wife's nimble fingers. And so she vows to change her life. She determines to become strong and learn how to protect herself. A revolution swirls inside her blood.

As Blanca grows, her fears begin to dissipate. An itch sparks in her, a yearning to be more than she is. It starts in her back, where all the wounds and cuts and nails have gathered, and spreads throughout her body. She puts up with her father's wife for her brothers' and father's sakes, nothing more. Surprisingly, she has become friends with several wild creatures. She can see them more clearly now, see the beautiful things that they are. They come to her asking for more than what they have, as if she holds the secret key to a fairer world. If only she did.

Many times she even sends a dove from the garden to offer an olive branch to his father's wife, and every time, the bird is thrown back with the branch for its head. Blanca grows tired of trying, and she attempts to cast the woman out of her mind. Blanca's father tries to intervene and apologise for his wife, but Blanca explains, "I have crossed a crocodile-infested river to meet that woman on the other side many, many times before, and I'm done with being bitten." Her father takes no action to remedy his wife's behavior.

As time goes on, Blanca studies her brothers' and their mother's interactions. She realizes that, while the woman boasts about them and brings them many treats, her words toward them are not very sweet. She says, "Get out of here! You don't love me like I do, otherwise you'd be listening to me!" when they refuse to do as they're told. The boys' faces fall, unsure of what they're doing wrong. Have they not being raised to do whatever they please while I was the one obeying her commands? thinks Blanca. Getting their way is all they know, and for that they can hardly be blamed. Her unveiled eyes show her an image of the woman's insides, and Blanca isn't surprised to see her heart is cold as a tomb. Why else would she say that to her own sons? With present after present, she buys their affection, foregoing real love from the heart (a love she cannot sustain for very long) and providing, instead, a new computer or two.

Blanca's determination expands and shields her like a thick coat of armor. She takes action. The itch in her back grows with a vengeance. She is not the half-sister anymore. With her newfound powers of truth and fierceness, she makes sure that word is erased from everyone's vocabulary. She is simply Blanca, the sister from another mother who makes friends wherever she goes. (This irritates her father's wife, but at this point, what the woman says bounces against Blanca's shiny armor and falls to the floor.) Her brothers' family is her family because she made herself a place in their midst, and they allowed it. She has cousins and aunts galore, and she is happy.

She can be joyful because she doesn't live in her father's house, and she has learned to stand up for herself when she is with her mother. Her brothers, however, live full time in a home where love is kept in a jar, hidden behind locked doors. The tension in their house grows as they search for the right keys to reach their mother's love, yet they all pretend the boys aren't suffering the lack of this emotion—except for Blanca.

She wails and screams and prays to be heard. Her thunderous voice echoes to the corners of the house, blasting out the windows with the force of a hurricane. Yet all she encounters is a sturdy wall of denial that keeps pushing her farther and farther away. Her father's wife, the main force behind the wall, holds her head high and looks down at Blanca in disgust. From her fingers hang the puppet's strings. On her chest Blanca sees a pouch labeled "Love," small as a raisin, and inside the woman's skull, she discovers the wiry connections that make a human care have been disconnected. This is how Blanca learns she can't blame her for being broken, but that doesn't mean she will forgive her for years past. The icy woman doesn't grasp, doesn't want to see, the reality behind Blanca's words.

Even though Blanca's coat of armor is strong, the wall is stronger. Blanca hopes the woman will strike down that wall on her own, and finally step up and own to all the messes she has made. But, of course, that doesn't happen. Just when Blanca's hopes are lower than they've ever been, her itching intensifies. She grows even more motivated. She prays each night for a way to save her brothers. Then one morning, she sees that wings have sprouted from her shoulder blades. They are still like a baby eagle's wings and she is afraid they won't work. But it is time, she knows. So, for her family's well-being, Blanca tries one more time to get through to her father's wife.

Standing in the small kitchen of her father's house, Blanca listens to the woman harangue her sons, "Don't you see I'm doing this because I love you?" she says. But the pouch in her chest remains empty, and Blanca doubts the sincerity of her words. The itch in Blanca's back intensifies, her power fluttering under her clothes. And, finally, in front of her brothers, her father and his wife, her wings strengthen and outstretch, taking up most of the kitchen's free space. And she rises up off the floor.

Everyone looks at Blanca in awe as the roof opens up, and Blanca's mighty wings take her up into the sky. "I'll be watching you," she calls down to her father's wife. This time it's the woman who cowers.

Blanca still resides there, high above slashing words and petty thoughts. However, no matter how far away she flies, when she hears her brothers' cries, she swoops down and covers them with her wings for a little while. Her brothers love her wings—so soft and warm, but at the same time, strong and hard as steel. Blanca prays the woman's cold heart will thaw one day, releasing kindness long trapped within her depths. But she doesn't fear for her brothers as much as before, for their own shiny armors are starting to show.

· · · · ·

Ella Preuss is a 22-year-old writer from La Plata, Argentina. When she's not reading or creating stories, you can find her with her camera in hand, capturing life's sweet, brief moments. Ella's writing a dystopian young adult series titled The Black Comet Chronicles, *and* The Darkness That Haunts Us — *the first new adult novel in her* Into the Light *series — is getting ready to be published soon. Visit Ella's Facebook page at facebook.com/AuthorEllaPreuss.*

Dear Rachel

Ruth Stotter

Dear Rachel,

I took the day off and am at the beach, sitting on Grandma's old quilt, watching the wild and wooly whitecaps riding the waves. As I spread the quilt out on the sand, I remembered how much you wanted it when Grandma died. Then I started to think about other things I've taken from you. Do you remember Popeye, your little turtle that I took out of his bowl to play with and we found him months later, dead, behind your bookcase? And your Schwinn bike with the basket that you wove from red willow branches that I left somewhere in Golden Gate Park, and it was never found? I suspect you never realized that, when you were packing for college, I stole your baby blue cashmere sweater set. And, then, of course, there's Ned. That's when you stopped talking to me. Now he's left me for that woman running for supervisor. Did you hear about that? So, with Ned no longer in my life, I feel I owe you an explanation. I guess I'll begin at the beginning, as that's the advice I give my playwriting students.

Well, Rachel, it started at Shelly's confirmation party, when Ned raised a glass to toast my getting the part of Claire in Dürrenmatt's play *The Visit*, and I said (God knows why), "Drink to me only with thine eyes." He walked over, scooped me up and took me out on the dance floor. When he squeezed me and whispered, "I'm going to Dayton on a business trip next week. Come with me," well — my body turned to pie dough. After Dayton, I went on all his business trips. It took a year and a half before you found out, filed for divorce, and stopped talking to me. Rachel, do you remember when I was nine years old and said, "Close your eyes and open your mouth," and when you did, I put a teaspoon of cayenne pepper on your tongue? I guess losing Ned must have hurt like that. Your friend Marcy told me that you told her your wedding night was your first sexual experience. I guess you bought into Mom's maxim, "If you pierce your ears or let boys fool around, you are a slut." (I was laughing as I wrote that. Mom tries so hard not to look at the three piercings I have in my left ear.)

But now — the real reason I am writing. Haven't you wondered why we are so unalike? Oh, not just little things, like my loving to sleep until noon while you're up at the crack of dawn. We don't even look like we are related. I know you resented it when we were growing up and everyone commented on my striking appearance. No one knows better than me how hard you tried to scale down with diets and exercise, but you've remained, to put it in a politically correct way, a "big" girl. Unfortunately, when people are overweight they look a lot older. To be perfectly honest, I think you're almost pretty when you smile, but you hardly ever do. Ned used to say your expression "imparts a perpetual doomed appearance."

Anyhow, the reason I'm writing is because I think you should know these differences are the result of our having different fathers—biologically! Mom told me last week that Dad refused to pay your portion for child support after their divorce because he claimed you weren't his child. When I asked Dad about it, he shook his head and said, "That's not true. I never would say anything like that. From the day of Rachel's birth, I decided to accept her as my daughter. It's your mother's guilty conscience that made her even bring that up."

I know you'll refute this, like you did when I told everyone at Shelly's baby shower my theory about Zinfandel and chocolate soufflé being health foods. You should google before you speak. If you ask me, your four years at Wellesley were a waste of money. At least I dropped out of Marin Junior College my freshman year when that stupid English teacher refused to take my paper because I turned it in a day late. I didn't need a degree from an expensive, fancy, Eastern college to achieve fame. Did you know that three years ago I was in *Who's Who in America*, and last year I was awarded a trophy engraved with my name for the summer school theatre program I developed? I put an addendum on my will to leave the trophy and my copy of *Who's Who* to Shelly.

Oh, while I'm reaching out and writing to you, I want you to know I don't mind that you copied me to start that summer program teaching kids to cook—although I find it hard to believe people pay money to have their kids learn how to make apple pie or a loaf of bread!

Anyhow, I'm sitting here in the sun, listening to the crashing waves, watching families gathered together on their private blanket islands, and Rachel, I'm missing you. I hope you are well.

Your little sister,

Abbie

* * * * *

In addition to creating the Dominican University Certificate-in-Storytelling program, Ruth Stotter has performed and conducted storytelling workshops on five continents, authored and contributed to numerous books about storytelling and folklore, and for six years, produced The Oral Tradition—*a storytelling radio show on KUSF-FM. In 2011, Ruth received the Oracle Life Time Achievement Award from the National Storytelling Network. She is also the author of* Little Acorns: An Introduction to Marin County Plant-Lore. *The youngest of three sisters, Ruth is currently a competitive croquet player and kayaker.*

Sisters

Janie Emaus

Jealousy scratches my skin
Like grains of sand between bed sheets.
Dead writers awaken me.
I sit up inside my dreams
Lie back and listen.
Dust settles to the floor.
I write you letters
From cellophane wrapped motel rooms,
Wondering if I'll ever have
a deliciously worn couch,
a baby in my belly.
I describe the sameness in faces
From Durango to Kalamazoo,
Thinking will I ever have
my seat at a kitchen table.
I don't want your happiness to sadden me.
But each day I want to be you.
And yet, you follow me
with yearnings on your skin.
You scorch your flowered apron.
You stir envy into home-cooked meals.

· · · · ·

Janie Emaus is the author of the time travel romance, Before the After, *and the young adult novel,* Mercury in Retro Love. *She has an essay in the best selling humor anthology,* You Have Lipstick On Your Teeth. *Janie is also a prolific blogger appearing on In The Powder Room, The Huffington Post, Better After 50, and Midlife Blvd. She was proud to be named a 2013 BlogHer Voice of the Year. Janie believes that when the world is falling apart, we're just one laugh away from putting it together again. To learn more about Janie visit her website www. JanieEmaus.com.*

Set Four

. . . .

Mana – memoir, Fabia Oliveira

Ripened Apricots – poem, Anne Tammel

Sisters in Scribe – memoir, Diane Sismour

The Day Mel Tormé Died – short story,
Mercilee M. Jenkins

After Curfew – poem, Karen Benke

The Pretty and the Strong – memoir, Lisa Marie Lopez

Her Name is Belinda – memoir, David Lucero

Meeting in the Ring – poem, Susan Ford

Sisters of an Only Child – memoir, Eva Kende

Paper Cranes – poem, Gwynn O'Gara

Darkling River – short story, Nancy Pogue LaTurner

Asha – poem, Elaine Webster

Mana

Fabia Oliveira

The house on Columbus Avenue felt sprawling. A front living room, dining room with a china cabinet, and three bedrooms off the narrow wood-paneled hallway were like branches on a scrawny tree. The kitchen faced the back of the house and led to a sloping deck where we sometimes hung our clothes to dry, when weather in Massachusetts permitted.

My mother cooked beans and sautéed rice in garlic and salt before she boiled it. The deep sink held casings and fat from cheap cuts of meat on days we had dinner parties with church members who substituted for the relatives my parents were used to being surrounded and held up by, substantiating who they really were: Brazilians with heat in their veins, a smoldering love that made no one just an acquaintance.

My brother and I knew nothing of this world of cousins and aunts and running on red earth. We lived in Somerville; we raced bikes on cement sidewalks and trooped down in groups of kids from Nepal and Greece and Haiti to the nearest park, unsupervised, unguided. These kids missed, too, the heat of our own land; the soil beneath belonging to you so that nothing felt distant no matter how far spread and inaccessible to you, the poor and shoeless children. Instead, we learned a roughness you needed to keep up with a world that does not want you there.

We made a tribe of our own, my parents and my older brother and I. Everywhere one needed to go the others came along. On a trip through East Boston to get to the nearest Brazilian embassy to register to vote (a patriotic right my parents have still not lost some twenty years after leaving their country) we laughed in our rusty Camry that Mama was the only white person in the car and outside too. I wanted to look more like my mother. I thought every daughter should. Instead I got my father's thin legs and pointed chin. My father and my brother and I had the warm brown look of sand at sunset, but this was not something we would know was beautiful until later in life. For now it was a marker, a red line through a price tag that placed you at much lower value.

My parents made their own Brazil around them. We went to video stores to buy the VHS of the week's news from the old country. We had journals and newspapers of what was going on in the world, their world far away. Our car dealers, our restaurants, our shampoos, our nursery rhymes were of that land, not here. No one around us thought this strange. Rallied together in a sinking net of the mainstream culture's ship, we saw nothing wrong with how we swayed like silver fish down and away from the surface of American life.

Until my brother and I learned that we would have to merge the two worlds and live in them well—a foot on each, like glaciers sliding farther and farther apart, it seemed. Our tongues were the first rebellions. We used our new language to assuage the sting of our strict parents' reprimands by voicing insults they could not quite place, though they gathered from our tones what we had intended. Then it was the music. It changed us and formed us. The bones underneath our skin felt vibrations that meant we could no longer be of the old world, now that the words we needed to tell us what we felt were found here, here in the new world.

Soon it was the company we kept. The friends with freckled skin, whose words came out lazy and sideways sounding, not upright and neat like the ones we heard in our parents' English lesson videos. These friends didn't have the heat in the veins that bound you to an earth, to solidarity, to family. When they roamed the streets they were not expected back, and when they were back they were not greeted with boiling rice and a little bit of coffee with milk. With this new alliance our parents were no longer on our side. It was like my brother and I slid across the ocean and landed in America when our parents weren't looking.

You cannot make this trip alone. For this migration to work, you need to build your own community, one that beckons like a lighthouse safely guiding your arrival. My brother was that lighthouse for me. He was older and he ventured the to parts of the neighborhood I could not yet. It was harder for him than for me to get along. Girls don't have to prove themselves so much. But on one afternoon at the public pool where our parents had left us for the day while they went to better neighborhoods and swept up the dust that gathered in the fine houses, I ran into the pain of finding I was not welcome. A small, pink-skinned girl sat next to me on the wading pool's edge and my curious fingers worked up the courage to borrow her shiny blue goggles, which could make you a mermaid in a two-foot deep ocean. "Stupid Spanish girl!" she said, before she walked back to her lounging family under the shade of the tree to drink Kool-Aid.

Whistles blew, and everyone took their pruning selves out of the pool so the guards could check the chlorine level and remove trash. I cried and cried as I ran up the black asphalt to where my brother was coming down the ramp with new friends he was making, the ones with cigarettes behind their ears and harsh laughs. I tried to tell him what had hurt, but I could not know then that I was not a Spanish girl. I only knew that being called one meant I wasn't okay. He tugged me along and brought me to the truck with the hot dogs. He bought me two. He sat with me on the grass and watched me eat. Then he got up and went to the ice cream truck and bought me a chocolate dipped cone so crunchy and sweet I could not eat it fast enough as it melted down my wrists. He spent all the money our parents had given us to share that day on me.

There would be other days like this, when we were living in a small apartment on Highland Avenue with only two rooms and the dark blue rugs that ran through it. Italians next door, with their deviled eggs and gold chains, did not like us. And my brother was told by a grown man with no hair on his head and plenty on his chest that he would fucking kill him if he did not return the video game his niece had claimed my brother stole. On the day the video game was found, forgotten but placed there by the niece herself in his work boots outside of their door, no one came to apologize.

Sometimes, our loyalty was tested and I cannot say I recall every incident, but I do know I didn't always pass. Once, when we were very small, my brother filled a balloon with water, against my mother's wishes. I sat at the table in the kitchen with dough she had made for me to play with while she cooked and cooked and cooked. He held a big green balloon against his belly, and it was straining him. He waddled into the kitchen, and my mother promised him a beating if that balloon were to burst on her floor. "Help me," he said. He looked right at me, but my mother promised me a beating, too, if I helped him and the balloon burst. The tears in his eyes came suddenly; the fury of my mother's quick hands was something we knew too well. I did not move. I cried at the table and waited until he dropped the big-bellied balloon and it broke apart, splattering water on the floor. Her hands came crashing down over and over on the back of his neck. He slipped. When he recovered he glared at me, betrayed. "Thanks a lot!" he grumbled.

Years later, as sometimes happens in youth's flickering light, I took an unexpected trip into parenthood. Also unexpected was the fierce support that came from my brother. With fists at the ready, he confronted the man who was supposed to support me but abandoned me instead. He insisted the deadbeat provide what I deserved. When my son arrived, my brother's bond with his nephew was immediate, and has since grown over cars and engines and things of power.

We're long grown now and can laugh at the foibles of having immigrant parents, but we always remember we have this to thank for our strong connection. I cannot imagine a life without my brother's presence; because of him I am someone's sister. I met my mother's little sister two years ago on my first trip back to my parents' old world. "Mana," my mother called my aunt when we phoned her long distance about the trip. I had never heard that word.

"It's like little sister," my mother said when I asked her, "only sweeter."

* * * * *

Fabia Oliveira is a first generation Brazilian immigrant raised in Somerville, Massachusetts, and surrounding cities. She recently completed her undergraduate studies at Lesley University in Cambridge, Massachusetts, with a bachelors of science in expressive arts therapy. She has been published in her school's literary magazine Common Thought. *Fabia is the proud parent of two wonderful children and continues to chase her dreams through the pursuit of a master's in creative writing with a focus on nonfiction at Lesley University Graduate School.*

Ripened Apricots

Anne Tammel

Young apricots hang from an early branch
in April light. If they knew
they had no weight

would they swell with all
they thought they wanted…would they fall
back to soil to wait, to live again?

Mom would reach for them in her
Saturday morning skirt. We would gather
the swelling ones at the soil.

"Why is this one brown and wet?" They're
spoiled, she said then reached for
higher branches.

My sisters waited for babies. But when
swelling seeds visited, they were tossed back
to soil. "It's a bud." I was told.

Mom served marigold tea
in bed. "A period," they said.
When later buds ripened, these women

swelled, dreamt of singlehood, of bursting
with all they had thought they wanted, one feigning
a marriage, the other flailing

unpredictably toward many lives, trailing trees
of brazen leaves, cracked at the soil, gaping
at hapless young saplings for life.

No longer weightless, both wish for less.

* * * * *

Anne Tammel, author of the collection of poems, Endless: a Literate Passion, *(March 2015, Aldrich Press), has been published in* Poydras Review, Annapurna, 3Elements Literary Review, Mediterranean Poetry, Saint Julian Press, *and many more. A news correspondent, professional speaker, and editor for literary journals, Tammel is also owner and founder of Poets and Dreamers, the author's network featured on CBS Los Angeles. Tammel earned her MFA in creative writing and her BA in English lit/career writing. www.annetammel.com.*

Sisters in Scribe

Diane Sismour

A text screams from the cell screen. HELP!!! Fumbling with the phone in my urgency to call, I drive past my exit. "Damn, the next turn off isn't for another sixteen miles," I mutter. At this point, I'm too upset with myself for adding a half-hour more driving to speak with anyone. I pull off the road and text a response. What's wrong?

I stare into the side mirror, and read the warning message firmly adhered stating, "Objects in the mirror are closer than they appear." The ramp still doesn't look that far away. I could put the Santé Fe in reverse and back up to make the turn. A string of eighteen-wheeler trucks roar past my SUV. By the time the fourth trailer passes me, my vehicle is swaying hard. I abandon that idea.

Flashing red and blue lights reflect off the driver's side mirror. I watch as a state trooper dons his hat and tucks the chinstrap in place before exiting the car.

"Oh, boy."

I remove the registration from the dash, pull my driver's license from my wallet, and roll down the window. The cell vibrates in the console cup holder notifying that there is another message. Hoping the disaster has changed to a false alarm, I lift the bane of my latest mistake to the steering-wheel arch, and open the message, just as the officer arrives at my door.

SHE'S GOING TO KILL HIM!!! blips onto the screen.

In my peripheral vision, I notice the officer tense, then reach for his radio. "We have a 10-67 for a 217 in progress."

I let go with both hands, and catch the cell with my knees before it plunges to the floor. It takes two seconds for me to realize who the she is behind the impending murder.

The radio rapping on the roof breaks me from the distraction. I give him my most please-don't-give-me-a-ticket smile. "Hello, officer. Did I do something wrong?"

"No, ma'am. Is there a problem? Is someone in trouble?"

"No, sir." I recall the code given to dispatch. "This situation is not a person calling for emergency assistance or an assault with intent to murder."

He looks at me as though I've sprouted a second head. "And how do you know this information, ma'am?"

"I'm a romance writer," I say, as if that should explain everything.

He still appears concerned, so I attempt to assure him further. "My last novel involved a murder, and I was fortunate to have the assistance of several Upper Macungie police officers in authenticating details. Codes were part of all that material."

"The message I glimpsed on your cell screen was about an imminent murder."

I pick up the phone and consider calling her so she can explain the position she put me in by making me miss that exit, but I try further persuasion instead. "No, it's nothing like that. The person who texted is just over excitable."

I know he has no reason to hold me, but his ice-blue eyes tell me he is contemplating whether to question me further. After a long pause, he says, "Ma'am, be careful reentering the highway."

"Yes, sir. And thank you for stopping to help me." He shakes his head before he returns to his vehicle, and mutters "Romance writers." The lights stop flashing as he drives past me.

After plugging in my headset, I engage the turn signal, press the button to connect the call, and then merge into traffic. I intend to tell her exactly how much trouble her inopportune message caused.

The phone rings once before she answers. "What should I do? She wants to kill him." Her anxiety is palpable.

My hostility vanishes, "Why does she want to kill him?"

"Because the idiot slept with her sister."

I recall all our conversations over the past three months, and there was no sister ever spoken of before now. "Her sister! Since when does she have a sister?"

"Since chapter five. I added her character to give Lucy someone to talk to about the attitude from her friends at school."

"Then write that scene out. There's no way he would cheat on her. Especially with a sister."

"But the middle is slow, and I wanted to spice things up."

"Right out of a happy ending! Isn't your novel a romance? I have thirty minutes to brainstorm. Tell me what you have."

By the time I returned to my proper exit, we'd figured out a new approach to the saggy middle, and saved the heroine from committing a heinous felony.

Assisting each other in the normally isolated process of novel writing creates a bond like no other. We share a vested interest in each other's characters and root for the romantic conclusion in every story. We celebrate victories, and console when rejection letters arrive. Maybe we just have big hearts from writing all those romances, but this was just another day, replete with writing emergencies and pitfalls, with my sister in scribe.

◦ ◦ ◦ ◦ ◦

Diane Sismour has written poetry and fiction for over thirty-five years in multiple genres. She lives with her husband in eastern Pennsylvania at the foothills of the Blue Mountains. Diane is a member of the Romance Writers of America, the Bethlehem Writer's Group, and the Liberty States Fiction Writers. Contacts: www.dianesismour.com; www.dianesismour.blogspot.com; http://facebook.com/ dianesismour; http://facebook.com/networkforthearts; Twitter @DianeSismour.

The Day Mel Tormé Died

Mercilee M. Jenkins

"Chestnuts roasting on an open fire ..."

It is June 1999 in France, the Dordonge region. I pause at the threshold of a patio overlooking a meadow shadowed by sheer limestone cliffs. My oldest, dearest friend, Julie, is softly singing *The Christmas Song* as she looks into the distance. The last time I was here, seven years ago, I had just gone through having breast cancer at the ripe old age of thirty-nine. Julie and Manny, whose patio this is, brought me here. I was hiking in those very cliffs when I understood I wasn't going to die after all.

"Don't you feel his spirit?" Julie says. "I feel his spirit. Let's toast him."

"I feel your spirits," Dan says hoisting his glass in her direction indicating he knows she has not waited for cocktail hour to begin drinking.

I step across the threshold. "Hi everybody. Who are we toasting?"

"You're here." Julie opens her arms to welcome me and kisses me on each cheek in the French way. Her husband, Manny, and Dan, their old friend from our San Francisco neighborhood, rouse themselves from their chairs and do likewise.

"Hello, Leslie. How was your trip? Isn't this great? I'm glad we finally got you here again. Just in time to enjoy the view and a glass of wine." Manny plops himself back in his chair. "You like white, right?"

"Come on into the kitchen and I'll get you some chardonnay." Julie is playing hostess, as usual. "We're toasting Mel Tormé. He died today. You know he wrote *The Christmas Song.*"

"I didn't know either of those things," I say as I follow her into the kitchen. "But I met him once in Florida when I was a kid."

"Really?"

Julie has a way of seeming interested in whatever you have to say, while the attention of others might drift away mid-sentence.

"Yeah, that was the vacation Vicki decided not to go because she was too busy being a bratty teenager, so I got to be an only child for once. It was heaven—the whole backseat of the car to myself. Never mind that on the way down the Smokey Mountains, our brakes went out and we had to coast in second gear, ready to use the emergency brake, and, of course, there were no seat belts ..."

"What does all this have to do with Mel Tomé?" Julie says, laughing and pouring the wine.

"Whoa. That's enough for me. He was staying at the same motel; we met him at the pool. He was very friendly and chatted with us. My mother loved his voice. They called him "The Velvet Fog." I can still see her posing in her black one-piece bathing suit and large brim hat on the ..."

"That's it?"

"Well, did you ever meet him?"

"No, but I feel his spirit now. Don't you feel his spirit?"

"Not yet." I pick up my wine glass and take a sip. "But maybe I will. To Mel Tormé." We toast.

"So Dan's here, you know," Julie says.

"I know. I saw him."

"Well, what d' you think?"

"About what? He's a confirmed bachelor with bad habits. And he always backs away whenever I show the least interest."

"This time might be different." She gives me a twinkly smile and moves her head in the wobbly way my mother did when she'd been drinking.

"I very much doubt it. Besides, I'm here to spend time with you and I can enjoy being single for a change."

"You mean single, lonely, looking for love?"

Like dear old Mom, Julie could play rough after a few glasses of wine. We'd known each other since we were 10.

* * * * *

"Everybody knows a turkey and some mistletoe ..."

Now I'm hearing the song in my head.

"Come Y2K, I don't think anything's going to happen," Dan declares as Julie and I return to the patio.

"What? The world's not going to end?" I say as I help myself to some Brie and crackers.

"Who knows," Manny says. "Something might happen, a glitch or something. I sure don't want to be up in a plane."

"You know, I think we need to do something," Julie says with conviction as she paces around the patio.

"Yeah, back up your computer," Dan comments as he spreads pâtè on a slice of baguette.

"No, I mean for Mel Tormé. We need to do something to honor him."

"What else can we do, Julie? We've already toasted him a few times." Manny pats the chair next to him. "Come on, take it easy, sweetheart."

Julie sits down. "There must be something else we can do."

"Why Mel Tormé?" I finally ask.

"I don't know. I like jazzy blues singers with silky voices. ... And I'm a Buddhist, so I feel his spirit." Julie gestures from her heart chakra to the crystal blue sky.

Dan counters, "You're not a Buddhist."

"I do yoga."

"Well, we did go to one of those Buddhist places around here," Manny adds in her defense. "And Julie got to go into the inner sanctum or something. They gave her a white scarf and the rest of us had to wait outside."

"Wow, that's cool, Julie." I'm genuinely impressed.

"She likes the idea of being a Buddhist," Dan interjects.

"So do I. Just not the outfits and cuisine." I can't help defending her against his barbs.

"You're as bad as she is sometimes," he continues.

"We're writers. We get to be. We need to experience a lot of different perspectives, put ourselves in other people's shoes or chakras."

Dan utters a sort of snort that makes me laugh, damn it.

The conversation drifts along like the river below. "I can't believe you have this to look at every day," I say. "This place really healed me last time I was here."

At the far end of the meadow, you can't quite see the green Vezère river running along the variegated grey limestone cliffs, but you know it's there. On either side, small farms operate as they have for hundreds of years, with a few horses and cows lazily grazing. Up above, the swallows and peregrine falcons cruise over the valley, probably eyeing our spread of food.

Dan makes a sweeping gesture: "This is the most beautiful view in the Dordonge. Better than the Esplanade restaurant in Domme or anywhere else."

We all murmur our assent and sip our wine, taking in the evening summer light.

Julie calls us out of our reverie, "You know, he was born in Chicago, but he's been living in Canada for years. That's his adopted home."

"No, I didn't know that." I'm wondering where she's going with her latest obsession and how it's going to involve me.

"Are we still talking about Mel Tormé?" Dan turns his attention back to the group.

"Who else?" Manny is getting annoyed. "I'm starving. Let's go to dinner."

. . . . .

"They know that Santa's on his way ..."

Julie is singing more loudly as we arrive at the restaurant. Of course, the maître d' knows Manny and Julie. There is much greeting, shaking hands, and kissing of cheeks and welcoming in combinations of French and English.

"Julie, Manny, Madame. Monsieur. *Bienvenue.* Welcome. We are so happy to see you again tonight. And you have brought your friends. That is *trés bon.* We have a lovely table for you. Please come this way."

Julie takes my arm as we go to the table. "People will think we're sisters or lovers," she says.

"Well, I certainly hope so, " I say, realizing she is leaning on me to walk straight.

"I believe you will find this satisfactory, *n'est pas?*" He stops at a round table in the midst of a room full of diners, deftly pulls out the chairs for Julie and me and delivers the menus. This placement strikes me as unfortunate, since Julie will be able to command the attention of patrons all around should she wish to do so. Her French is excellent, despite an odd accent from having spoken a special twin language with her sister, Jenny, when they were small children. I always fancied myself the third twin when we were growing up.

"Don't you think he's good looking?" Julie points out a man around our age at the table to our right.

"Yes, he is, but so what? And don't point so loudly. I'm not really interested."

"Is that because you're still in love with Jeff?" Julie asks.

This is the problem with having old friends. They remember things. "Really, Julie, he's more of a hobby—it's been twenty-five years. ... Besides, I don't speak French." I look down at the menu. "What the hell should I order?"

"Look on the other side. It's in English."

"Oh, *merci*, Julie," I say as we both laugh at me. "How gauche."

The waiter approaches. We order from the prix fixe menu. Soon, our wine arrives, followed by the food. Manny and Dan talk politics and tennis, and Julie and I talk politics and writing. She says she doesn't write about this place because it is too beautiful.

"Beauty is no excuse for not writing." I say.

"It is because you can't improve on it. Can't really capture it. I don't know. It's not what I do."

"It's a mystery and that's what you write," I counter.

"But it's not political."

"It could be."

"You think everything is political, even love."

"It is."

Throughout our conversations, like a refrain, Julie reminds us we should do something to honor Mel Tormé's passing. Then she advances a suggestion: "Why don't we sing? I know. Leslie, you could sing his song. You have a good voice. I've heard you sing in some of your solo performance pieces. What was that one about your student who died of AIDS?"

"You Made Me Love You." I don't remind her that she came in late, drunk, and started talking to me on stage. "I just sang a few lines here and there as part of a spoken word piece. I'm not going to stand up and sing an entire song in front of all these people."

"Why not. I think they would love it. Wouldn't they absolutely love it?" She turns to Manny and Dan for support and accidentally knocks over her glass of wine. "Oops, I guess I need another." She laughs.

129

"People are enjoying their dinner." Manny says. "Let them eat in peace."

"Besides, I don't know all the words," I interject.

"I think you should." Dan says egging Julie on.

"Dan knows all the words. He knows all the words to every song pra'tically there ever was. Don't you? You could sing it with her," Julie says.

"I might know the words but I'm not singing a duet," he says, suddenly very serious, but it's too late.

"We could all sing together," Julie suggests. "Not just our table but everybody." Julie is beaming now with this revelation of how we will honor Mel Tormé. Dan excuses himself from the table. Manny looks around for the waiter to ask for the check, but the place is very busy; the check probably won't come soon enough. Julie gets up to go to the table behind us, where a Canadian couple is dining. They have overheard us talking about Mel Tormé and toasted with us a few times. But I divert her. "Let's go to the ladies room first. Come on. It's through the garden."

"Good idea. I forgot how much I have to pee. By that time Dan should be back."

We proceed through the restaurant to the garden.

"Look at that line," Julie says, gesturing extravagantly to indicate its length.

"Let's sit down," I suggest, so we settle on a wooden bench near the WC.

"Wish I brought my wine."

"I'm glad you didn't."

"I know, I know you think I drink too much just like everybody else."

"Dan makes fun of you to your face. You're not writing. Your personality changes when you drink so much all the time. You're not as smart. And you don't really listen."

"Like to your boring Florida story?"

"Yes, that's what true life-long friends do. I love you like a sister. You were really there for me when I didn't even realize how much I needed someone and you brought me here. But now, you remind me of my mother when she'd had too many martinis."

"Well, your mother was a lovely, lovely woman." Julie hiccups.

"Not when she'd been drinking martinis all day."

Julie looks at me through her oversized tinted aviator glasses that she has worn since they stopped being popular. "You don't think I can do it, do you?" With that she gets up and weaves toward the bathroom. "'Scuse me. It's my turn."

"Julie." I follow, but when I come out she's gone.

Back in the restaurant, she is at the Canadians' table leaning heavily on the backs of both their chairs. I hear her talking to them about singing the song. To my dismay they are all for it.

Just then, Dan comes back. Julie waves him over. "Dan, Dan, come here; they want to sing with us. You must lead the song, since you know all the words and so does this woman." She pats the Canadian woman on the shoulder. "She will help you, if you forget anything."

By now, everyone is looking at us. Dan and I exchange nonverbal condolences as he walks across the room. I want to scream:

"Although it's been said
many times, many ways."

YOU DRINK TOO MUCH!

But I stand up next to Julie, along with Dan, and sing.

Amazingly, the whole restaurant joins in. The final "Merry Christmas to you," rings out, followed by much clapping and laughter—a sense of joy fills the air that only Christmas in June can bring.

As parties at each table congratulate each other on their successful rendition of the song, Julie begins to droop, her mission accomplished. Manny and I scoop her up, one of us at each arm. We are an awkward threesome making our way out of the restaurant, me at five feet and Manny at six, with all the patrons watching our slow progress and wishing us well. Dan wants to take my place, but I hold tight to her arm. "I've got her, thanks."

I am smiling, too, and trying hard not to cry, thinking anyone who can get a roomful of French people to sing *The Christmas Song* in English in June will probably never stop drinking too much. Why should she when she can accomplish such a feat while enjoying something she loves? That's the beauty of broken people. I should know. I am the third twin.

* * * * *

Mercilee Jenkins is a playwright, fiction writer and performance artist. Her one act play, Winning, *was a winner of the Redwood Writers Play Contest. An excerpt of her latest full-length play,* The House on Norfolk Street, *was performed at CounterPULSE in San Francisco and was published this year. Her play,* Spirit of Detroit, *was produced in Detroit at The Wright Museum of African American History. Her new solo piece premiered at Stage Werx in San Francisco.*

After Curfew

Karen Benke

Let's sneak back—
past our parents' bedroom, tiptoeing
over the creak of another Saturday night.
Out front, we'll slip the spare key
into Dad's dented pickup
and coast the highway, counting the horses
grazing the August hills.
We'll find the appaloosa we called our own
that summer we didn't know
she belonged to anyone but herself.

Later, laughing in the upstairs bathroom,
we'll slide the pocket door closed,
pull on bathing suits, and examine
the souvenirs our boyfriends left
across our flushed necks.
We'll worry over when they'll call,
when we should say I love you.

Finishing each other's sentences,
we'll whisper into the dark river of our futures.
This time we'll hold on tight to our childhood,
to the secrets we swapped—my life
moving out to greet the horizon,
yours remaining safe
on the rocky shore.

* * * * *

Karen Benke is the author of Sister *(Conflux Press, 2004) and three* Creative
Writing Adventure *books from Roost Books/Shambhala:* Rip the Page! *(2010),*
Leap Write In! *(2013), and forthcoming in September 2015:* Uncap That Pen! *A
writing coach and a poet with California Poets in the Schools, she lives north of
the Golden Gate Bridge with her husband, son, and two literary assistants: a cat
named Clive and a dog named Rasco Roon. Visit her at www.karenbenke.com.*

The Pretty and the Strong

Lisa Marie Lopez

Life was unfair. As I stood in front of the bathroom mirror struggling to cover up a mountain-size pimple on my chin, my sister was preparing for a weekend of royalty.

"So, what do you think of my gown, Jaymee? The lady at the store said it would make the perfect Prom Queen dress."

Prom Queen. The words made me cringe. I was sick of hearing about it: gowns, limos, corsages and, of course, Cassandra's new jock boyfriend, Brian Lieberman, who was most likely to be crowned Prom King.

I shrugged. I felt about as pretty as a dead rose standing beside my sister. Her gown was out-of-this-world-gorgeous—long and sparkly, the same shade as her blue eyes. "It's nice," I forced myself to say. "I'm sure Brian will like it."

"It's going to be perfect," Cassandra went on. "Wait until you see the necklace Mom's lending me." She trotted downstairs, and I heard Mom sigh and fuss over how beautiful she looked.

I spent the rest of the evening curled up in bed, listening to The Rolling Stones with my giant headphones. The music drowned out the chatter downstairs, and I was able to fall asleep without having bad dreams about long, smothering gowns and glittery acne cream. Sometimes, it's not easy being the pretty girl's sister.

The next day, Mom gave me money to buy new clothes. She said, now that I was thirteen, it was time I stop wearing the same old T-shirts and shorts everywhere. But I couldn't care less about having a nice collection of floral tops and stylish jeans like my sister. I went to Kmart and bought the cheapest clothes I could find. Afterward, I called up my best friend, Nikki, and told her we should go to Zandie's Records.

"Everybody says your sister's going to get Prom Queen for sure," Nikki said. "Is she nervous?"

We were rummaging through used CDs in the back of the store. I raised one eyebrow but didn't look up. "How would I know, it's not like we talk about those kinds of things."

We used to talk about everything, my sister and I. But once Cassandra started high school, all she wanted to do was hang out with her trendy cheerleader friends and kiss boys. Suddenly, the three years between us felt like ten.

Nikki didn't have any sisters, just three brothers. "You must be so happy for her," she said.

I merely smiled. "Cassandra excels at everything she tries for," I said. "She'll probably end up being President some day." That's when I came upon a CD by The Rolling Stones that I'd never seen before. It was like finding a diamond ring at a garage sale. "I can't believe it," I said. "This one's imported from England. It includes a bunch of live tracks and B sides."

Nikki agreed it was a must have. It was only eight dollars, so we went ahead and picked out two more. At the counter, a girl with a pierced lip stared at me and asked, "Hey, aren't you the Prom Queen's sister?"

I glanced at my dirty Converse shoes. Suddenly, I wanted to grab the girl's silver hoop piercing and drag it across the fabric of my sister's prom gown. But it wouldn't matter; Cassandra could make even the ugliest pair of sweat pants look pretty.

"Cassandra hasn't been crowned Prom Queen yet," I told her, as if she'd said something offensive. "She might not even win. Danielle Hanson might."

The girl didn't seem the least bit swayed by my suggestion; neither did Nikki. Who was I fooling? Even I wasn't convinced. I guess I was just tired of hearing my sister's name. I spent the last of the money on goodies from 7-Eleven.

"If I hear one more person mention Cassandra and the prom, I'm moving to another state," I informed Nikki. We were sitting on a bench outside 7-Eleven, munching on Doritos and sipping cherry ICEEs.

"It's not like the prom's going to last forever," Nikki reminded me. "Right now, everybody's excited because it's getting so close. Once it's over, all everybody's going to be talking about is summer vacation."

"Maybe," I said. The kids might forget, but come Thanksgiving, the relatives would be admiring her prom pictures. Talk around the dinner table would be all about Cassandra and the upcoming senior ball.

When the big day arrived, my sister was so excited, she broke a saucer at the breakfast table. I found it amusing but kept my laughter inside and focused on fishing for red hoops in my Fruit Loops. Cassandra was too nervous to eat multicolored cereal, so Mom made her toast with grape jelly.

A half-hour before Brian was to arrive, the house became a photo shoot. I was mesmerized when I first saw my sister in her gown and blonde hair in an elegant up-do. She looked more beautiful than ever, but I didn't tell her that. Instead, I watched briefly from the top of the stairs as she smiled and waved in front of flashing cameras, like a movie star. Then I holed up in the bedroom for the rest of the night and, with my giant headphones, listened to the new CDs I'd bought from Zandie's.

I woke up five hours later to the sound of my sister crying. I flicked on the light and found Cassandra lying face down on top of her bed, sobbing into her pillow. My initial thought was that she didn't get Prom Queen.

"Cassandra, oh my gosh, I'm so—"

"I got it," she said, but wouldn't look up at first. "I'm the Prom Queen."

I sat beside her, perplexed. "So then, why are you crying?"

She sat up and sighed. Her face was smeared with black mascara mixed with tears. "Brian ruined the entire night. Of course, he got Prom King, but it didn't matter. He's a jerk, Jaymee. All he cared about was getting me out of there and ..."

Her upper lip began to tremble, and I suddenly found myself fuming like a volcano about to erupt. I was sure, if I tried, I could make a hole in the wall with my fist. I wanted to punch Brian in the face and tell him he was a worthless creep, more scummy than the floor of a gas station restroom.

I lay beside Cassandra the whole night. I told her she was too good to let some jerk bring her down. We talked about boys and music and what we hoped our husbands would be like. She assured me I would make a guy very lucky one day. She told me I was a great listener and a fun person to be around. She also said I was strong, the stronger of the two of us. I told her I didn't realize just how strong I could be until I saw how much she needed me.

I congratulated her on making Prom Queen and told her she looked beautiful in her gown. She smiled and hugged me tight, and I started to cry. Sometimes, it's not easy being the pretty girl's sister.

* * * * *

Lisa Marie Lopez was born and raised in Northern California, where she still lives today. She has a twin sister, who along with her husband, is her best friend. When not writing, Lisa enjoys reading, playing her bass guitar and rooting for the San Francisco Giants. She's had several short stories published in various anthologies and magazines. She completed a course at Long Ridge Writers Group in 2012 were she was fortunate enough to have author Lou Fisher as her mentor/instructor. Visit Lisa Marie at http://www.lisamarieworldoffiction.webs.com.

Her Name is Belinda

David Lucero

I must have been in my early teens when I asked my mother if she wished she had a daughter along with my brother and me. I asked this question while she was preparing dinner in the kitchen. I sat at the table waiting for her to answer.

My mother lifted her head in thought, and a quick second later she said without further hesitation a flat, "No."

She was not adamant about it, but I knew my mother's word to mean what she said, as always.

I was surprised to hear this. I believed up to that time a woman preferred to give birth to girls. Girls were supposed to be more fun than boys. A mother could relate to girls growing up, and guide them much in the way a father guides his sons, or at least how a father should guide his sons.

I asked my mother why.

Again, without hesitation my mother answered, "If I had had a girl, your dad would have spoiled her rotten, and she would have grown up hating me for trying to keep her in line."

I was too young then to understand, but something about the way my mother answered told me she was probably right. Still, from time to time I wondered what it would have been like to have a sister.

In our household it was only my brother and me, and Mom and Dad. We had a dog and cat, too, and traveled a lot because my father served in the U.S. Air Force for twenty-three years.

Everywhere we went I made friends with people who had brothers and sisters. It was fun enough having my brother to hang out with. We were best friends. This was especially true when my father accepted a transfer to a new post, and my brother and I had to make friends all over again.

I was the oldest, the protector and, I am embarrassed to say, sometimes the bully. What caught my attention about boys with sisters was how protective they were of them, especially the younger sisters. When we hung out and played baseball, football, or went hiking, their sisters always joined us. Not once do I remember the girls being asked to leave us boys alone. They were part of the team. And that was that.

Sisters touched my life in a new way when I got married. My wife, Martha, had two sisters. The oldest was Becky, who lived with her husband in Mexico. The distance between her home and San Diego, where we lived, did not afford me the pleasure of meeting her often. Sadly, she died in a tragic accident in 2001.

Thus, I am grateful Martha's youngest sister, Belinda, has been integral to my life for a long time. From the start, I could see she was special. She was going to college in Berkeley, had her future planned out, and was a lot of fun to hang out with. She also had a very special relationship with Martha and my son, Carlo. He grew up with her babysitting him and introducing him to many of her friends. And when Carlo had difficulty in school, I always reminded him how doing well in school had benefited his Tia Belinda, and he would be wise to follow her example.

My proudest day came when my son received his bachelor's degree from San Diego State University. He worked long and hard, and deserved this honor. His graduation also took place on my birthday, the best present I could have received. I thanked Belinda for all she had done for Carlo to help him get his degree, and she asked what I meant by that. I told her when Carlo was a senior in high school there was a particular essay he needed to complete. Belinda had visited us that evening and Carlo had gotten distracted. When it was time for bed, Carlo said he would just explain to the teacher he was unable to complete the essay due to family obligations. Belinda told him how when she was in college she stayed up late many nights completing homework due the next day. It was just part of life, sucking it up and doing what had to be done. Carlo got the point. The next day he turned in his essay on time.

This was the best piece of advice an aunt could have given her nephew. I believed then, as I do today, that her encouragement directly resulted in my son's determination to be the best he could be. When I told Belinda this, to my surprise and disappointment, she had no recollection of having had that conversation with Carlo. I blame myself for waiting so long to tell her how much her remarks had meant to Carlo and me.

I have always admired my wife's sister for her work ethic, for being a loving mother to her two sons and a devoted wife to her husband. But I especially admire her for giving my son a piece of advice that has helped him become a successful man in every sense of the word. Belinda's words were and still are to my son what they were, and still are, to me today: Inspiration.

I have a sister. Her name is Belinda.

· · · · ·

Award-winning author David Lucero lives with his wife, Martha, in San Diego, California. He is a U.S. Army veteran and has worked in the home improvement industry for more than two decades. His first novel, The Sandman, *was Military Writer's Society of America's 1st Runner-Up for Best Fiction in 2009.* Who's Minding the Store *is his second book, released in 2012. He is currently working on his third novel. Follow him at www.LuceroBooks.com.*

Meeting in the Ring

Susan Ford

My younger sister, Paula, feels
it's her job to let me know I'm not
doing it right, not doing it her way.

It's Saturday. She's had enough of my niceness,
challenges me to a fistfight.
My mother's at work, my father
watches the Red Sox, while
my two younger brothers, Bobby and Kevin
build the longest bridge in
the world with their erector set.

I ignore her
but she will have none
of it. It is time to settle
all the mountains and mole
hills that stand between us.
Fist fighting does not come naturally
to me. Paula eggs me on,
excitement brews, my father
lets us go at one another.
We've all had enough of her bossiness,
there's rooting and hollering
for someone to stand up to her.

She jumps on the bed and pulls me up.
Swinging pillows at each
other, pulling hair, we dance
like the wrestlers
on TV. Surprisingly,
I am a natural
swinging wildly. Our fierceness
builds, turns to laughter. Each
time the peanut gallery roots
against her, she throws a punch. I
match it. The rhythm of our dance

slows, we grow exhausted, land
on our backs, tears
streaming freely with pure
laughter washing the slate clean.
My brothers and father want more.
But we called it quits. She is finally satisfied
that I showed her what I am made of.

* * * * *

Susan Ford, originally from Boston, Mass., has resided in San Francisco since 1975. She is a professional storyteller and teaches gentle yoga in the San Francisco Bay Area. Susan is working on a group of family poems and a collection of short stories focusing on age discrimination, war and belonging.

Sisters of an Only Child

Eva Kende

As a child in Budapest, I had neither siblings, nor a father to protect my mother and me from the vagaries of war and communist dictatorship. I didn't feel the impact of the situation, because most of my friends and schoolmates were in the same circumstances. Many were only children, who, like me, were growing up without fathers in an oddly created, but quite typical post-war family where mother, grandmother and often an aunt or great aunt formed the nucleus of the family, with a regularly visiting male relative fulfilling the surrogate father role.

For unquestioning sisterly companionship, I had my best friend Marianna, with whom I shared a pram at the beginning of our friendship. Often, after a play date, the mothers couldn't separate us when it was time to go home. We clung to each other fiercely, hugging and kissing.

To look up to and admire as an older sister, I had my distant cousin Zsuzsa. I have a picture of her as a young woman with a note from me on the back: "I love this Zsuzsa very much." Roughly sixty years have passed since I wrote that, but the sentiment has not changed. Once, about fifteen years ago, she was asked at a small party how we are related. She replied, "You'd need a pair of binoculars to track that."

Sadly, I did not come of age in the company of Marianna and Zsuzsa. In the early afternoon on October 23, 1956, I was sitting in our sunlit Budapest bedroom, peacefully listening to the latest pop hits on the radio and doing my homework. Hours later, my life was turned upside down when the Hungarian Revolution broke out. Several days of huddling inside with news dominating air waves and shots ringing out in the distance were followed by a tentative peace and the hope that the country had gained its independence. Peace and optimism were short lived, because the Russian army returned to claim the country. In less than four months, I was a refugee in frozen Winnipeg, adjusting to a totally different life.

In time, Canada gave me many good things, including a caring stepfather and two stepsisters. My new family supported me and cheered me on. Ruth, the older of the two sisters, was anxious to help me become "Canadianized." She taught me to shave my armpits, pick raspberries, and encouraged me to participate in activities appropriate for my age, like horseback riding, which until then, I only read about in books. In return, I entertained her young daughters when she visited us, allowing her free time to gossip with her Winnipeg friends before she returned to her small-town-Saskatchewan life at summer's end.

I had a much stronger bond with my other stepsister, Shirley. She lived in Winnipeg at the time and would visit us with her husband and two boys on Sundays. They owned a discount department store, and she would often arrive with an armload of new clothes and order me to model them. I pirouetted through the living room to the disinterest of male eyes and mother's confused gaze, for she didn't understand current western fashion, or Shirley's critical assessment. When the show was over, she would choose six or seven garments and then ask her father to pay for them. When he would hesitate, she'd put on her sweetest smile, her head cocked to bridge the distance between her five foot frame and his nearly six foot height. This was guaranteed to melt her gruff father's heart. Then she would say, "But Daddy, Eva can't wear hand-me-down clothes to University!" I vividly recall how he would shrug his shoulders and put his big hands into his pockets to come up with a fist full of dollars to give her. He didn't believe in wallets. He often said that only "tight"—meaning cheap—men used wallets.

Shirley did the same thing with shoes. We both wore size five, the size salesmen carried for samples. Twice a year, one company would release all the samples for a fraction of their value in the basement of the Hudson's Bay Company. Shirley would buy a bunch for herself and for me. Anything neither of us liked she would return. One day I was accidentally in the Bay when they brought out the shoes. I headed to the phone booths lining the wall, next to the gleaming brass elevators operated by smartly groomed women with white gloves and uniforms. I was disappointed when I got no answer at Shirley's home. Coming out, I contemplated whether I should chose a few pairs for her, when the door opened on the adjacent phone booth, and Shirley came sailing out. She had been trying to call me. We had a good laugh as we headed to the basement, where we spent the afternoon companionably, digging through the mountain of shoes in every color imaginable.

Although she was more than a decade older than I, we developed the closeness of sisters without the competition that causes friction among "real" sisters. She was the matron of honor at my wedding, a natural choice, since I wore her wedding dress.

Later, while I was living in Edmonton, caring for a young child, working full time and supporting my husband's career, a big rift developed in the family. I should probably have tried to smooth things over, but my life was too busy. My mother was on the warpath with my stepfamily, for reasons that are not clear to me even now, and I lost Shirley, who was deeply wounded in the process. I felt guilty, but powerless for years.

Finally, decades later, I mustered the courage to call her. At first, she was her old self. She sounded cheerful and interested in my life, just as she used to be. Then, as if a curtain had descended, she became distant and suspicious. She asked why I called. I told her it was just to say: "I love you and miss you, but I understand your feelings."

Shirley and I never talked again, but I kept regular tabs on her through my niece. She passed away a few years ago, and while I understood, vaguely, what came between us, it didn't make losing her easier. Marianna and I are not especially close now, but we both know we are there for each other and always share in each other's milestones. Thanks to the Internet and cheap long-distance packages, Zsuzsa and I are closer than ever in spirit. Looking back, I must say I am very fortunate to have had these "adopted" sisters and their love in my life.

* * * * *

Eva Kende was born in Budapest and came to Canada as a refugee in 1957. She earned her BSc in 1963 and worked as a biochemist in medical research for over twenty years, before starting to write in English. After the success of her cookbook Eva's Hungarian Kitchen, *she published another cookbook,* Eva's Kitchen Confidence, *the memoir* Snapshots... Growing up Behind the Iron Curtain, *and several articles. Eva lives in the beautiful Canadian Rockies.*

Paper Cranes

Gwynn O'Gara

Every day since her sister died
the woman folds paper into birds.
Dozens of cranes dangle from beam,
molding and mantel, crowding
her house with her sister's absence
and prayers for safe passage.

While she folds, the woman sees her sister
abandon a ragged tent beside a glacier,
climb beyond the visible world
and ascend in light to the fiery dark.
She remembers bubbles in the tub,
pleasure in her sister's pliable nature,
impatience with her ambivalence,
pink Chinese pajamas at Christmas.

She's lost count of the birds,
the rends in time and space.
She feels her way along folds
she no longer needs to see,
pushes needle and thread through
each bird's heart and tethers it,
her fingers know the knots.

One day the needle breaks.
She means to get a new one
but life claims her back—son,
husband, work, the comfrey
in the side yard that just won't die.
Coming home one evening
the cranes bother her.
She doesn't need reminding.
Grief has settled in her bones.
She yanks one down, the pin
flies out of sight. She'll call a friend,
take them all down tonight.

． ． ． ． ．

Gwynn O'Gara served as the Sonoma County Poet Laureate from 2010 to 2012 and has taught with California Poets in the Schools for over twenty years. Her poems have been published in Spoon River Poetry Review, Calyx, The Evansville Review, *and the* Beatitude Silver *and* Golden Anniversary *anthologies. Her books include* Snake Woman Poems *and the chapbooks* Fixer-Upper *and* Winter at Green Haven.

Darkling River

Nancy Pogue LaTurner

I lived in solid obedience to God's will until an onrushing stream of events washed away the roots of my faith.

In my reckoning, Jasper's journey to Bermuda provided the wellspring for what followed, although Jasper himself played a minor role. He went to the islands as a missionary for our church, but he came back home to Minnesota in less than a year with a wife.

Everyone whispered behind his back. When I first laid eyes on Flossie, I understood. A halo of magic surrounded her. Her brown skin glowed with it. Her dark eyes sparkled with it. Her bright teeth glinted with it in an ever-present smile. Flossie bubbled with joy. She sang songs that weren't hymns. She had music inside her and she danced to it as she swept the floor or hung her washing on the line. Flossie was unseemly, dangerous, irresistible—and my sister-in-law.

Jasper brought her home in 1895, the same year I married his younger brother, Elmer. I witnessed the birth of their first child, fetching towels and water for our sister-in-law Ella who so capably took charge. When my own angel, Francie, was born the next year, Flossie stayed by my side all through the long, painful hours. Her ministrations touched me in the most intimate places, with precious tenderness and reverence. She encouraged me to accept the functions of my body during childbirth no matter how shocking or unpleasant. She showed me how to embrace the slippery, blood-streaked infant and encourage her to suckle.

Flossie's sturdy Serena was nine months of age the day my sweet baby Francie passed into the arms of Our Lord at the tender age of seven weeks. It was Flossie who nursed me back to health and gave me courage. Her gentle hands soothed my wretched headaches and her sprightly cheer sparked hope in my ravaged heart.

Our husbands worked side by side in the oat fields and barnyards while Flossie and I kept house and gardened and brought forth our children. We attended each other's lying-in and had no need of midwife or doctor. Flossie's buoyant outlook carried me through the long hours of labor and my gratitude overflowed into fervent adoration of her flawless, magical persona.

Flossie saved me again when the Lord took my delicate Dulcie at age five. The typhoid fever struck my darling girl and no amount of tender loving care could save her. Beloved Flossie held me in her arms and sang her favorite lullaby to balm my wounded soul.

Baby's boat's the silver moon,
Sailing in the sky
Sailing o'er the sea of sleep,
While the clouds float by.
Sail, baby, sail,
Out upon that sea,
Only don't forget to sail
Back again to me.

A year later, the Lord blessed me with rosy Cora, my fourth-born daughter. Flossie's laugh tinkled when I asked how could I be so full of babies.

Soon after that, Flossie celebrated her own blessed event when Reggie's first cries burst forth on a blustery March morning like a cockerel's crow at daybreak. Flossie was as full of babes as I was, but hers came out as easy as an egg from a hen and all lived in robust health thereafter.

My life ripened, rich with love, hard work, and laughter—until that inevitable day, the second day of August 1905, when Flossie wished to join the Tichenor youngsters on a berry-picking expedition. As always, she included me in her plans. Young Everett Tichenor had a boat, she said, to take us to the raspberry patch on the east bank of the Swan River, and he'd bring his younger sisters, Goldie and Edith, who were twenty and seventeen years old. It was a small boat, she told me, so we'd leave our combined seven children with our sister-in-law, Ella, for the day.

I never could say no to Flossie, not in the ten years I knew her, no matter how fanciful her desire. So I said yes, even though a familiar queasy feeling in my stomach told me that I had another baby on the way and I might not be at my best for a frolicsome day in the berry patch. I could have insisted we stay home, but I knew my reluctance would be no match for Flossie's gay enthusiasm.

We set off from the Tichenor place at eight o'clock in the morning. Everett and Edith took the boat up the lagoon to its mouth where it emptied into the river. Flossie, Goldie, and I walked through the fields so we could pick onions and radishes to add to our lunch basket.

When we were done, Everett helped us back into the flat-bottomed boat and we wedged our baskets beneath the rough plank seats. I tucked the hem of my shirtwaist behind my lower limbs but Flossie and the younger girls let their skirts flutter in the breeze. Flossie threw her arms wide and tilted her face toward the sun as she sang a bright tune in her sparkling voice:

> Row, row, row your boat
> Gently down the stream.
> Merrily, merrily, merrily, merrily,
> Life is but a dream.

She taught us how to start singing, one after the other—she called it a "round." I prayed for God's forgiveness of such worldly frivolity. All aglow, Flossie lifted my hand in both of hers and brought it to her lips. I died inside at the rising heat that filled my chest and blazed my cheeks. The others didn't see, but I knew that God watched.

Everett called a halt to the singing and pointed out that the boat had sprung a leak. He rowed toward the nearest bank where we could land and tip the water out before it got deep enough to wet our shoes. It didn't look like enough water to worry about, and I trusted Everett's experience with boating. In a trice, we gained the shore and Everett planted one foot on the grassy bank.

Flossie, Goldie, Edith, and I, eager to help Everett bail, all stood up at once, all on the same side of the boat. I've asked myself a thousand times: Why? Why didn't I step to the opposite side?

The boat capsized, dumping us into the swift current of the chill river.

I floundered in the murky water, flailing and kicking, dragged down by my sodden skirt. My hair tore loose from its tidy bun and swirled across my eyes and cheeks. I spluttered to the surface and saw the desperate tableau of Everett holding Goldie in one arm and Edith in the other while pushing Flossie ahead of them in the direction of the riverbank.

Not knowing how to swim, I bobbed and sank like a fishing cork. I went under many times before I realized I could use my hands like boat oars to push my head above water for a breath. But the cruel current fought my efforts to stay afloat. Roiling water pushed me hither and yon. My saturated shirtwaist pulled me down, down, down.

I felt the ooze of muck under my hands and used all my power to crawl like an infant on the bottom until I reached the shore. Pulling on fistfuls of long grass, I dragged myself half out of the river and lay prostrate, lungs agonizing for breath, coughing up dank water that tasted of organisms long dead.

When I turned toward the river, there was Flossie! She floated serenely with her face barely visible above the water. I called her name through my raw throat. I clutched the nearest stick of useful length and thrust it out as a lifeline. My dear one stared straight up at the clouds above as the flow carried her away. Flossie!

I summoned the strength to stand upright. Dizziness almost brought me down. One step at a time, I stumbled downriver with hopes of catching up with precious Flossie and saving her from drowning. The raspberry bushes stopped me. The branches and thorns ripped at my clothes and tore jagged, bloody stripes along my arms. Why, oh why, couldn't I forge on through the thicket and find my beloved?

I cried out once more for Flossie and then turned 'round upriver to drag myself in the direction of the nearest farm, the Roshalts' place.

The Roshalts ran to greet me as I staggered up the path. My story gushed out in ragged bursts. Immediately, Mr. Roshalt organized a search party and sent word to town where Flossie's husband, Jasper, and my Elmer were working on repairs to Jasper's wagon. When Mr. Roshalt left to carry the news to the Tichenor family, I collapsed in the arms of Mrs. Roshalt and succumbed to delirium. I thrashed and moaned and reached for Flossie, whose face shone above me more glorious than the sun. My eventual return to consciousness struck like a slap. Where was my darling Flossie? Did she survive?

The searchers recovered Flossie's body that same Tuesday evening along with Edith's a few minutes later. On Saturday, they found Everett floating in a tangle of driftwood. They discovered Goldie's corpse on Sunday. All of them dead while I still breathed. My mind curdled with visions of pale, bloated bodies, sightless eyes, twisted limbs.

I couldn't bear to go to the church service or the burials. Jasper's grief fueled my own. I lay in my bed with curtains closed, eyes closed, heart closed, unable to pray, isolated in sorrow and guilt, estranged from my Lord God and Savior.

Elmer came to me, his face lined with worry and exhaustion. "Think about the children," he said. "Flossie and Jasper's as well as ours."

I reached out for God to give me strength and purpose. I vowed to devote myself to the care of my children and Flossie's children until they grew to adulthood. I pledged to bring as many more children into the world as God saw fit to give me. And I begged God's forgiveness for loving Flossie too much.

Now, seven months have passed since the accident. The child within me kicks with vigor and never rests – he'll be a boy, I'm sure. As first-born son, he'll get his father's name. I'm afraid to birth him without Flossie by my side. I long for the pleasant rasping of her calloused fingers that massaged the back-pain of my laboring. I yearn for the of Sen-Sen licorice fragrance of her breath as she whispered, "Push, dear Hazel, push now." Dare I hope that God might bless me with an easy time? I keep my Bible open to the Twenty-Third Psalm: "Yea, though I walk through the valley of the shadow of death …" in earnest hope of living in His light again.

Flossie consumes my thoughts, and the pain of her loss hangs heavy on my shoulders like a leaden shroud. When I'm alone, I bring out the newspaper clippings from the day of the accident. I keep the well-worn papers inside the back cover of my Bible, where they're easily at hand.

I weep when I read the verse at the end of the article in the Grand Rapids Independent:

> There is a river we all must cross
> > A river whose darkling storm
> Within the depth of eternity
> > Buries its silver gleam.

> With tearful eyes, we bid farewell
> > To those we knew of yore.
> Waiting the hour when our hands shall join
> > Upon time's deathless shore.

The darkling river calls to me in Flossie's voice. Tomorrow, I shall visit her shores to discover which part of me is stronger – the torn heart that yearns to reunite with beloved Flossie or the tortured soul that struggles to accept the healing power of God's love.

· · · · ·

Nancy Pogue LaTurner cherishes life-long membership in the sisterhood of writers. Her stories and essays have been published in The Albuquerque Almanac *as well as in several anthologies—*Wisdom Has a Voice, *the* Writers' Shack Anthology, *and all four volumes of* Seasons of Our Lives. *She is also the author of* Voluntary Nomads: A Mother's Memories of Foreign Service Family Life. *Besides writing, Nancy loves hiking in the mountains and kayaking in calm waters.*

Asha

Elaine Webster

Asha found me
perched atop a stoop —
two friendless children
one from Turkey
both in Queens.

Hot summertime streets spurred
trips to the schoolyard. Cool water
sprinkling from a pole brought us
barefoot giggles
soggy beach suits.

Hopscotch numbered boxes defined
our path. Spinning tops
hula hoops jump ropes traded
for swings and monkey bars.

With unbridled giggles we braided
our pigtails tied them with bright
colored ribbons dazzling
against our worn dungarees
our ice cream stained shirts.

I fell in love with Asha
couldn't let her go
yet she left.

A memory tastes of
blueberries, sour cream
sweet in Asha's kitchen
sour as my youth.

. . . . .

Elaine Webster writes fiction, nonfiction, memoir, essays, and poetry. Her memoir of the 1970s, Balanced on the Edge of the Crowd, *employs the same memoir-style writing as the author's nonfiction works:* Jesse's Tale: Overcoming Fear Aggression and Separation Anxiety in an Adopted Greyhound *and* Heartfelt: Caregiver's Guide to Cardiomyopathy and Mitral Valve Surgery. *Elaine's poetry has appeared in Redwood Writers anthologies,* The Sound of a Thousand Leaves, *and* And The Beats Go On.

Set Five

· ·

From None to Many – memoir, Jan Boddie

First Medicine – poem, Gwynn O'Gara

Picker Sisters – memoir, Diana M. Amadeo

Lucy and Ethel Break In – memoir, Debra Ayers Brown

Celebrating Flo's 60th Birthday – poem, Nellie Wong

Groovy Sisters – memoir, Nadia Ali

Hero – memoir, Pamela Taeuffer

Born of a Chill Wind – memoir, P. H. Garrett

Light Show – poem, D. A. (Daisy) Hickman

A Time of Magic – essay, Patricia Jackson

Quilts – poem, Mark Wisniewski

Sisterly Tribes of the Modern Age – essay, Erica Brown

The Science of Sisterhood – poem, Sue Kreke Rumbaugh

From None to Many

Jan Boddie

I grew up with a brother five years older than me in a family that relocated often. I ached for an older sister, one who would tell me things my parents shared in whispers and my brother refused to discuss. A prayer I repeated almost daily was, "Please God, give me a sister."

When I was seven, a second brother was born. I loved him very much, but begged for a younger sister. Each time we moved, I was snatched without warning from my friends. No chance to even say goodbye. Usually we landed in a different city during summer vacation, and when fall came I was the new kid at school. I wanted to kick and scream every time the packing began, but didn't dare until the months between my fourth and fifth grades. Empowered by circumstance, I yelled at God, "I want my sister! Now!"

After that move, the attic in our new home became my personal playing field until school started. I explored boxes of toys and games, old clothes and lots of cartons with papers. I found some of my older brother's schoolwork and was breathless when I saw his last name, Cabelus. Our name was Chartier. Suddenly, everything looked fuzzy. I felt cold, almost numb, and knew I had uncovered a secret, part of a shadow that had haunted me for as long as I could remember. I wanted to know what the other name meant, but braced myself before I ran downstairs and called out to my mom. I knew she would not be pleased. She never welcomed my questions.

My hands shook as I held up that single sheet of paper and asked, "Why is Ray's name different?"

Mom looked down, speechless, then spoke in a stern tone, "It was a long time ago, my first husband's name. He's Ray's father, your father too. But that's in the past; my husband today is your father now. He's the one who supports, takes care of us. That's it. Don't ever bring this up again, to me or your brother."

She grabbed the paper and walked away. As soon as I could get him alone, I implored my big brother to tell me what he remembered. But he had been sworn to secrecy. He looked angry, shook his head and left the room.

Our moves to new cities fostered more isolation. I needed a trusted, caring sister the day I sat on the toilet and saw blood on my underwear. And there was more when I wiped myself. I looked up and silently screeched, Why am I being punished? What did I do? and Please! Don't let me die!

I had no sister, no solace. I was alone with my fear and grief, my confusion and self-blame, until my mom opened the door. I felt ashamed, wished I was dead and wondered, How did she know? Mom was uncomfortable and matter of fact as she told me the bleeding was normal. She called it my period and said I was no longer a child but a young woman. I cringed when she said the blood would return every month, and was furious she had never warned me.

When I was nineteen I tracked down my biological dad, Ray Cabelus. After a brief phone call we met for dinner. It did not go well. First, I declined his invitation to order a cocktail. Second, he began to tell stories that made my mother the problem in their relationship. I knew he had left for another woman and told him to stop blaming my mom. Next he wanted me to meet his second wife and their kids. Fearing a third refusal would guarantee I'd never see him again, I agreed. As it turned out his wife wasn't home. He introduced me to four young and noisy boys and one girl. Overwhelmed, I wondered, Is she my sister? My evening with dad ended soon after and he promised to stay in touch. Silly me, I never thought he'd abandon me a second time, but he did. I found solace elsewhere.

Throughout my twenties, thanks to college friends I met before dropping out, the Boston-Cambridge folk music scene, and a job I loved at a small publishing house on Beacon Hill, I experienced the camaraderie of sisters. My best friends were young women with open hearts. They spoke their truth and shared their knowledge. Instead of yelling or fleeing from disagreements, they stood strong and worked through them. They weren't afraid to cry, and were generous in giving and receiving apologies. Their presence in my life helped me to catch-up and grow-up. My words and actions became less guarded, more spontaneous. My greatest victory was being able to talk during shared meals. Long before I entered high school I had learned to hide in the safety of silence because my step-dad turned all my attempts at conversation into arguments and insults. He even succeeded in teaching my younger brother, his son, to do the same.

During my Boston days I met Eddie, now deceased. He was black; I'm white. When I told my mom we were getting married, she disowned me. Eddie wanted me to tell my dad about our engagement.

"He doesn't care," I said.

"All dads care," he insisted.

After a few days, I made the call. When I told him the news, the first words Dad uttered were, "Does your mother approve?" When I responded in the negative, he asked, "What's the problem? Is he black or something?" A long pause folllowed. Finally, my dad said he had no right to judge, he was an alcoholic, his kidneys were failing and his wife had left him for another man. Then he said, "I'd like to meet him."

When I returned to college in my late thirties, I had more confidence and social skills. For the first time, I shared family secrets with my friends and talked about my yearning for a sister. Later, I met my true sister of the heart, Marystella, now my beloved partner of twenty-one years. She knows all my secrets. We play and work together, share clothes and trade treasures. Sometimes we argue, and we always make up.

Marystella and I knew we were soul mates the moment we met. A week later she came to my place for dinner. After hours of asking each other questions and sharing stories, I invited her to spend the night. That was a first for me. My life-long pattern was to spend months getting to know someone before I would engage in a first kiss. Marystella responded by jumping up from the couch and running to the stairs, "I brought a toothbrush just in case. It's in my car. I'll be right back!" That night the two of us joined the sisterhood of lesbians.

In my sixth decade my biological half-sister, Raelene, found me after a long search on the Internet. Though she was one of the children running around my dad's house years earlier, she didn't remember our brief encounter. We communicated by email, then phone, and soon after Marystella and I flew from San Francisco to Boston. Lenny, Raelene's husband, and Marystella shook their heads and chuckled as they watched Raelene and me interact. We had the same mannerisms, similar speech patterns, and even had the same favorite drink. Back East it's called a Sombrero, a mixture of coffee liqueur and cream. Diabetes was Raelene's downfall. A year after we met I returned to the East Coast and stayed close when she had her left leg amputated below the knee. When she died the following year my friends were heartbroken for me. Of course I mourned my loss, but my gratitude for the time we had shared far outweighed my grief. I did have a younger sister. She was born eight years after me.

Now in my seventh decade, with old wounds and worries healed, I have far more sisters than the one I prayed for long ago. Thank you, Goddess.

* * * * *

Jan Boddie PhD, a Massachusetts native and former psychotherapist, wrote the-atre reviews for Broadside *folk music magazine throughout the 1960s. She later moved to San Francisco and was one of the original counselors on San Francisco General Hospital's AIDS Unit. She self-published* Circle Left to Enter Rite *in the '90s and has had several articles and stories published in magazines and anthologies. An active member of Redwood Writers, Jan is completing her spiri-tual memoir,* Lessons from Earth & Spirit. *www.vortexjourneys.com and www.vortexgreenjewelry.net*

First Medicine

Gwynn O'Gara

You get the kids to practice,
cook and get to work without
imploding and becoming a burden.

Yet grief catches up with you,
the missed appointments only postponed.
The safety pin on the floor appears
incredibly sad like the night heron's
rasp flying home at dawn.

Tears, mess, mysteries
about a brassy woman afraid
of a hip replacement. You want
to go down to the dark, die
a little, join the one you lost.

The red-shouldered hawk cries out
her longing, grief and hunger.
Poppies close at night. So can we,
till dawn's noisy light.

* * * * *

Gwynn O'Gara served as the Sonoma County Poet Laureate from 2010 to 2012 and has taught with California Poets in the Schools for over twenty years. Her poems have been published in Spoon River Poetry Review, Calyx, The Evansville Review, *and the* Beatitude Silver *and* Golden Anniversary *anthologies. Her books include* Snake Woman Poems *and the chapbooks* Fixer-Upper *and* Winter at Green Haven.

Picker Sisters

Diana M. Amadeo

We started out as nurses at the same hospital, although never in the same unit. The night shift has a way of unifying NICU and gerontology nurses, just by virtue of being fellow night stalkers. Later, we found ourselves on the same bowling league, although not on the same team. Through the years, we discovered that we shared similar religious upbringings and had complementary ideas on how to live in a world that sometimes seems otherworldly. Mutual pregnancies and raising children solidified our bond. Over our thirty years of friendship, we've seen and lived it all while dealing with chronic diseases: mine, multiple sclerosis; hers, systemic lupus erythematosus. We supported each other through wheelchairs, crutches and hospitalizations with teasing and laughter. But it was our mutual love of picking—finding funky, eclectic, unusual, artsy-fartsy beauty in objects most people see only as mundane—that made us related.

We are picker sisters. And we dubbed ourselves this long before the History Channel embraced the notion.

Usually, Marion's style is decidedly different than mine. When she taught me the fine art of jewelry making with Swarovski crystals, her style was big and bold; mine much more understated. Yet we appreciate each other's "eye," or lack thereof, with a keen sense of humor.

After the kids had grown, our families seldom had the opportunity to spend time together. Yet, barring bouts of illness or other calamities, Marion and I would meet over coffee once a month and then visit one or two haunts to pick over the goods.

"Oh, look at this!" I said one day at a local thrift shop, while holding up an old, wooden perpetual calendar.

"You have one," she replied wryly.

"It would look good on my new porch," I said, ignoring her.

"This would look good on my new porch," she said ironically, picking up a gaudy wicker basket filled with faded dusty plastic flowers.

"You don't have a new porch," I said.

"Exactly my point," Marion said. "Now back away from the calendar."

Instead, the calendar went into my cart.

Marion found a limited-edition Barbie in impeccable shape. She slipped it into her cart, hoping I don't see. But I saw it, and so began my tale of finding the perfect, limited-edition Ballerina Barbie for a ten spot, yet worth triple digits, given to my two-year-old granddaughter. My grandbaby bonded with it immediately, called it "Bah-bee," and let it dance on the tabletop at a Mexican restaurant. When the server brought out chips, Bah-bee did pirouettes smack dab in the middle of the salsa.

Marion grunted. She'd heard the Barbie story many, many times.

I found a storage box in the shape of a book. "Oh look! *War and Peace*! It will go great on my book shelf."

"You have three of those," Marion reminded me.

"But I don't have *War and Peace*," I said, while placing it in a cart.

"What do you do—hide money in those?"

"Its function will be determined," I said defensively. "It has yet to speak to me."

Down another aisle, Marion picked up an antique rose-patterned jacket with brass buttons. "This baby is saying, 'Rescue me, Mommy.'" And it went into her cart.

And then I saw it, hanging on a distant wall. Marion looked up and spied it too. "On your mark, get set—" she began, But I'd already taken off with my cart, at record speed, despite my gimpy legs.

I beat her to the wall and carefully retrieved the black, white and red purse. I gently ran my hand over the faux leather pattern. The sexy figure on the bag looked back at me with big eyes and a familiar pout. It was a gently used, vintage handbag I'd researched many times online, but just couldn't justify the money spent. This, on the other hand, was priced just fine.

"Let me have it," Marion begged.

"Finders keepers, losers weepers, "I replied.

"I'll give you my Betty Boop bedroom slippers if you give her to me now."

"Your feet are bigger than mine," I said, placing the leather softly next to my cheek. "The lady belongs to me."

A third shopper cleared her throat. It was apparent that we were being watched.

"Don't mind us, "I said, with a smile. "We have no life."

Our observer tilted her head. "Quite the contrary," she said. "I had a friendship like yours once. It was sad when she moved away. What you two have is quite the life."

I looked at my long-time friend—this sister from another mother—and we simultaneously broke into infectious grins.

Indeed. We've had a wonderful life.

* * * * *

Multi-award winning author Diana M. Amadeo sports a bit of pride in having an excess of 500 publications with her byline in books, anthologies, magazines, newspapers and online. Yet, she humbly, persistently, tweaks and rewrites her thousand-or-so rejections with eternal hope that they may yet see the light of day.

Lucy and Ethel Break In

Debra Ayers Brown

Oprah has Gayle. Laverne had Shirley. Lucy had Ethel. I've had Joyce since the day we met. From the get-go, our bond felt more like family than friendship. Everyone mistook us for sisters, with our blonde hair, big smiles, and similar style. I'd never been happier to have a "sister" than when I pulled an all-nighter to meet marketing deadlines for the coastal community where I worked, and needed a partner in crime.

Everything moved according to plan until daylight, when I got ready to leave the two-person office to go home, take a shower, and then rush the booklet to the Savannah printer. That's when I realized my keys were nowhere in sight.

"This can't be happening," I moaned as I dumped the contents of my pocketbook onto the conference table. Pens and paperclips pinged against the table. My cell hit with a thud. Lipstick, compact, mints, and gum splayed out like a fan.

I dug into every hidden pocket in the cavernous purse. No car keys. I searched my desk, the kitchen, and finally the bathroom. No keys. I stared at the office where we housed our copy machine and financial records— the one I'd just turned the knob to lock as I pulled the door closed. Could I have laid them down inside when I turned off the light? I was so tired; anything was possible. Probable, even.

Panic replaced fatigue as I realized I had no office keys, no car keys, and no way to leave. Since we were in the early stages of selling lots in an isolated community, few people were nearby. To make matters worse, my boss, Ren, and my husband were out of town.

I glanced at the clock. I knew Joyce rose early, so I made the call. In no time, she arrived at the scene.

"Good morning, Sunshine," she said, looking perfect—well rested, dressed for the day, and ready to go. Even this morning, her smile made me feel better.

I didn't want to think about my appearance—sleep deprived, rumpled, and grimy. I couldn't be a pretty sight.

But Joyce overlooked it. She'd done it before. She's the one who always insisted I see the doctor when sick, take a fun break when stressed, and speak up about little annoyances before they got out of hand. She'd been the first to arrive when my father passed away. Through the years, we'd discussed dreams and disappointments, talked every day, and spent most holidays together. Joyce had definitely been more like a sister than a best friend. Truth be told, she'd been both. As an only child, I'd really lucked out when we made our sisterhood connection.

So, on this early Saturday morning, we shared my dilemma.

In an instant and with a Lucy-esque gleam in her eyes, Joyce announced, "I've got an idea."

"What?" I asked with Ethel's hesitant hope.

"We can break in."

"Have you been into the *vitameatavegamin*?" I asked her, remembering Lucy's attempt to sell the alcoholic tonic in a TV commercial. "We can't break in. We're not strong enough to break down the door." Maybe we did need a little *vitameatavegamin* to put some oomph behind our muscles. Maybe I needed to hit the gym more after this desk job.

Wide-eyed and eager to get started, Joyce said, "Don't be silly. I have tools in the car."

I waited at my desk. Joyce was always prepared. Once on an eco-tour, she happened to have the tweezers to pull out the prickly pear cactus stuck in my ankle. At a cancer walk, she had blister Band-Aids ready to go when I needed one. No doubt she'd come up with something to help us break in. But what would Ren think when he returned to find we'd taken the hinges off the door? Or broken the lock? We had lots of deadlines and pressures at work, so I wasn't sure how he'd react. He might get testy, and quite frankly, I wasn't in the mood to deal with it. So I started back-pedaling.

The front door slammed. Joyce whirled into the room. "I can't find even one tool."

"No problem," I said, relieved.

"We can't stop now," she insisted. "You need your keys. I'm sure we can get them."

Joyce rummaged in the kitchen drawers, crumpling papers and clanging through junk. Drawers slid open and shut. Cabinet doors creaked and then slammed.

While Joyce plundered, my fatigue started to get to me. Maybe all I really needed was a shot of *vitameatavegamin*, whatever it was. With blurry eyes, I decided to face reality before we went too far. We were heading for trouble.

"It's okay, Joyce," I said, brushing my hair away from my face with both hands. "Don't worry about it. I'll be okay."

"Don't be ridiculous. We can do this," she assured me. "Just give me a minute." One more door slammed shut. "Aha, this should do!"

Joyce spun around, wielding a paring knife and a plastic spoon, and handed a pair of scissors to me. Immediately, she pulled up on the door knob. "Stick the scissors in there."

I gulped, but followed her instructions. I inserted the scissors into the narrow opening between the door and the frame near the lock, twisting to find something to release it. My pulse raced.

Meanwhile, Joyce poked and prodded with her knife and spoon. "Push!" she ordered, and I automatically pushed. "Push again!" My knuckles ached, but I pushed harder.

Click.

I looked at Joyce. She turned to me with a grin inching across her face. I beamed at my Lucy with her devilish smile, big eyes, and a look that said, "We did it."

"Ren will never need to know," she said.

"Not unless he tries to lock the door."

I had to laugh. Just what would Ren think about our break-in? Would he appreciate Lucy's nerve and inventiveness? Or Ethel's "Okay, I'll give it a try," attitude—as long as Lucy didn't go too far? I'm sure I'd have some 'splaining to do.

I discarded my scissors and stared at Joyce's battered paring knife.

"Oops," I said, "That's Ren's favorite fish fillet knife."

Even so, I realized how lucky I was to have my own Lucy in my life. Joyce pulled me right into whatever she was doing—from trying a new diet to getting dressed up for a fancy event. She eased me out of my comfort zone. Think Zumba, Italian cooking classes, and even a mild case of breaking and entering.

But, who would know? Unless, of course, Ren noticed the tip of his knife was missing.

I looked at Joyce, my ally for life, with a twinkle in my eye.

"How are you at sharpening knives?" I had a little sneaky Lucy in me, too. "If we sharpen this, he'll never know what happened," I assured Joyce. "We can do this ... and then we'll go get breakfast."

The breaking-and-entering escapade reminded me sisters at heart and partners in crime could accomplish anything when they put their heads together—with or without *vitameatavegamin*.

* * * * *

Debra Ayers Brown is a creative nonfiction writer focusing on humor and inspiration as well as an award-winning marketing professional and social media trainer at Your Write Platform. She is published in numerous magazines and anthologies including Chicken Soup for the Soul, Not Your Mother's Books, Guideposts, Woman's World, *and more. Debra graduated from the University of Georgia and earned her MBA from The Citadel. Visit www.DebraAyersBrown. com and connect via www.About.Me/DebraAyersBrown.*

Celebrating Flo's 60th Birthday

Nellie Wong

Flo, Lai and I reunite at Lark Creek Restaurant
On a warm sunny day in San Mateo on October 29th
We greet each other with warm hugs
Sorry that Li Keng could not join us

On a warm sunny day in San Mateo on October 29th
Flo's 61st birthday is the special occasion
Sorry that Li Keng could not join us
We three sisters nevertheless eat with pleasure

Flo's 61st birthday is the special occasion
She looks grand in beige with a jade-green scarf
We three sisters nevertheless eat with pleasure
We still remember when we children ate on credit

She looks grand in beige with a jade-green scarf
Happy to know that Roger is slowly recovering
We still remember when we children ate on credit
"Lai," I say, "you ordered crab cakes last time!"

Happy to know that Roger is slowly recovering
We three sisters in our 60s are alive and well
"Lai," I say, "you ordered crab cakes last time!"
And Lai replies, "but it's a different restaurant!"

We three sisters in our 60s are alive and well
Flo opens gifts, a book of Inuit women artists and a Beany Baby pig
And Lai replies, "but it's a different restaurant!"
Gilbert Dair, restaurant manager, stops by to say hello
vFlo opens gifts, a book of Inuit women artists and a Beany Baby pig
Lai tells us that Allison has moved to her new house
Gilbert Dair, restaurant manager, stops by to say hello
On November 4, Li Keng speaks about her immigrant experience

Lai tells us that Allison has moved to her new house
Alex, Lai's youngest daughter, will help to commemorate Angel Island
On November 4, Li Keng speaks about her immigrant experience
The Gees will gather to celebrate our ancestral history

Alex, Lai's youngest daughter, will help to commemorate Angel Island
Our mother, Theo Quee Gee, emigrated over 60 years ago
The Gees will gather to celebrate our ancestral history
Flo sews and embroiders immigrant history on American flags

Our mother, Theo Quee Gee, emigrated over 60 years ago
The paper sister of our father, Seow Hong Gee
Flo sews and embroiders immigrant history on American flags
Our mother, Suey Ting Gee, reclaimed her real name

The paper sister of our father, Seow Hong Gee
Ma and Bah Bah would beam if they were here
Our mother, Suey Ting Gee, reclaimed her real name
Even though her grandchildren have different surnames

Ma and Bah Bah would beam if they were here
On a warm sunny day in San Mateo on October 29th
Even though her grandchildren have different surnames
We greet each other with warm hugs.

* * * * *

Nellie Wong is the author of a chapbook and three books of poetry, the most recent being Breakfast Lunch Dinner *(2012). Her work has appeared in numerous anthologies and journals, including* This Bridge Called My Back: Writings by Radical Women of Color, The Iowa Review, American Working Class Literature, The Haight-Ashbury Journal, The Paterson Literary Review, Voices of Color *and* Speaking for my Self: Twelve Women Poets in their Seventies and Eighties, *among others.*

Groovy Sisters

Nadia Ali

Two sisters wearing exactly the same groovy outfits with pride can only mean one thing: it's the Seventies! My sister, Shireen, and I were only two years apart in age, which enabled our mom to sew outfits for both of us. Yes, you read right, I said sew.

Back in the late Seventies, when we were teenagers, our mom sewed us long dresses that sported some really sweet patterns, not to mention far-out colors. She also made us elastic pants with huge bell-bottoms that were all the trend at that time. But the bigger thing was that our mom insisted on making us both exactly the same outfits in the same material. For people who knew us, we were cool sisters; to those who didn't, we must have represented a clothing buy-one-get-one-free sale.

Shireen and I were proud of our wardrobe. We especially liked to accessorize with huge platform shoes and adorn our hands and necks with big, chunky jewelry. We had a sense of what was trendy, suggesting to our mom that she add that extra bit of lace or ribbon to complete an outfit. We could rival any other sisters that came our way in looks and fashion. We had flower appeal, and we knew how to work it with our funky headbands. We were the ultimate "groovy chicks."

Now, as mothers of our own daughters, when we share our memories of these delightful times from our past, their reactions are less than favorable. Sherma, the eldest daughter, who is in her late 20s and was part of a drill team, laughs discreetly while trying to disassociate herself from us. Shari and Shazara, who are in their mid 20s, try a controlled laughter approach. Our younger daughters, Shanice and Raisah, don't pull out any stops and just laugh out loud. They all agree that "groovy sisters" we were not, and label us "geek sisters" by today's standards!

They especially dislike it when we put on our digitally remastered CDs with hits of the Seventies and show them what a dance move really looks like.

"Ewww! Mom, that's just embarrassing!" they say, rolling around in laughter as Shireen and I bop around the kitchen.

But, despite what they say, we knew that, back in the Seventies, if we had pursued it, we could have been high-fashion models asked to walk on the runways of Milan and Paris, because we were the ultimate Groovy Sisters!

· · · · ·

Nadia Ali is the smaller sister of Shireen Solomon who grew up in London, UK. Their mom kept them hip and happening in the '70s with psychedelic prints, bell bottoms and long flowery dresses. They always dressed to impress as the ultimate … Groovy Sisters!

Hero

Pamela Taeuffer

The day my sister's life changed forever, I came home from middle school at the usual time. Jenise, three years my senior, generally arrived a few hours behind me. She liked to hang out with her high school friends, talking, drinking soda or the occasional beer, and doing other things that occupy typical teenage girls. So when she was late, no one gave it a second thought, that is, until dinner came and went and she hadn't called.

My father was drunk, as always, and without his sparring partner at the table, he ate dinner quietly and went upstairs to bed. Our parents had bought my sister a cell phone so they could reach her, and she them. But that day, she didn't answer her phone. When my mother began cleaning the house after dinner instead of reading one of her romance novels, I knew something was very wrong.

"Did you hear from Jenise today?" Mom finally asked me.

"No, I came right home from school and then went up to my room to study," I said.

"Have you phoned her friends? I have some of their numbers if you don't. She's friends with Patty's sister."

"I've called them all," Mom said. "As far as they knew she was coming right home."

A sinking feeling filled me. It seemed my mom was walking a fence, trying to decide whether to call the police, look for Jenise, or stay put. In a way, she was trapped. If she went out searching for Jenise, I'd be alone with an inebriated father who wouldn't be able to help if my sister called.

I did the dishes and then sat in the living room, where my mom and I watched TV and ate ice cream. At about 9 p.m., Jenise walked through the door. Her clothes were rumpled, her face was drained of color, her eyes distant. The first thought that crossed my mind was, She looks dead.

"Where have you been?" Mom accused. "I was so worried."

With eerie calm, Jenise answered, "I was raped."

Mom's face was still as stone.

"I want to take a shower." Jenise's voice betrayed no emotion.

That snapped my mom into action. She stood up and ordered, "Just stay right there. Don't move, wash, or take anything off. Don't even comb your hair. We need to go to the hospital first." She knew the protocol for rape victims; part of her job working with troubled teens was to take care of girls at "Juvie" who'd been attacked.

I don't know if Mom wanted to take Jenise into her arms and tell her she was sorry for what happened and that she loved her, but she didn't. As always, Mom pushed her emotions down and said to me, "Watch your sister." Then she rushed up to her bedroom to change clothes.

Jenise stood motionless.

Soon she came back downstairs, dashed to the kitchen and phoned the hospital. I heard her ask for a "SANE" professional—someone trained in rape trauma—to be present with a rape kit. After hanging up, she came down the hall and grabbed her purse and keys off the small table by the front door.

When Jenise finally lifted her head and looked at me, her sad eyes screamed, "Why did this happen to me?" I turned away. Her blank expression said it all. Her spirit was gone, and I didn't know how to process the pain of seeing her that way. She'd been my hero. The one who always stood up to Dad. I didn't want to hear about her violated body, the joy ripped from her, or her innocence taken by some power-crazed, sick man.

"Do you want to come to the hospital or stay here?" Mom asked me.

"I'll stay." I was eleven and already knew too much of what was to come. I had overheard my mother's conversations about her work and didn't want to be at the hospital where my sister's legs would be spread, where medical professionals could gather semen, hair and blood samples, and where law enforcement would wait or even watch. I envisioned my mother aching for her hurt baby girl, as Jenise, exposed and probed repeatedly, closed her eyes and detached emotionally.

My mother, sister and I had endured, and hidden, years of abuse at the hands of my father. Now we had another trauma to bury. I was already an adult in some ways. I took care of myself because I had to; I could handle that. As long as something bad happened to me, I was prepared. But watching my sister's face, even for just that instant when her desperate eyes burned through my heart, I realized how vulnerable we still were.

Days after the rape, I learned it wasn't one man who raped Jenise; it was three high school seniors who lived nearby and attended the same school she did. They'd followed her for several weeks, knew what time she went home, and the distance from the streetcar stop to our house. When one of the boy's parents went on a business trip, the trio carried out the attack. Jenise thought she was safe among neighborhood friends when they lured her into their car.

Knowledge of the boys' depravity turned on a switch deep inside that closed my soul to sex. I thought, "When you come of age and flirt, go to parties, show off to boys, it kills your spirit. If my sister, my hero—the strongest person I know—could be so hurt, how could I ever be healthy?" Jenise was the one who took the belt for me when my father was on a rampage. The one who challenged him, kept him away. She was my friend, my power, and the only one who guarded our family secrets with me.

For the next few weeks, I heard my parents talk about the rape every day. And my sister had to relive her trauma again and again as she answered questions from law enforcement, medical professionals, and even our mom and dad. They interrogated her, as though her attackers were the victims. They asked why she had gotten into the boys' car in the first place, what she'd been wearing, whether she was already having sex. When police officers asked her, for the fourth time, to name the boys who had raped her to make sure her story "stood up," Jenise stopped cooperating. She must have gone into a deep shock in which her brain sent a message through her body to shut her voice down.

Jenise stayed home for a while after the attack. Her innocence gone, never to return, she was left on her own, trying to figure out how she could enter her life again, a life that included seeing her attackers saunter down the halls at school. But what Jenise's attackers hadn't counted on was that her friends had big brothers who took care of those three boys. After the rapists were beaten, they transferred schools, ashamed to face their classmates.

I didn't talk with Jenise about her return to school, or the details of her rape, until several years later. But my friends heard from their older siblings that she became introverted after it happened. A school counselor who knew her story took notice, and through the counselor's urging, Jenise sought professional therapy. For nearly two years she learned how to recover from being violated.

Even shut down and broken, my sister forged ahead, helping herself silently and powerfully. At the time I didn't understand the strength it took for her to do that. What was my reaction? I was angry she let her attackers take her down. I don't mean the rape. I was angry because she "let" them become such an influence upon her afterward that she withdrew. I thought she had let them conquer her soul.

I took it to such bizarre lengths, that if the door to her room was open when I walked by, I moved past as fast as I could. At the dinner table, I hardly looked up, even though I sat next to her. I turned my back on her and blamed her for being weak. I believed she gave in, gave up, and subconsciously embraced being a victim. My feelings were so strong that I withheld forgiveness—as if it were mine to withhold.

I also thought she was taking too long to recover. Didn't she know she had to get out of our house as soon as she could? Didn't she know she had to watch out for me, too? There was no time for therapy; she needed to get on with it. And how could she talk about our secrets with anyone but me? It was an unwritten rule that we never shared our family troubles with outsiders, and she was breaking the rule. As siblings often do when one betrays family secrets, I saw her as a traitor for opening up to strangers. She disgusted me. I believed she should've been able to control herself and remain strong. I was sure if those boys raped me, I'd press charges, put them in jail and make them pay. And I'd sue their parents for everything they had.

All of this changed our relationship for years. Not because Jenise didn't reach out to me, but because I wasn't receptive nor I suppose mature enough to understand. I felt like she'd left me on my own to deal with our family, and I resented her for it.

But because of her therapy, Jenise recovered and saw her life in a way I couldn't for many years. She refused to be swallowed up and forever be defined by the violence of her youth. I should've admired the way she overcame her challenges and the courage she had in asking for help. Not only did she overcome darkness, she became fearless. In time, I realized how misguided I had been. Jenise became my hero again, and for the rest of her life, which ended far too soon, I was her champion. She was, and will always be, one of the great loves of my life.

* * * * *

A San Francisco native, Pamela Taeuffer has lived in Sonoma County since 1975. She is the author of Shadow Heart *and* Fire Heart, *the first books in the* Broken Bottles Series, *a love story detailing the trauma of growing up in a family battling alcoholism. She has been published in the poetry anthology* And the Beats Go On, *and has written the first book in a series on business networking for introverts. Learn more about these and upcoming projects at http://pamelataeuffer.com.*

Born of a Chill Wind

P. H. Garrett

I was eight years old in the winter of my discontent. Every school day at 7:30 a.m. my sister Emily and I reluctantly trudged down the porch steps, and shivered our way four Brooklyn blocks to P.S. 99. Five days a week we struggled along the slippery sidewalks, our backs hunched against the cold. Clumps of snow clung to our mittens and dusted our faces before we'd gone half a block. Icy winds skidded up our skirts, stinging tender flesh. And every day I watched the boys cavort and carry on, warm and dry in their long pants, tucked into boot tops.

By the time we stepped through the heavy, double doors, which guarded our institution of learning, my knees were burning with the cold. Wet socks chafed where slush had splattered into rubber galoshes that covered my saddle shoes. My little sister cried. Her nose was beet red. Her hands shivery against the metal Howdy Doody lunch box she carried.

At 3 p.m. we bundled up and made the trip home, hand in hand, damp mitten clinging to damp mitten as we negotiated the freezing afternoon streets.

"It's not fair," I informed my parents one night over dinner, and described our daily misery. "Why can't we wear pants to school?"

They blinked and wiggled their eyebrows at one another in some silent conversation.

Dad swiveled his blue eyes toward me. "You are not boys," he announced, as though that explained everything. He nodded to indicate the subject was closed, and returned to his skirt steak and potatoes.

Mom shrugged. "Eat your dinner, girls," she said, picking up her fork for emphasis.

The flame of feminism began its long, slow burn that night.

* * * * *

P. H. Garrett embraces life in the American West. Her writing includes press releases, articles, short fiction, and a first novel currently in rewrite. Her work has been published in the Nob Hill Gazette, Marin Independent Journal, USA Today, FYI San Francisco, Horse Journal, Family News, Up Beat Times, Petaluma Post, Call of The Wild, San Francisco Chronicle, *and online at* Tiny Lights, *and gutsyliving.com. In 2014, her stories were published in two new anthologies. Contact her at wordwranglingwoman.com.*

Light Show

D. A. (Daisy) Hickman

Did you see the moon around midnight,
absorb its persuasive glow, its brilliance,
its assigned place in the sky, and did you

recognize that snowy sphere from years
ago, the same one that left us wide-eyed
as children, dancing in the dark by its light

on a damp summer lawn, and did you feel
a sudden tug, almost like the earth shifting,
when a thick night sky captured that moon,

hiding it from us, with us so certain it was
gone forever? It was new then, the sights
before our eyes, the myth of days and nights.

* * * * *

D. A. (Daisy) Hickman, author and poet, is the founder of SunnyRoomStudio: a creative, sunny space for kindred spirits. Hickman is also a member of the Academy of American Poets and the South Dakota State Poetry Society.

A Time of Magic

Patricia Jackson

The impact of lesbian militancy in the Seventies can be understood in the historical context of lesbian lives prior to that time. While male homosexuality was stereotyped, lesbians were practically invisible. Our few portrayals in popular culture were of loneliness in literature—*The Well of Loneliness*, for example—or despair and self-sacrificing suicide in such films as *The Fox* and *The Children's Hour*. For my generation, movies had provided an escape. However, these anti-lesbian films in the early Sixties dredged up conflicting feelings about our sexuality and our place in society. Thankfully, youth today have films such as *Pariah*, which depicts contemporary dykes of color dealing proudly with challenges in their lives.

After the 1969 Stonewall Rebellion in New York City, lesbian, gay, bisexual and transgender people became more out front about our lives. My coming out caused the loss of my teaching career, so I became a full-time organizer and searched for other militant lesbians. At a Gay Liberation Front conference on the Berkeley campus in 1969, I heard Judy Grahn read her position paper, *Toward the Development of a Purple Fist*. Her words reflected my politics as a lesbian. At the end of the conference, Judy and her lover, Wendy, invited me to spend the night in their small apartment in San Francisco. My life changed paths.

Judy and her writings embodied all we strived for in making a new movement of lesbians—women loving women in all our ways of being. I have loved Judy since that night in 1969. When I mention her name now, many young women recount how reaching that place inside of being a lesbian opened with a poem given to us by Judy.

At Maud's bar, in San Francisco, I met other lesbians, and after becoming friends with women from a Berkeley household, I moved into their home on Benvenue Avenue. Berkeley in those years was home to numerous women's collectives. We lived together not for economic survival only; we communed for sharing political beliefs. This household became a gathering place for lesbian feminists.

Weekends spawned impromptu parties with dancing and debates. Discussions on theories of socialism, feminism, and the causes for woman's oppression took place in the kitchen and on the hallway stairs. We planned presentations to straight groups, organized sit-ins about child-care in work places and banks. We shocked patrons by proudly wearing our East Bay Queers T-shirts on trips to the local ice cream parlor. We produced the first West Coast Women's Dance, patterned after one held by sisters in New York. This bold action of a women-only dance event jarred the Berkeley male counter culture, but delighted all the women. We attended the North American Homophile Conference to confront sexism within that organization and called for lesbians to form our own groups. We believed that, as lesbians, our unique oppression linked us intrinsically to the oppression of all women.

Our eruption of female energy evolved into the creation of Gay Women's Liberation. Challenging the dominant gay culture of the day, we emerged from different places, backgrounds, races, and ages. We fell in love with ourselves as women. For that special time in the Seventies, we converged to make magic.

The roots for a woman's bookstore grew in that house on Benvenue. We collected small books of poetry and short stories from the few women in print at that time. The only grassroots woman printing and publishing in our area was Alta, who only went by her first name, with her Shameless Hussey Press. We gathered copies of her works along with other writers in her stock, contacted bookstores in the entire Bay Area, and placed women's writings on consignment. Each week we headed out in our household car to canvass bookstores from Berkeley to Santa Cruz. A few stores agreed, and we returned to find out if any sold. I believe that, due to our efforts and Alta's publishing, people experienced their first exposure to writers and artists like Susan Griffin, Judy Grahn, Red Arobateau, Pam Allen, Wendy Cadden, Pat Parker, and other sisters.

We printed the première publication of *Woman to Woman*, on a hand-cranked Gestetner mimeograph machine. We delicately peeled off paper-thin artworks and created a collection of poems. We folded these treasures within heavy, blood red construction paper covers and in the mode of that era, did not credit each individual piece, but added all the names collectively at the end of the book. This book launched future works of poetry and art published by women for women. *Woman To Woman* helped launch the Women's Press Collective in 1978.

In the fall and winter of 1970, a group of us teamed up with the San Francisco Mime Troupe, the Tony-award winning acting troupe started in 1959, known as "America's theater of political comedy." The Mime Troupe still performs free, outdoor musical plays taking on the political issues of the day. The 1970 season production included a double billing of a feminist melodrama, *The Independent Female: Or A Man Has His Pride*, and an epic play, *Seize The Time*, about the Black Panther Party. We caravanned with the Troupe across the country, set up our literature tables at each performance, hawked our women's pamphlets, and engaged playgoers in conversations about feminism.

In Lansing, Michigan, we met women who had formed the Horse-Back Anti-Rape Patrol. We spent an afternoon with Robin Morgan, who wrote *Sisterhood is Powerful*, and met with Rita Mae Brown, activist and member of Lavender Menace, a lesbian-feminist group protesting NOW's exclusion of lesbians. Later, in 1973, Rita Mae published the bestselling lesbian novel, *Rubyfruit Jungle*, which is now a classic. In New York, we participated in meetings of women forming a women's party. In New Haven, we attended a trial against Erica Huggins and Bobby Seale, part of the FBI's Cointel Program of harassment and killings of Black Panther Party members. In Washington D.C., we witnessed the historic Black Panther Party conference, The Revolutionary People's Constitutional Convention.

Back home in the "People's Republic of Berkeley," our collective household scored the rent with combinations of odd jobs, including hawking papers on the street corner of Telegraph and Shattuck. One night my housemate Connie and I set out before dawn to secure our corner and joined other alternative folks who made their living selling the *Berkeley Barb* and *Berkeley Tribe* newspapers. At dawn, an incredibly loud noise erupted and shook the very corner we had claimed. It turned out someone had planted a miniature, homemade bomb by the Bank of America (BofA), which blasted a large hole in the sidewall. No one was inside at the time. In those late-Sixties days, BofA and Safeway symbolized corporate capitalism. Our grape boycotts supporting the United Farm Workers helped shut down one Safeway store in Berkeley, which we replaced with a locally owned community store. I still feel disloyalty crossing over a Safeway threshold.

To our amazement, the police and a repair team cleaned and patched up the hole in the bank before the sun rose that day. No one else ever witnessed this particular people's revenge. Connie and I figured the police would blame us. Undercover officers had already recorded our faces in their regular drive-by-picture-shootings from the windows of unmarked cars. Whenever they aimed their cameras at us, we proudly and prominently displayed our paper, *It Ain't Me Babe*, which sported some anti-patriarchal headlines. After *Ms. Magazine* obtained and published FBI files on the women's movement, Gay Women's Liberation Berkeley, our group of lesbians, registered high on the subversive list.

Small rebellions happened all the time, but never made the six o'clock news. The media often ignored demonstrations. I remember marching in October 1983 with thousands of people in San Francisco against President Reagan's invasion of Granada—no news coverage of that resistance either. However, a wedding took place that morning, and as we marched past the church, the bride, groom, and the entire wedding party, with fists in the air, stood on the church steps and cheered us on. We returned blown kisses and wishes for their future together.

Eventually, the shenanigans at the Benvenue house led to an eviction. Women pooled money, placed a down payment on a house in Oakland and formed Terrace Street, another women's collective. The women in this collective founded ICI: A Woman's Place bookstore and The Women's Press Collective.

My Berkeley years back-dropped momentous times of the Seventies. One morning, we awoke to a sun submerged under an ominous yellow brown haze — a fire in the Oakland Hills. It seemed to be an omen. Later in the day came news of the invasion of Cambodia and that the Ohio National Guard had shot and killed student protesters at Kent State. The killings at Kent State have been well documented. Not as well recognized are the police killings of African-American students just days later at Jackson State College in Jackson, Mississippi. As protests against the war continued, police brutality escalated. After the takeover of People's Park in Berkeley, the city erected concrete barricades in our streets to contain and coral descent.

No walls, barricades, tanks, or broken promises, ever end a movement of people for justice.

* * * * *

Patricia Jackson, a seventy-three-year-old dyke, eco-feminist, and communist, walked her first picket line in 1964—a wildcat teacher strike in Louisville, Kentucky. In 1969, she organized as a Gay Liberation Front activist. Currently, she continues social activism and serves as Convener for the Gray Panthers of San Francisco. Her passion is co-facilitating intergenerational workshops with outLoud Queer Youth Radio and openhouse services for seniors in San Francisco. More in her memoir: www.takesanuprising.com.

Quilts

Mark Wisniewski

"nearly every morning" she told Bill "they're the first thing I think
of: all those depressed women
all those angry women
all that goodwill they put into gathering to sew while sharing their oral
    histories—plus
seeing to it that one of them actually came
to hear me read & presented me
with their work? I mean to what end really? me up here alone
on a mountain unable to sleep under even one of these 200 things?
because every time I've tried
I remember my ex-husband & get ticked off & feel more awake than I
    have all day"

maybe Bill thought she wants us
in bed
& for me to be aggressive in making
that happen
wasn't this how it always went? right woman right place wrong time by
    maybe a minute?

"I mean what kind of end is that?" she said "I mean
for me personally
what has all this sisterhood led to?"

now Bill was sure she wanted him
to try but the skin above his lips went stiff
assuring him he'd prove
worthless to her

"I have no idea" he said "about sisterhoods"

"well I just don't know" she said "about anything"

then they both stood facing the quilts but not completely
nor were they really facing the National Forest
as if two strangers could be teamed
to face nothing & everything
by simply dropping that subject
& staying there

. . . . .

Mark Wisniewski's third novel, Straightaway, *was sold at auction to Putnam Penguin Random House. His second,* Show Up, Look Good, *was praised by Ben Fountain and Jonathan Lethem; his first,* Confessions of a Polish Used Car Salesman, *was praised by the* Los Angeles Times. *Wisniewski's fiction has won a Pushcart Prize and appeared in* Best American Short Stories. *His poems are published or forthcoming in magazines such as* The Iowa Review, Prairie Schooner, *and* Poetry.

Sisterly Tribes of the Modern Age

Erica Brown

My sense of sisterhood is a throwback to communities of ages past, when women were gatherers and men were hunters—a tribe, all of us in a garden of sorts. Only the world got smaller, and communication is now via instant Internet messages. And the nuclear family system of everything being insulated is turning powerful women into beings who suffer from isolation, depression and questioning everything important in their lives.

We get that we're alone on this planet, we're born into this world alone. We grow up fighting for our survival among our siblings, school peers, authorities, and society while learning to love and to fear. And somewhere along the line, we meet someone, maybe get married and have more little beings, and then we die. Basically.

But along our paths, we meet other girls who understand us. It's like heaven brings an angel to our confusion when we say, "I feel so ... blah, blah, blah," and another person says, "Gee, I know exactly how you feel. Just the other day ... blah, blah, blah." It's not like she has magical, mist-lifting powers. It's that together, we can dance, play and forget that the mist even is there. And then it isn't, and the sun shines again.

Girlfriends, especially soul sisters, can feel your mood from a thousand miles away. They don't always say what you want to hear (mostly because you don't even know what you want yourself) but they'll be empathic, and that's all anyone can do. Instead of saying, "I told you so," or constantly stealing the attention, they make you a cup of tea, send you a funny photo, or just sit quietly, taking in the space, surrendering to what is happening in the present instead of trying to make it something it isn't.

Sisters walk in a relationship far more honest and truthful than I've felt within a sexual relationship. There are no expectations, no limitations; there's no possessiveness. Someone loves me exactly the way I am: pimples, orange peel cellulite, and hair growing in places it really shouldn't. All these things we can tell our girlfriends. And they, more often than not, are willing to help squeeze those hard-to-reach pimples, discuss cellulite like it's not a disease but a reality of getting older, and tell you when you have a stray hair that needs to be plucked.

Sisters of this kind know when to butter the bread thick with compliments and when to say, "That's enough Vodka Red Bulls," at the second bar on a night out. We know we can call anytime, day or night, to discuss boys and their serious lack of understanding and sensitivity. Quite frankly, how are guys supposed to understand us when we only show them what we want them to see? Let's face it; there are some things lovers shouldn't see or know about. It keeps the mystery alive. A woman once said, "Always hold a few secrets from your man (or men); it keeps the intrigue and chase alive for them. You will never be replaceable then." I have found this to be a true slice of wisdom.

Girlfriends together often create a mystical state of goddess energy. Any man will tell you being with two or more girls is like being in Venus' heaven. Girlfriends talk openly with each other, giggle and hug, share the same spoonful of vanilla ice cream, undress to knickers, and sometimes beyond, without a question of how they'll be judged.

Being a boy growing up with girls is living in heaven and hell at the same time. Girls tease them, beguile them with open sexuality, and enthrall them with a powerful sense of belonging and understanding. It's seduction of the highest form.

So, can sisters live balanced lives without each other when we grow up? Without sisterly companionship, we may live our lives, but they're rarely balanced. Women need other women. We gather energy and wisdom among each other to share with the rest of the world. Together, we find solace and a sense of deep belonging, and we fill our vats with love to give, heal and dream with.

Sisters of the modern world hold the key to connection. We guide each other's children to their futures in a state of neutral grace and unconditional love. We encourage each other to dream unfathomable dreams and remind each other of those dreams—and of each other's worth—during times of struggle. The sisters in my life hold the fabric of my world together. Without asking, begging, pleading, or discussing the hows and whats, they just do. And I know I do this for each one of them, too.

* * * * *

Erica Brown is a sensitive and passionate womyn. Born under South African skies. Child of the world. Creative and charming. Inspired by laughter, food, wine, great sex, nature, traveling and people with a magical spark. From professional cheffing to working in the film industry, teaching snowboarding and photographing bungee jmpers, her heart belongs to the river of life's changes, and she isn't afraid to swim the rapids and the oceans to feel alive. goldensunflowers@hushmail.com.

The Science of Sisterhood

Sue Kreke Rumbaugh

From the same atoms,
we look alike, we move alike,
we share a taste for music and art.

As crystals,
we grew – out, away from center's warmth –
into space,
exploring the world: a magnet.

The cleavage of sisterhood: we are separate, together.

With time's subtractions, additions –
our universes expanded,
we, the nuclei, anchor
and repel like-charges,

sending us into orbits,
each on the courses we have set:
we are sisters
on trajectories we call home.

* * * * *

Sue Rumbaugh, MPM, MFA, is Associate Professor of English at Carlow University, where she teaches creative writing. Her work has appeared in Washington State Reflections, Western Pennsylvania Reflections, Travel Writing Handbook, the Bicycle Review, Story Circle Network, *and the* Pittsburgh Post-Gazette. *Her book,* If I Could Tell Her—a daughter's memoir, *is a work in progress. She has publicly performed in Pittsburgh, Pa., Ohio, Washington, D.C. and Carlow, Ireland. She and her husband, Larry, live in Glenshaw, Pa.*

Set Six

. . . .

White Rose – short story, Gaurav Verma

Barbie-girl – memoir, Karen DeGroot Carter

The Girls From Byron's Corner – memoir,
Gloria Beanblossom

Come Hike with Me – poem, Wilda Morris

Zori Sisters – memoir, Barbara Toboni

Sister to Sisterhood – essay, Lynn Millar

The Warp and Weft of Sisterhood – memoir, P. H. Garrett

Flowers for Leslie – poem, Nellie Wong

Twinkies for Breakfast – essay, Elspeth Slayter

Devora's Changes – memoir, Marie Judson-Rosier

Crossing Over – poem, D. A. (Daisy) Hickman

We Always – memoir, Tanya Savko

After – poem, Nina Tepedino

White Rose

Gaurav Verma

Vandana plucked the last rose off the only bush in her garden, pure white in color—as white as the several feet of thick snow spread for several miles, as white as her long cotton dress before it became stained with blood, as white as sun waking up lazily after a long hibernation at the horizon, covered with fog—with tiny drops of dew glistening on petals crumbling and ready to wither away.

. . . . .

War raged all around her. Gunshots thundering, intermittent sniper hits, continuous, indiscriminate blasts from machine guns—all bringing death to her door. Clouds of dark grey smoke rising from charred bodies; the smell of salty blood oozing from burning flesh mixed with gunpowder; the cries—shrill and sobbing—of pain and of victory, of command and of reconnaissance, of new widows and of new orphans. All this had taken its toll.

Alone at home, with her husband, Mithilesh, out on patrol again, Vandana was dazed and confused. Her ears felt deafened by the sound of her soul shrieking, her eyes blinded by salty lakes erupting from within, her nose blocked for want of breath. Then, she sensed someone in the house, but before she could turn around, strong, rough fingers gripped her face from behind; the hand was cold and smelled of sweat. Slowly her assailant turned her around; his face was covered. Only his dark, kajal-clad black eyes were visible, revealing a confused, cold heart.

When he was certain no one else was nearby, he dropped his hand from her face. "I'm hungry," he growled, averting his eyes.

"You look Pakistani," she whispered.

"Yes," he replied. "I have been hiding for days. Your soldiers are bloodthirsty; I haven't eaten anything for a long time."

Raising her voice, she said, "Go away. My husband will kill you for stepping on our land." She shoved him in the chest.

"Don't shout, you foolish hound." He gripped a knife stuck in his waistband.

A soldier's wife, she didn't flinch. "Leave immediately, I command."

But when their eyes locked, his expression shifted from cruel to kind.

"Sister." He spoke gently this time. He took out his knife and threw at her feet. "I'm hungry. I will leave after eating."

"Don't dare call me your sister; don't defile such a pious relationship. You are my country's enemy, and mine, too," she said, anger rocking her body.

His eyes moistened. "Sorry," he said. He turned, stepped across the threshold he had just stealthily breached, and entered the courtyard. Vandana watched him trudge away and, to her surprise, felt her heart turn heavy.

"Wait!. What's her name?" she called from behind.

He stopped but didn't look back. "Shazia," he replied, then resumed walking. "Your eyes are like hers."

"Wait! It's time, our soldiers will be marching this area. Come inside," she said.

"Let it be. I'm a fighter. I can face them." He moved on, but his pace slowed.

"You need something in your belly to brave them. Come. Eat. Leave when it's dark," she said in a softer tone, aware he was listening.

He stopped, turned around and asked, "Why?"

"I was a single child. I don't know what it's like to have a sibling." She moved closer to him. "Where is your sister?"

"She died six years ago; kafirs killed her. She was brutally raped before that." His eyes held both anger and tears. "Apparently, she had crossed the line of control while herding the goats." He sat on the ground and covered his eyes with his hand. "Her eyes were wide open when her body was found; tears had dried in them; it seemed she was pleading, and no one listened."

"I'm sorry. I don't understand why men cannot fight like men. Why do they have to act so cowardly?" She stared at him intently, her heart pulsating with the current of his sobs.

He wept for a long time. When he stopped he looked at her and said, "When I turned you around to face me, I felt like my sister was looking at me."

"Let's eat something, brother." She reached for his hand, unable to deny the strong kinship she felt for him. "What is your name?" she asked.

"Shabir," he replied.

. . . . .

"Why did you come today? I told you Mithilesh would be coming in at noon," Vandana said with concern on seeing Shabir at her house when she wasn't expecting him.

"I had to, Sister. Today is the festival Shazia adopted of tying thread for me like you Hindus do. I didn't want my wrist to be bare." He handed her the colorful thread that symbolizes the unbreakable bond of brother and sister.

"Ohh." She took the band of thread from him. She was proud he looked so different than when they met four months ago. His clothes were now cleaner; his hair was neatly trimmed, and he carried not even a small knife as weapon. "Now let me tie it before he comes," she said.

He held out his hairy arm. As she wrapped and tied the threads she asked, "How's your work?"

"It's doing great. The cloth shop I opened is wonderful. And people from nearby villages are coming to get their dresses sewn by me," he replied with a twinkle in his eyes.

When she finished, he raised his arm, and as the thread rolled around his wrist, tears rolled down his face.

"Hey, hey, hey, now, you can't cry. Your sister is back. See in my eyes. Aren't they of Shazia?" She tried to console him.

"It's cold here; let's go out in the sun together," he said, rubbing his eyes.

"No. Mithilesh could be back anytime. Please leave now," she said, her heart beating fast at the thought of her husband's imminent return.

"Okay." He stood to leave, but stopped when he saw a fierce looking man in khaki dress blocking the door.

"Mith... Mithilesh, you? He ... he is Shabir. He lives in a nearby village," Vandana stuttered.

"Which village?" Mithilesh asked. He pointed his gun at Shabir. "And what are you doing here?"

"I live across the border; I came to meet my sister," he replied.

"How did you cross to this side of border?" Mithilesh asked, gun still pointing at Shabir.

"I was trained in how to move undetected at Madarsa, but I left all that behind months ago. I am a merchant now," Shabir replied, no trace of fear in his eyes.

"What, you are feeding a terrorist?" He accused his wife in anger. "And you, straighten your arms and bend on your knees," he commanded Shabir.

"No Mithilesh. What are you doing? You cannot shoot him; he is my brother." She stepped in front of Shabir, becoming a human shield covering him.

"And I'm your husband. This is your country; you cannot betray your land." He aimed his gun at her.

"He became a terrorist on losing his sister. Now he has found one," she said. "Don't repeat it. If a brother can turn into a terrorist upon losing his sister, so can a sister. I pray you don't repeat the history." She grabbed the barrel of his gun.

"My nation, my army is my first religion. You are insane," Mithilesh said. "These Pakistanis are not to be trusted; he is using you to get our confidential information. Ask him how he missed a full village just a few miles away and found our solitary house here. Now get out of my way, Vandana." He pried her fingers from his gun. "I am not going to kill him; he could be of use to us. I will hand him over to military police."

"No, he is no longer what he used to be. His whole life will end in prison. He deserves a second chance." She pleaded, furious.

"Terrorists die as terrorists; they can't be reformed. Let the court decide his fate. Now get out of my way, and let me do my duty." He pushed her.

She held onto the gun and shouted, "Shabir run!"

Shabir paused momentarily, trying to understand what was happening as Vandana and Mithilesh tousled. Then he lurched out of the door.

"You bitch! You have gone insane." Mithilesh shoved his wife aside and ran after Shabir, who was less than two hundred meters away. He aimed his gun and pulled the trigger. Just one shot pierced Shabir's back. He ran few steps farther and stumbled like a racing horse. Birds fluttered into the sky. A red river flowing from his body smeared the white snow. His last word, "Shaz ..." vibrated through the pine trees. Soldiers hiding nearby ran toward the gunshot.

Vandana, aware of Shabir's fate, came out sobbing, her limbs heavy with grief. She plucked the last rose off the only bush in her garden, pure white in color—as white as the several feet of thick snow spread for several miles, as white as her long dress before it became stained with blood, as white as sun waking up at the horizon covered with fog—with tiny drops of dew glistening on petals crumbling and ready to wither away.

She waved soldiers who had gathered around him to let her pass. In silence, she looked at Shabir's open eyes, his lips curled at the sound of Shaz, his broad forehead streaked with vermilion, and his wrist bonded with woven threads.

"This should go with him in his grave," she commanded in somber voice to no one. And she placed her last rose on his chest.

· · · · ·

"Who am I?" he thought for a whole day and night. A month passed, and a year, and many thereafter. No answer came. So he did engineering and short-circuited between resistors and transistors; he turned to IT and turned zero among bytes; he got an MBA, but crunching financial numbers crunched him. Finally, he picked up a pen and paper, and he felt elevated. So that's all about Gaurav Verma: born in Dehradun, India; writer by passion; voracious reader; art lover.

Barbie-girl

Karen DeGroot Carter

When I was a kid, my big sister, Lisa, led the way. She was the boss. Never mind that she was the sixth of eleven kids with five older brothers. Never mind that she knew better than to talk back to our parents—until she was in high school, anyway. As far as I was concerned, Lisa was more dynamic than I could ever hope to be. She also happened to be taller, and louder, and just a tad opinionated.

By sixth grade, I'd accepted my place as the skinny, freckle-faced, brainy little sister who did not even try to compete with Lisa. In our Catholic school, she'd been a blonde cheerleader. I played every sport and had stick-straight brown hair. Lisa would tell me to do something with my hair and I would tell her not to look at me if she didn't like the way I looked. This was tricky, since we shared a room for years, but she got the message. She still tried to style my hair with a curling iron that sent plumes of smoke into the air followed by tons of aerosol hairspray. Sometimes, the result resembled the classic Farrah Fawcett flip, which I would soon attempt on my own. One time, I was given a Toni Tennille inverted bowl 'do, which I loved.

What I loved most, though, was having Lisa's attention, as long as I was doing whatever she told me to do.

In high school, Lisa blossomed into a stunning, tan, long-legged beauty. One year, she dressed in heeled boots and a silver-sequined leotard and carried the marching band banner with a friend in a matching outfit. As band drum major for two years, she wore a cool cowboy hat, boots, and shorts that showed off her legs. Senior year, she won our town's beauty pageant.

Fast forward to January 1985, when I was a returning freshman at Syracuse University, not far from home. I remember walking off the elevator of my floor with my dad, who carried some stuffed animals as he followed me through the lounge and toward my dorm room. "You'd never see my dad carrying a stuffed turtle for me," I heard one girl say. Dad was proud of me and was smiling. I'd had a challenging previous semester (a straight-A student through high school, I cried when I got my first college grades). I'd studied during the break, though, and was confident I'd improve my GPA ... even while I continued to work nights driving a van full of students to the next town over to paste up the student newspaper the old-fashioned way, with glue and X-acto knives.

Within weeks, I'd be a mess once again, but hanging in there, determined to finish what I'd started without admitting I needed help on many levels. One of the editors of the paper announced in an early-morning meeting of the entire staff, when everyone else was bright-eyed and I'd barely gotten any sleep, that the production work of that day's paper matched the weather word for the day: brutal. It was the middle of winter in upstate New York, in case you're wondering what kind of weather could possibly warrant such a description. I'd wanted to say something, but I was a freshman running herself into the ground. What did I know? So I did what I normally did that semester: I remained silent, and wished I was sleeping.

Sometime that same semester, I became aware of Barbie-girl. She looked like Barbie and seemed to enjoy parading around campus with her tight jeans and long hair. She probably also reminded me of Lisa, though I don't remember making that connection right off the bat. They did both have blonde hair and got a lot of attention wherever they went. I just felt the familiar certainty that I disappeared briefly when this girl walked by, that if she—or anyone else on campus—considered me at all, it was with disdain and just a little pity. "Nice jeans," Barbie-girl said to me once in a distinctly insulting tone. She stood in an elevator full of other students. The elevator had stopped on my floor to let someone on or off, I don't know. But for some reason, she felt compelled to say this to me as the doors were just about to close. I was walking through the lounge from one hall to the other. I wore relaxed-fit Lee jeans and had gained more than my fair share of the typical freshman fifteen.

One day, so exhausted I thought I was seeing things, that same elevator had opened and closed with no one inside but a poster of an extraordinarily overweight girl in some skimpy outfit with those dreaded words—"Freshman Fifteen"—plastered above her head. I remember pausing in the blessedly empty lounge at that moment, certain I'd imagined the whole thing and taking it as a sign that I needed to cut back on the starch-laden meals and desserts in the dining hall, the donuts at the printing press too many nights during the week, the four-for-ones at a campus bar. And then I went to my room for two more hours of desperate sleep before my first class.

This time, though, the time Barbie-girl sneered at me, the one time she deigned to say anything to me, I immediately pictured how silly I looked with my permed hair, my shirt tucked in, my jeans billowing below. I paused for a humiliating moment and decided this girl was mean, much more mean than Lisa had ever been. Lots of big sisters pick on their little sisters, but most manage to do this in private. I was nothing to Barbie-girl, and yet she'd picked on me in front of an elevator full of people.

I decided I could take her comment as just a vicious jab at my ego, which it certainly was intended to be, or accept it as yet another message from the universe that I needed to get a grip on who I was and what I wanted to accomplish. I also eventually acknowledged that working nights and making donut runs for the newspaper production staff wasn't exactly the best way to achieve much of anything besides sleep deprivation, elevated sugar and cholesterol levels, and depression. It took a while for the planets to align and for me to actually make any progress on these fronts. At the moment of Barbie-girl's comment, I wanted only to make it clear that I couldn't afford any other jeans than the ones I had on, that I worked all hours of the night, and who was she, anyway? If the sight of me in my pathetic, size-thirteen, relaxed-fit Lee jeans sickened her so much, she should just not look at me. So there.

But then I'd be back home arguing with my sister. Not that we fought much by that time. Lisa had moved away from home and was on the brink of marriage and becoming a stepmom and a new mom. Eventually, she would reach out to me more and more and we'd become good friends. Years later, when she read a draft of my first novel, which includes the loss of an older sister, she emailed me: "Whatever I did to you, I'm SORRY, OK?" Lisa's not taller than me anymore, and I'm probably just as opinionated as she is, but she's still more outspoken, more dynamic, more courageous. A multitalented businesswoman who's reinvented herself many times over, she's also still leading the way. And I'm more than happy to follow.

*   *   *   *   *

Karen DeGroot Carter of Denver has had her nonfiction and poetry published in small literary journals and on sites such as BlogCritics, The Compulsive Reader, Literary Mama, Imagination Soup, and MixedandHappy. Her blog, Beyond Understanding, highlights resources that celebrate diversity. OneSister's Song, her first novel, is available on Amazon in print and Kindle editions, and her second novel is on submission. She is currently writing a collection of short stories and works as a freelance copyeditor.

The Girls From Byron's Corner

Gloria Beanblossom

On the outside, I have it all: a big house with expensive furnishings, a faithful husband, and time to do what I love, which is writing. I'm a novelist. I sit for hours, thinking, fantasizing, and dreaming of lives that exist only in my imagination. And yet, I am haunted.

My ghosts don't howl in the night and rattle chains forged from past lives of sin. They come to me in the twilight: two pale little girls with black owl eyes and tangled, dirty hair. They creep into my consciousness, sit by my side, waiting, pleading to be set free. I want to cry out to them, scream to the rafters: it wasn't your fault! But they can't hear me. And soon they return to their hiding places, until another twilight, another day.

I want to banish these ghost children from my life. And, sometimes, I think they're gone for good. But all too often, when I close my eyes, there they are, saying, "Mommy left us, and she didn't come back. She didn't come back. She didn't come back." The clinging spectres are my sister, Stephie, and me, exactly as we were when our mother abandoned us shortly after our father left the family.

My parents' divorce had terrified me. I was thoroughly in love with my daddy. He was handsome, tall and dark. Mommy always said he could charm the birds right out of the trees. When he left, I was afraid I'd never see him again. And what really broke my heart wasn't the fact that Daddy had left Mommy, but that he'd left me. Without him, the three of us— Mommy, Stephie and I—moved into a shabby, two bedroom, furnished apartment on the lower west side of Carbondale, Illinois. It was dark and cramped, infested with water bugs and cockroaches. The only thing to recommend the dump was the cheap rent.

Mommy stood for eight hours a day, six days a week, on the concrete floors of the local Rexall drugstore. When she wasn't waiting on bitchy old ladies, or fending off the advances of her obnoxious boss, she stocked shelves, lifting boxes of merchandise that strained her back, and bruised her ego, for the grand salary of sixty-two-fifty a week. Daddy promised to pay a hundred bucks a month in child support, but he never did. I remember Mommy sitting at the kitchen table long after Stephie and I should have been asleep. She would stare at a heap of unopened bills, afraid to tear into the envelopes, afraid to see what was inside.

Life with my parents had never been easy or predictable, but when Daddy was around, there seemed to be enough money. The lights didn't suddenly flicker out, because the electric bill was three months past due. Mommy didn't hide us in the closet when a string of bill collectors came pounding at the door. We didn't go hungry.

Mommy had a quick, sometimes violent, temper and mercurial mood swings. One minute everything would be fine, and the next, she'd be crying and cursing. She would march out of her bedroom, tugging a brush through her hair, kicking our shoes and toys out of her way, screaming about nothing and everything, mostly just wishing her life had turned out differently. An abusive, womanizing husband and two kids she could barely afford to clothe and feed wasn't what she'd bargained on when she ran away from home to marry my father.

It was just too hard for her to go it alone. I know that now, but as a little girl, all I knew was that she was so angry she frightened me. And it was always something Stephie and I did that set off her fury. Mommy left for good on a Friday. The minute she walked through the door after work that evening, I knew there would be trouble.

"Didn't I tell you girls to have this house picked up by the time I came home?" she screamed, tossing her purse and jacket on the sofa. "What the hell do you do all day while I'm at work? Just once I'd like to be able to walk into this apartment without tripping on garbage!" Her rant escalated. I could almost feel the tension and frustration boil and churn inside of her. I knew there was no appeasing her, especially when Stephie started to cry. That invariably made Mommy worse.

"For God's sake, shut up Stephanie! Stop that bawling!" Mommy ordered, jerking Stephie's little hand away from mine. "I can't be expected to put up with this the minute I walk through the door." She shook Stephie like a rag-doll. "You lazy brats are going to have to start helping out around here!"

"We're sorry," I whined.

"Just look at this mess," she screamed, releasing Stephie.

"I'm sorry," I repeated.

"Sorry. Sorry!" She turned toward me. "That's all I hear from you and that damn father of yours."

Mommy's hand struck my cheek, my head snapped back, and my eyes clouded with tears, which had nothing to do with the red handprint on my face. It was my pride, my dignity, and my heart she had injured. Mommy grabbed me by the neck and thrust me in front of the mirror. She was like a wild animal trapped in a corner.

"You're just like your father, just like him, aren't you, Dorie! " She shrieked, thrusting my face close to the mirror.

"Mommy don't," I whimpered. "I'm sorry. I'll be good. Mommy, don't." I stood still, afraid to move.

"Well, you can tell that father of yours that I hate him," she hissed, her lips so close to my ear I could feel her breath stirring my hair. Then she stalked to the couch, grabbed her purse and jacket, and stormed out the door, slamming it so hard that the noise made us jump.

"Jesus Christ," I whispered. The echo of Mommy's words still thundered in my ears. I stood frozen, facing the mirror, my reflection staring back at me. "How ugly you are," I said to the sad creature in front of me. "How ugly you are."

Stephie sank down on the floor next to me. The house was suddenly very quiet except for the sound of her plaintive sobs. The light from the lamps gave the room an unnatural yellow glow, casting elongated shadows on the walls. It was mid-June, but it felt cold and lonely.

I sat on the floor next to my sister. I didn't know what to do. Stephie was so little, so fragile, and I was supposed to take care of her. Before that day, I had often thought she was demanding and spoiled. I had resented that so much of my time was spent taking care of her. I was also more than a little jealous of her blonde curls and big, brown, doe eyes. Despite our petty rivalries, though, Stephie was my baby sister, and I loved her. When Mommy would fly into one of her rages, it was Stephie who received the brunt of her anger. And it broke my heart to see her cry.

After Stephie's sobs died down, she said, "Dorie, I wish Mommy hadn't left, but she doesn't like me anyway. When she gets pissed off, she says, 'Stephanie, you're just like your dad, and he'll never amount to a tinker's damn'!" Stephie was a wonderful little impersonator, and she had Mommy down pat. In spite of myself, I laughed, and so did Steph. Here we were alone and abandoned, stranded in a second-rate apartment in a third-rate neighborhood, waiting for God knows what, and we were laughing.

"She doesn't mean that Steph; you know how she is," I said, suppressing a giggle. "She's always shooting her mouth off. Mommy doesn't mean anything by it." I tried to sound mature and reassuring, the way I thought a big sister should.

The little smile that had been playing on Stephie's lips remained, but the sparkle in her eyes faded. "She may not mean it, but it hurts my feelings all the same, Dorie."

A suffocating pain seized my chest. I hugged Stephie to me, and all the sadness that was my life came spilling out. I cried until I was sick from crying. I cried because I wanted Mommy to come back. I cried because I wanted to be a little girl, not a mother to Stephanie. I cried because Mommy and Daddy didn't love me. I wanted so desperately for them to love me. I tried to smile for Stephie's sake, but something in me withered and died there on the floor as we waited throughout the night for Mommy to return.

After that terrible Friday, I never brought up the subject of my mother. I tore up her pictures. I wanted no reminders of her. I couldn't stop thinking about her, though, and wondering where she was and what she was doing. I wanted to see her again so I could ask her why she hadn't even said good-bye to us. More than anything, I wanted her to look at us and say good-bye.

I was broken and didn't know how to put myself together again. Little by little, a wall formed around my heart. I stopped longing for love. Nothing really touched me. I felt only as much as I chose. The pain and angst were gone; in there place was something cold and numb. Gone forever was the little girl who believed fairies lived in morning glory vines, and knew the old oak tree outside our window watched over us while we slept.

For years, Stephie and I blamed ourselves for our situation. We believed we were worthless creatures and deserved nothing. We berated ourselves thinking we should have done what we were told, we should have cleaned that crummy little apartment. In reality, Stephie and I were just two little kids doing the best we could, without really knowing how. We weren't old enough to be on our own for the long hours Mommy was at work each day. And I wasn't prepared for the responsibility of raising a younger sibling.

However, we could have gone the way of so many abandoned children. But we did not. After our mother's departure, our grandparents learned of our plight and took us in. They loved and nourished us to the best of their abilities, and we became known as the girls from Byron's Corner. But what really saved us was the way we cared for each other. No one will ever understand me or love me more than my sister because of our shared experiences. We have laughed and cried our way through this world. But still the questions remain and, occasionally, ghosts from the past linger. When memories of lonely days and hungry nights rear their ugly heads, my sister and I cling to each other, both of us warmed and reassured by a love and tenderness only the two of us can know.

. . . . .

Gloria Beanblossom grew up in a quaint farming community near Robinson, Illinois, the home of noted author James Jones and the James Jones Literary Society. It was in this atmosphere of literary excellence that she developed her passion for storytelling and writing. Gloria's works entertain while also speaking to the Everyman in all of us. Her published novels include The Tamarisk Tree, Byron's Corner: A Child's Story of Abuse and Survival, *and* The Wishing Stone. *Gloria and her husband, John, reside in both Peoria and Stanford, Illinois.*

Come Hike with Me

Wilda Morris

Come, Sis, let's follow the path
of the old Interurban train, walk
the rusted tracks like we did as children.
This time, we'll hike northwest
'till we find a landmark to tell us
we're close to Goat Hollow.
We'll watch for rattlesnakes,
try not to rub against poison ivy.
We'll blow dandelion seeds,
mimic their airy dance, stop
to watch monarchs flitter on milkweed.

We'll pretend chickens still
run free in the yard, and the goats,
fenced in their enclosure,
gnaw on weeds and grasses.
They'll come to the gate,
and we'll gentle them
with our murmurs, feed them
apple slices until Aunt Irene calls us
for goat milk and cookies.
We'll curl up in blankets, listen
as Uncle Norman tells tall tales
as if they were gospel truth.

• • • • •

Wilda Morris has three sisters by birth and two by marriage, and several found sisters. Workshop Chair for Poets & Patrons of Chicago and Past President of the Illinois State Poetry Society, Wilda has led poetry workshops for children and for adults in three states. Wilda's book, Szechwan Shrimp and Fortune Cookies: Poems from a Chinese Restaurant, *was published by Rockford Writers' Guild Press. Wilda Morris's Poetry Challenge, at http://wildamorris.blogspot.com/, provides monthly contests for poets.*

Zori Sisters

Barbara Toboni

The summer I was seventeen, my older sister moved out of the house, and my best friend left Guam, the island where my family had lived for several years. Concerned that I would be lonely, my parents bought me a puppy, a beagle I named Mellow. I loved owning a dog and enjoyed our long walks together. On one of these walks I met Sunny.

"How adorable!" Sunny knelt to pet Mellow, a smile blooming from the point of her chin to the tip of her nose.

"Thanks. I'm trying to teach him to walk with a leash."

"Cool. You live around here?" The pup leaned against Sunny's leg, a paw catching on one of her rubber shoes.

"The end of the street. Wanna walk with us?" Maybe she had other plans, but I hoped not, because I wanted the company, and she liked my dog. I tugged Mellow off her foot and noticed our sandals matched, same color, bright orange.

Sunny gathered long strands of her unruly hair and twisted it all into a bun. She pointed to our flip-flops. "Look at us, The Zori Sisters."

Matching sandals, wild hair, we could have been related. Sunny filled my sister gap as we flip-flopped all over Apra Heights, the Quonset hut Theater, Navy Mini Mart, and the neighborhood park.

I told her all about myself, and vice versa, only her versa was immensely different than mine. Other than the thrill of learning to drive—with my father, not so thrilling—my life up to now seemed dull, but Sunny, only two years my senior, had been married and given birth to a stillborn baby. Then her marriage was annulled. Wow! In a short expanse of time Sunny had lived, really lived. I wanted to know all the details but shied away from asking. Our friendship was too new, and nosey wasn't my style.

Sunny's name matched her personality, and her cheerful chatter eased my loneliness. I had begun writing poetry, depressing stuff with lines like Love dies as machines blacken the world. Breaking my own privacy rule, I allowed my new friend to see my writing. She said my poems were sensitive and honest. She would know because her mother also wrote poetry.

Gradually, Sunny confided in me about her ex mother-in-law, saying the woman had demanded an end to her marriage. She blamed the girl for cursing her own pregnancy and causing the child's stillbirth. I couldn't imagine such cruelty, but my friend told me the woman didn't approve of her, a white girl, marrying her Guamanian son.

Sunny said the woman taught her to cook. One dish, chop steak, I liked so much she shared the recipe:

> *Ingredients: 1 pound sliced steak, 1 clove garlic, 1 carrot, 1 small onion, 1 stalk of celery. For sauce, equal parts of soy sauce and water, lemon juice to taste. Add garlic to oil and stir fry steak till brown. Remove steak. Add sliced carrots, onions, and celery to the pan and stir fry. Pour in sauce and steam a few minutes. Add beef back in and heat.*

"Be careful of the curse," she warned.

"Really? How silly." I didn't believe her.

Because my own mother taught me the old adage that the way to a man's heart is through his stomach, I served the dish to Kenny, the boy next door, my secret crush. It worked. Kenny raved about the meal the first time I cooked it for him, and he proceeded to get me drunk on a bottle of wine he had acquired somewhere. We went for a walk after dinner. I carelessly left the empty bottle on the kitchen table. When I returned home Dad lectured me about having boys in the house without parental supervision and underage drinking.

The more I stir-fried steak, the more it seemed Sunny's warning had merit: more stubbed toes and sidewalk stumbles, rainy days and lost umbrellas, and the final row that broke it off with Kenny. By now, I had lost track of Sunny. Her plan had been to buy a cheap car, find a job, and move out of her parents' home. I tucked the recipe away along with my Zori Sister memories.

A few years later, when I married J.R., I changed the recipe by adding ginger and sesame oil. I renamed the dish Sunny's Stir-fry Steak. Would my luck change too? J.R. loved it, and ate it all the time—until the divorce.

· · · · ·

Barbara Toboni is a writer, blogger, and poet. Her work has appeared in newspapers, literary journals, and anthologies, including Wisdom Has a Voice, Vintage Voices 2011, *and* Cup of Comfort. Undertow, *a chapbook of poetry, was published in 2011.* Water Over Time, *her most recent collection, was published by MoonSkye Publishing in 2013. www.barbarasmirror.com.*

Sister to Sisterhood

Lynn Millar

Hair-pulling? Shin-kicking?

If you asked what "sister" meant when I was a child, those might be the words I'd have used. I felt kicking protected me from a sister who was six years older, bigger and stronger. I raged with frustration.

Of course, she also taught me how to read before I started first grade. Most of the things I know about daily life come from her. I hear her voice in my head and out of my mouth every day.

For me, "sister" also came to mean "sisterhood" in the 1960s. A time of change for young people like me, we shivered with things frightening and exciting, silly and deadly serious.

After watching the civil rights movement on television, from people being fire-hosed and burned out of their churches to seeing the March on Washington, things changed for me. After marching in anti-Vietnam War demonstrations in Boston and New York, things changed more.

Finally, a modern feminist movement arose. I stopped wearing makeup and it saved me twenty minutes every day. I stopped wearing high heels. I tried to quit thinking about my flaws and started thinking about what I could be.

Reading Betty Friedan's *The Feminine Mystique,* Simone de Beauvoir's *The Second Sex* and Germaine Greer's *The Female Eunuch* taught me different ways to look at my "sisters" and myself. Words seemed so important, as in adult females called women—not girls, gals, ladies or even chick and bitch. "Libbers" instead of "feminists" rolled out a new insult. Thinking of females as "women" signified a new level of respect. I still cringe when I hear "ladies." Unfortunately, suggesting a different word is no better understood today than it was forty years ago.

More than thinking differently or having discussions with friends and co-workers, sisterhood meant doing something. Just as the civil rights and anti-war movements taught me, one had to participate in the change. I felt a great need for the women's movement.

Bra-burning?

The bra-burning, though not an ongoing type of outrage, became a media hit. A protest against the packaging of "beauty" at the Miss America Pageant, the term "bra-burning" discredited all the varied demands of the women's movement. Pageants go on today. Our sisters continue to participate in contests including very young girls trussed up to be "beauties."

Equal pay for equal work?

Professions for women seemed limited to teacher or nurse, not professor or doctor. Newspapers listed job ads by gender in the late Sixties, when I started looking for work. In the early 1970s I worked in a large office where my male co-worker made $700/month and I made $425. Then I got a union job on the railroad and made several hundred dollars more his $700.

In 1963, women's pay was $0.59 on the dollar compared to men. Today, it's about $0.77. An improvement, I'm not sure how to judge given that higher paying jobs for working people—construction and manufacturing—have severely declined.

Figuring out equal pay for equal work seemed way too difficult for sophisticated economists. It's been debated before and after the Equal Pay Act of 1963. How to compare secretaries to construction workers?

My union job on the railroad was equal pay for equal work. Railroad work, except for the hours, paled compared to all those other jobs I ever had for women's work. But discrimination came in daily harassment from male co-workers and the level of jobs women could hold. We were barred from higher paid jobs. Gradually, many of those higher-paid jobs opened to women, though not exactly proportional to the number of women in the workforce.

"Equality of Rights under the law shall not be denied or abridged by the United States or any state on account of sex." Simple?

By the 1970s I became involved in the Equal Rights Amendment (ERA). First introduced in 1923, a few years after women got the right to vote, it floundered for decades.

With little government support under the Equal Pay Act and Title VII of the Civil Rights Act, my sisters felt the need for something more. After the Women's Strike for Equality in the summer of 1970, the U.S. Congress started holding hearings. In 1971, the House, Senate and President Richard Nixon endorsed the ERA. The ERA quickly passed ratification in thirty states. An amendment to make the rights of women across the nation equal seemed so close.

Then the ERA got stuck. In the next four years, only five more states ratified it to become an amendment to the U.S. Constitution. Three more states needed to ratify and a deadline loomed ahead in 1979. States like Illinois required a three-fifths majority to pass the amendment. Living in Chicago, I joined with many women and organizations, NOW (National Organization for Women) and CLUW (Coalition of Labor Union Women) to try to get it passed. I went to demonstrations at the state capital in Springfield.

Without the ERA, if I should move to Arizona or Alabama, I would have different rights than if I moved to Wisconsin or Oregon. That made no sense. Didn't I have the right to whatever job I could do or own whatever property I could afford? Apparently not.

We couldn't make it happen. States started to rescind the ERA. We had lost the moment. I gained many sisters, but lost this war. We won some battles, we lost others.

The consolation was that we were in this together as we addressed other issues, such as access to birth control, which is elemental in freeing us as sexual beings. The right to abortion–to control our own bodies–had a victory. The U.S. Supreme Court ruled in favor of abortion based on a woman's right to privacy. It's been under constant onslaught and attack ever since, which includes killing doctors, bombings and attacks on clinics and women resorting to unsafe abortions in their desperation. And in 2014, the U.S. Supreme Court ruled in favor of a group of employers that refuse to include birth control in the health coverage they offer employees.

It baffles me that those who don't want the government involved in human rights, job and product safety, education and health, demand a say in what a woman does with her body and when.

By the time I came to California in the late 1970s, I was already active in an Anti-Bakke coalition. Allan Bakke's lawsuit against the Regents of the University of California claimed that preferential treatment in admissions contradicted his rights under the 14th Amendment. He decided to challenge California's Proposition 209 prohibiting race- and gender-based preferences in state hiring, contracting and state university admissions.

Commonly known as affirmative action, it provided a way to make up for the trend of discrimination against minorities and women. Eventually, the U.S. Supreme Court ordered UC Davis to admit him to school (denying specific quotas), but that race could be used in determining future admissions. I might have supported Bakke if he'd challenged his admission as discriminating against him as "too old."

It felt like a loss.

Today, I sense that women feel comfortable taking on any job and that they are in charge of their lives. Women dominate in college enrollment. But the top political and corporate positions are elusive. Why is the pay still uneven?

In my recent office work, women dominated in numbers if not in rank. Women's work remained in the office. Our husbands were laid off and could not find work again—as retail, manufacturing and construction jobs disappeared. Our daughters succeeded and our sons floundered.

Somehow, the right to work and be independent had turned out differently than we expected. So many other factors of politics and economics came into play than we could foresee. Our excessive consumerism and the cost of medical care meant women had to work–it wasn't a fight for the right to work. We needed to work or we lost economically.

The struggles of my "sisters" remain. Sexual harassment and job discrimination go on. Domestic violence and abuse with both male and female victims continue. Young people need to be counseled that violence is not acceptable within relationships.

While many conditions for women have improved in the United States, for women in other countries, life is often perilous.

Sometimes the battles are short and periodic. Sixty women challenged Saudi Arabian social convention by driving their cars one day in October 2012. They could own the car and work professionally, but couldn't drive. The last protest was eleven years ago.

Sometimes the battles are long. By age eleven, Malala Yousafzai of Pakistan started blogging about the rights of girls to attend school past the age of fifteen, when they were forced out. The Taliban, opposed to any formal education of the girls, closed schools in the Swat Valley where she lived. And in late 2012, when Malala, age 15, returned home on a school bus, the Taliban shot her. While she recovered from her injury, more than two million people signed the Right to Education petition. This led to ratification of the first Right to Education Bill in Pakistan.

The actions of one individual can inspire others to take action to improve the lives of many. I'm glad to call these women activists my "sisters."

I made a few personal choices in my youth responding to the injustice, violence and war I saw in the world. I felt empowered by my choices, understood the pain of my sisters more fully, and could act in the hopes of making a better life for all of us. The solutions are more complex than I ever imagined, but young women today are ready to go forward.

* * * * *

Lynn Millar is a child of the 1960s. The Civil Rights struggle and the Vietnam War deeply affected her. She became active in the anti-war movement and later in the fight for women's rights. While she wishes she'd written as those seminal events took place, she's been writing stories, poems, plays, and nonfiction for the last ten years. Not an active fighter today, she is encouraged by the young women who carry on the struggle.

The Warp and Weft of Sisterhood

P. H. Garrett

Early on, my sister and I were labeled and placed in categories carved out by our parents. I was my mother's daughter, and Emily, born with his blue eyes and dark hair, my father's darling. She was deemed the artistic child, I the smart one; she shy and obedient, I the wild child. In the fertile soil of division, jealousy, confusion and fury thrived in our home. Like an invasive weed, it poisoned our lives for three decades.

I was two-and-a-half when Emily arrived in my world. I don't remember much about the initial impact my new sibling made. It was only when my little sister became seriously ill that the arrangement took on momentous proportions. She was sick for two years. Dad had been Emily's champion since her birth. Suddenly, Mom deserted me, the object of her affections. All her time and energy went to my sister. Life buckled and curled.

On occasion, Emily and I played together peacefully during our grade school years. Often we battled. We laid yarn across the floor to divide our bedroom down the middle. Placing a toe over that line frequently brought us to blows. We tattled on one another. Once I pulled the head off my sister's favorite doll. I fantasized about losing her on the way home from school. She got me into trouble all the time. Later I stole her boyfriend. She snooped in my diary and spied on my friends when I had pajama parties.

But we were sisters, and our lives remained entwined, spinning out through the years on a tightrope of unspoken suspicion, envy, and yearning.

One fine day a phone call changed everything. Our dad had passed away some years before and I was calling on the anniversary of his death. We started to reminisce.

"I was always so envious of your special relationship with Dad," I told her, amazed to be saying it aloud. "You were lucky. No one ever noticed that that my dance was art too. Daddy hated that I loved to read, that I spoke up, that I used my brain."

"What!" Emily squealed. "Well, I may have been his favorite, but he never paid much attention to me except for criticizing my shyness. He never noticed my 'art'." Her words trembled with emotion. "They both let me know I wasn't much of an academic achiever and it was fine with them. I was always jealous because Mom liked you best. I wanted what you had—Mom."

Astounded, I explained how our mother was all mirrors and smoke, never there for me, too busy with herself, her career, impressing my high school boyfriend. "I was always desperately trying to get her attention and approval."

We started to laugh then. Our chuckles turned into howls and hoots as we shared our dashed parental expectations, and the craziness of wasting so much time wanting what the other had, when we both had had pretty much the same. Suddenly my world felt brighter with Emily in it. I heard it in her voice too.

Sisters are a living weave, a breathing tapestry. That's a good thing, because during our heart-to-heart, a new and lasting pattern in the dazzling colors of sisterhood, was woven into our lives. We are weaving it still. Emily is my best friend. She is funny, wise, supportive, and tremendously talented. My life is rich with all we share.

* * * * *

P. H. Garrett embraces life in the American West. Her writing includes press releases, articles, short fiction, and a first novel currently in rewrite. Her work has been published in the Nob Hill Gazette, Marin Independent Journal, USA Today, FYI San Francisco, Horse Journal, Family News, Up Beat Times, Petaluma Post, Call of The Wild, San Francisco Chronicle, *and online at* Tiny Lights, *and gutsyliving.com. In 2014, her stories were published in two new anthologies. Contact her at wordwranglingwoman.com.*

Flowers for Leslie

Nellie Wong

Hey, Sister!
Look, I've brought you these flowers,
Aren't they pretty?
Mums, iris, narcissus,
Ready for Chinese New Year,
We're celebrating, yes, with white-cut chicken,
Jai, Chinese chicken salad, fun see, a hot beef dish,
Mushrooms, stuffed dow foo and fresh orange wedges.
The whole family's gathering
To pay homage to our ancestors
To remember their battles
In Toishan on the land
Where cows graze and move
Slowly in the noon-day sun
Where on the soil
Our long-time Californ' forbears
Reclaimed the land in the Delta,
Built stone walls for the wineries,
Caught shrimp at China Camp,
Settled in the community of Locke
And others in the Mother Lode country.
Yes, those yellow men
Hoeing, plowing, digging, fighting,
Using their arms, legs and muscles
To create and build the transcontinental railroad
While our foremothers' sisters sold their bodies
In barracoons to feed their families, sold abalone shells
In Monterey, helped their husbands
In the only Chinese store in town
Where restaurants flourished
On the streets and in tiny storefronts
With meats and vegetables cooked
In wrought iron pans for hungry miners
And we, their descendants,

March, picket and sing
Our songs of love and struggle
Where your spirit, my sister,
And that of Ma's and Bah Bah's merge
As you feast in your finery of red and gold
In a land of sun-washed mountains
As I sit here by your side
Gazing over the skyline of Oakland
Missing you and loving you
With flowers blooming through these hands.

. . . . .

Nellie Wong is the author of a chapbook and three books of poetry, the most recent being Breakfast Lunch Dinner *(2012). Her work has appeared in numerous anthologies and journals, including* This Bridge Called My Back: Writings by Radical Women of Color, The Iowa Review, American Working Class Literature, The Haight-Ashbury Journal, The Paterson Literary Review, Voices of Color *and* Speaking for my Self: Twelve Women Poets in their Seventies and Eighties, *among others.*

Twinkies for Breakfast

Elspeth Slayter

Sometimes, I'm not just my sister's sister. I haven't met many others with such a problem. In our case, Amelia has an intellectual disability, and since our parents' deaths, I feel the pull between my sibling role and de facto parental role. The dictum in loco parentis never quite felt so real before. Navigating the waters between sister and parent has become a regular challenge for me—especially when it comes to Amelia's desire to eat Twinkies for breakfast. It all started three years ago when I became the "point person" for my sister's home visits as our father was nearing the end of his life.

We were in the junk food aisle at Stop n' Shop. I was not happy about this. The fruit aisle had been a total bust, as had been the cereal aisle. With her hand hovering over a package of Twinkies, Amelia turned to me with a dark look. Those pushing their shopping carts by us in the cramped supermarket aisle scurried away, sensing an argument in the air. People generally don't take kindly to those who look different; in this case, those with an intellectual disability such as my sister. And nobody likes a family argument in public.

As an adamant professional advocate for the right to self-determination for people with intellectual disabilities, there I was, struggling with my sister's food of choice for breakfast. In my head, I calculated the location of my line in the sand vis-à-vis the distance to a full-blown tantrum from Amelia. I chose the fruit route and made a plea for cantaloupe. "But I don't want cantaloupe. I want Twinkies!" she declared in an overly loud voice, her pointer finger standing straight up. "They taste good with milk and tea."

My counter argument came out as my arm angled to my hip. "But, Twinkies," I stammered, "that's, that's just not breakfast food!"

Both glowering, neither of us was likely surprised by Amelia's strident response. "It's my 'human right' and you can't stop me." Her back stiffened.

I recalled that Amelia was a regular attendee at her group home's human rights training sessions. The concept of human rights in day-today life choices is a central goal for all community-based people with intellectual disabilities who live in government-supported settings. In describing her activities at such meetings, Amelia acts out the role-playing she engages in. Generally, this involves standing up for one's rights in decision-making at all levels—from self-defense and job choice to food choice. "On the one hand," I thought, "this human rights training is totally right on. But on the other hand, how could they let a person with pre-diabetes eat Twinkies, of all things, for breakfast?"

I grew agitated. "It's my house, and my wallet, and we don't eat Twinkies for breakfast at my house!" My voice now met Amelia's in decibel as I attempted to impersonate a parent, now that our mother was dead and our father was so sick. The parental tone did nothing to further our détente.

Her voice, even louder now, became more adamant: "They let me eat it at my house. I went to my human rights advocate. I eat one for breakfast with tea and milk. It's what I eat for breakfast. I want it for breakfast."

Freeze frame. This seemingly simple incident in the grocery store is actually about the foundation of modern disability policy writ small and large—the implementation of the "dignity of risk" concept coined during the de-institutionalization era by disability studies scholar Robert Perske, who first used the term in "The dignity of risk and the mentally retarded," published in *Mental Retardation* in 1972. In the article, he challenged disability system workers about "going overboard in their effort to protect, comfort, keep safe, take care and watch ... this overprotection can ... consequently prevent the retarded [sic] individual from experiencing risk that is essential for normal growth and development."

By reflecting on the potential gain from experiencing day-to-day risk, Perske championed the need for people with intellectual disabilities to be able to take such chances as well. While I doubt that Perske thought much about Twinkies for breakfast, he did comment on the need for the acquisition of "prudent" risk taking to avoid what could be a "crippling safety." Perske's commentary has informed the disability service community to think deeply about how to best support people with intellectual disabilities living and working in the community. And yet, I wonder, have families really had the conversations we need to have about the nitty-gritty of the implementation of the dignity of risk, say, when it comes to Twinkies? Of course, the situation Amelia and I face is fraught with the sibling-as-parent confusion we navigate.

"Well," I thought, "here I am, on the front line of implementing this important principle, as it relates to Twinkies for breakfast." The cynical sister in me thought, "Somehow, we've taken a wrong turn on this human rights stuff." The disability civil rights professional shuddered in horror. Taking a deep breath—and a new tack—I posed this question to Amelia. "Okay, I understand and agree that it is your right to choose Twinkies, but will you at least also have some fruit, and think about how Twinkies impact those sugar levels the doctor warned you about last week, you know, because of how you've been feeling sick sometimes?" As her pseudo parent-figure, I felt compelled to lecture, and yet I also felt like a hypocrite, failing in my chance to effectively implement the dignity of risk.

Met with a studied and confident silence, Amelia turned away from me as she defiantly placed three packages of Twinkies in the shopping cart. So, as many parents have likely done, I bought the Twinkies to avoid a scene in the grocery store. And, needless to say, Amelia had her Twinkies for breakfast the next morning, with tea and milk.

While Amelia has since moved on from Twinkies to Count Chocula's best, we do continue our discussion of her "sugar problem" and the importance of healthy choices, but the process is slow. I find I'm often stumped about how to support my adult sister on making her own choices, as I believe a balance must be struck between supporting the "dignity of risk" with the need to support a person's health "security." Or, maybe that's just an overprotective sister talking. While many sisters may have such debates, when the power differential is so extreme the dynamics shift radically.

So, when I find myself struggling with Amelia over such issues as Twinkies, I look back to Perske to guide me. Recently, in looking over his seminal writing on the topic, I found Perske addressed overprotection in a way that challenges the reader to look deeply within: "Overprotection can keep people from becoming all they could become," he wrote in his 1972 article. "Many of our best achievements came the hard way: We took risks, fell flat, suffered, picked ourselves up, and tried again. Sometimes we made it and sometimes we did not. Even so, we were given the chance to try."

Drawing on my memory of this passage in my toughest moments with Amelia, I'm more able to step outside of myself. It's taken me too long to realize that much of the learning that needs to be done is learning on my end—not Amelia's. While my health-focused conversations with Amelia go on, I've learned to back off and respect my sister in ways I never thought I could. And in turn, Amelia has, on occasion, surprised me by asking for cantaloupe at breakfast.

* * * * *

Elspeth Slayter lives and writes in Provincetown, Massachusetts. She is a disability and family studies researcher and an Associate Professor in Salem State University's School of Social Work in Salem, Massachusetts. With degrees in history, social work and social policy, Ms. Slayter has worked in child welfare, juvenile justice and forensic social work, focusing on supporting populations with disabilities.

Devora's Changes

Marie Judson-Rosier

Devora. Straight-A student. Ballet, sports, crafting. She took everything further than I did. I begged for ballet lessons, then dropped out when the teacher demanded too many demi-pliés. She stayed with ballet until "toe," getting a part in *The Nutcracker*. I ran faster than anyone in my school. She wasn't as fast but stuck with track until she received ribbons in high school.

Devora was my big sister, second mama, the one who said, "You're the cutest, sweetest little Ruthie" (my childhood name). Without her compliments, fondness, and affection in those early years, I'd be a different person. No one else in my family deemed encouraging remarks to be important or even desirable. "Sing me to sleep," she'd say. "You have an angel voice." She sewed tiny outfits for my troll dolls. She baked cookies just for me.

Despite her achievements, Devora always got in trouble with our parents because she spoke her mind. She pointed out hypocrisy. If there was something not being said, she named it. The two youngest of five siblings, Devora and I were inseparable, playing dolls under the willow tree or running like horses, her favorite game. The three elder siblings steered clear of her moods, which could swing. I acted as arbiter, defending her from them, and them from her.

After high school, Devora put herself through nursing school. At twenty, she married a guy working in a lumber mill. They bought a cozy prefab house, and Devora filled it with her sewing and crocheting—neat curtains, afghan spreads on couches, handmade tablecloths. Then, out of the blue, she left her husband and joined me in Santa Cruz. I was twenty-one, she twenty-three. Soon I left to attend school at UCLA, where I met my future husband, Mark. She stayed in Santa Cruz and found a boyfriend: Rick, a crepe chef.

Devora moved to Oakland. When I visited, she told me she'd lost a nursing job. "They said I left the side of a crib down," she mumbled.

"So … the baby fell out?"

She was evasive.

I returned to Los Angeles. Correspondence with my sister was sporadic, usually with me the one contacting her. Years passed. Mark and I moved to the Bay Area. I became pregnant with my first child. At last, Devora called. She told me she'd met a guy named Jim at some hot springs, and they were shacked up together in San Francisco.

Not long after that, she phoned to tell me she was working at a strip club in North Beach.

"A what?!" This was so unlike my sister, the registered nurse, the straight-A student who'd also watched out for me when we were kids.

"It's okay. Jim wants me to."

"It's not okay," I said.

The next day, Jim called: "If you don't send money for our rent, Devora will be sleeping on a park bench."

Feeling threatened, I called my sister. "Dump that piece of excrement."

Devora slipped out of contact.

I had another child. Mark and I opened a café. One afternoon, I picked up the phone. It was Devora. "I'm living in Portland, Oregon. I'm marrying Gil," she said. Gil, it turned out, was in his early twenties, a decade younger than Devora, and just out of the army. They had known each other about a month. "He's my sweetie pie," she told me.

They married and moved to the Bay Area. I was glad to have my sister close by. She watched my kids and was a fun, affectionate auntie. They watched Babes in Toyland, ate home-baked cookies and healthy meals in her home, again filled with her handcrafts.

One night, in the wee hours, I heard a knock at the front door. Mark was out late, as usual. Throwing on my robe, I left the kids sleeping in their beds upstairs and peeked out. Devora stood on the front porch. I let her in, amazed.

"You have to help me get my purse back!" she said, wild eyed.

"Your purse?" We sat in the living room. "Did you lose it?"

"I have to find my car," she said, desperate. "They were shining lights in it. They chased me."

"Who chased you? We need to call the police."

She laughed in a strange way. "It was the police. They chased me all over."

I stared at her, uncomprehending. Then I noticed her bloody ankles.

The following months were dizzying as, slowly, I realized something was deeply wrong with my sister. She told the kids outlandish stories. "I dropped a thread and that's how the world started," she explained with perfect sincerity. "I have one hundred sons. My husband is Montezuma."

At Christmastime, with our café filled with customers, Mark asked Devora to watch our two-year-old, Sol, while I helped at the register. Knee-deep in shoppers, I noticed a disturbance outside and hurried to see what was wrong. A stranger walked toward us, holding Sol's hand. "I found him crossing the street alone." She pointed down the block to a busy intersection.

That was the last time Auntie Devora babysat.

After that, I received numerous late night calls from Devora or the police. One time, she was found sleeping on a family's couch in Salinas. Another night, she called telling me she was being followed in San Francisco. That time, she was beaten up and landed in a psych ward. They kept her for a ten-day observation. That was when she was finally diagnosed with paranoid schizophrenia.

But when the ten days were up, she was right back out on the street.

Meanwhile, I was going through a divorce. In the midst of this upheaval, I received a call from police at a homeless shelter in San Leandro. "Your sister was standing with her pants down in the middle of the street—at night, in the rain, on a curve. A car could have come around the bend and not seen her!"

The officers put Devora on the line. She exuded rancor for the lack of understanding she perceived on the part of the peace-keepers: "I was waiting to be punished by the gods. I did what they told me; I never cut my nails so they could leave messages under them."

Devora was admitted to a San Leandro psychiatric ward. I was relieved to know she was off the streets. But in a few short weeks, a call came that she was being released; an advocacy group bought her story that she was perfectly sane, because she sounded coherent when medicated.

I got the agency's number and called them. "Do you realize Devora gets beaten up, wandering the city streets at night? That the police can do nothing unless she's hurt or dead? Would you want your sister released under these circumstances?"

"We had no idea. She said—"

"She's very lucid when medicated. But she's a danger to herself," I insisted.

Despite my efforts, she was released. I picked her up and brought her to the condo I shared with my two kids, then five and seven. Once a health nut who juiced carrots and didn't touch alcohol or cigarettes, she'd taken up smoking nonstop. She stood outside our condo, rocking back and forth, puffing on her cigarette. She'd put on weight. But she was lucid; the hospital had injected her with a thirty-day dose of anti-psychotic medication.

"If you're going to stay here, you need to stop smoking, Dev," I told her.

She did not like the idea. "Send me to Portland." She had a friend there who would help her get settled, she told me. No one else in the family wanted anything to do with decisions regarding Devora's care. It was left to me, the youngest but the closest to her, to hold the terrible burden of decisions and their consequences. So I agreed to be the one to receive her disability checks and send her cash. My children and I put her on Amtrak for Portland. She sat with her two suitcases and some cash, her smile showing beautiful teeth that cost my parents thousands in braces. Occasionally, a shadow passed over her face—perhaps she listened to displeased gods.

Things went well at first in Portland for Devora. Her friend helped her get a flat she could afford, as promised, and assisted her with shopping. But all too soon, a call came from the Portland police. They had received a complaint that strangers found Devora in their car. The police returned with Devora to her apartment, where they found inches of grunge in her bathtub and wadded dollar bills in her pocket, despite the reports they gathered that she'd been begging for meals at the local restaurants.

When the police put her on the phone, she laughed hilariously. "Ruthie, if they'd only seen the limousine." She described the elegant vehicles her husband sent her, from Mars.

With a sinking heart, I called Oregon Mental Health. They promptly took over her case and provided her with assisted living. I signed custodianship over to them.

For a few years, she came by bus to my parents' home on the Northern California coast for the holidays. My kids searched for the auntie with the colorful stories and spontaneous affection. Her once-pealing laughter took on a hoarseness from constant smoking. She told fewer stories and stood outside rocking and smoking in a wonky beany hat, her breath puffing white in the cold winter air.

The last Christmas she bussed down to California, she didn't remember who I was. I suffered loss then, as if a mother had died. I was truly heart-broken as the meaning of her disease really hit me, as I contemplated a life in which no one would remember the hours we'd shared—the two of us—the closest relationship of my life in many ways.

After that, we exchanged letters. Devora sometimes sent drawings, among incoherent ramblings, mingled patches of wisdom, a poem, sometimes a literary reference.

When the kids were nearly grown, I flew to Portland for a job interview. There, I made my way down a tree-lined street to Devora's halfway house. Between the wings of the residential building, she stood swaying, back to me, heavy in a puffy ski jacket and baggy sweat pants. Her stringy, graying hair strayed from a ski hat. Cigarette smoke curled over her head.

"Devora?" I asked tentatively from several feet away.

She turned and gave me a gap-toothed grin, a smoker's wet cackle. Her face, once so lustrous, with glowing cheeks well into her thirties, had an unhealthy pallor. Her still beautiful hazel eyes looked out from a stranger's face.

"Ruthie." She hugged me, smelling of cigarettes, strange cadence to her voice.

Despite my shock at the missing teeth and gray complexion, so like the impoverished, drug-addled street people inhabiting every city, I felt a wash of relief that she'd recognized me.

She showed me her room. Stuffed animals lined the shelves, her paintings adorned the walls. My heart cracked when I saw the number of books stacked high against the walls. She still read voraciously. What part of her mind ate up the stories in those novels, while the rest found little foothold in our shared reality?

I suggested we go on an outing. I checked with the office staff and they were overjoyed. In the institutional bathroom, with its long metal hand bars, I helped her wash her greasy, tangled hair and put it in a French braid. She loved it.

On the MAX—the local light rail—we watched the billboards and city scenes pass. I started a song we loved as kids. "Christopher Robin is saying his prayers." Devora joined in, singing with abandon, dreamy eyed. We went on to, "Animal Crackers in my soup." Kids stared. Adults moved away. Teens snickered. Undeterred, we continued our songs.

In Pioneer Square, the sun shone and workers streamed out for lunch break. Devora was no stranger to this place. She bee-lined to Starbucks, then took up her stance near a lamppost, cig in one hand, latte in the other, rocking from foot to foot. I felt unnecessary.

On the way back, Devora wandered up to a rough-looking man on a bench and spoke to him. Within seconds, he'd risen, fist balled. I hurried over and steered her away. She infuriated several others before we finished our outing. To me, nothing she did seemed all that wrong. People lashed out because she didn't follow prescribed behavior. She unnerved them. On the MAX ride back, she told stories. These lacked the luminosity of her early tales about starting the world with a thread. They were morose and religious, about how she'd tried and tried to save Jesus from the beatings, went to the desert over and over with her helicopter, but he would not board. Panic flooded her eyes. It seemed her medications subdued her but turned her visions dark. Now I mourned not her loss of memory, but her happier illusions.

Back at her house, in a spontaneous gesture, I suggested she come live with me (though not without trepidation). However, she demurred, saying she couldn't leave David, a young man at the halfway house. He was her "cutie sweetie-honey." He was her husband. The young man sat, mostly oblivious to her, working on his computer.

At my hotel that night, I cried, for her and for myself. She was the one who had made me feel special, had doted on me, in a childhood with little attention from our mother. Ours was the most mutually caring, snuggly, belly-laugh relationship I ever had, until my own kids.

Devora died a few years later, of a cancer that swept swiftly through her. I have a photograph from our final visit, of her on her bed surrounded by her stuffed animals, and I know that, at least that one last time, we sang "lions and tigers loop-de-loop" together.

· · · · ·

Marie Judson-Rosier grew up in Northern California in a town that is now part of Silicon Valley. She loved to run in fields and orchards with her four siblings and spend summers reading under fruit trees. Marie has a background in education and is pursuing graduate work with plans to dedicate her future to healing individuals and communities, fostering a happier planet. The mother of two grown children, she resides in Sonoma County, California. She likes to grow her own food, sing harmony, and write fantasy fiction.

Crossing Over

D. A. (Daisy) Hickman

She mailed them to me in a
brown envelope, a clump of
roots with soil clinging to
their sides

I wondered if they carried
hidden life

I wondered how and where
to plant this gift, this daylily

red, she'd said the blooms
would be cherry red

an old pail filled with water
became a temporary home
a place for the roots to rest

it seems we all need this
kind of place

the blooms convinced me.

* * * * *

D. A. (Daisy) Hickman, author and poet, is the founder of SunnyRoomStudio: a creative, sunny space for kindred spirits. Hickman is also a member of the Academy of American Poets and the South Dakota State Poetry Society.

We Always

Tanya Savko

I've often wondered if there were many groups of siblings as different as my sisters and I are, yet also as close, and with as many shared memories. Too often I am saddened to hear of sibling rifts that never heal, and I think about how blessed I am to have loving siblings and many positive shared experiences. But perhaps it is our differences that create a healthy respect for each other. First there is myself, the eldest, a writer and special needs advocate who loves to go wine tasting. I'm often seen in suede Puma sneakers. The middle sister, Macrina, is a forester and wild land firefighter who brews her own tasty beer and wears rugged work boots. The youngest, Anastasia, an actress/craft food chef in Los Angeles, makes delicious raw chocolate and is often seen wearing platform heels.

Truly, I don't think we could be more different from each other. But we have a tradition that we all look forward to with equal enthusiasm: our annual Sisters Rafting Trip. Yes, every summer, for at least 12 years, the sisters have taken a three-hour rafting trip down the Rogue River in Southern Oregon.

The Rogue flows about 215 miles in a westward direction from the Cascades to the Pacific. I would venture to guess it's one of the colder rivers in Oregon, and I've been in several of them. And parts of the Rogue are quite wild, which make it one of the original eight rivers named in the National Wild and Scenic Rivers Act of 1968. Parts of The River Wild were filmed on it. Almost every year, people die on it.

The sisters don't raft those parts. No, we raft the three-to-four-mile stretch that is affectionately known as "The Booze Cruise." We laugh that there might be one Class Two rapid on that part. The wettest you get (unless you voluntarily get in or someone pushes you off the side of the raft, where you had been innocently lying in the sun, unsuspecting) is when your teenage son or one of his friends decides to start a water war with neighboring rafters and begins exchanging fire using the three-foot-long water gun tubes provided by the rafting company. And that's when you lean over to the sister nearest to you and say, "Next time we take that kid rafting, he's going in his own tahiti."

I probably don't need to explain this, but it's called The Booze Cruise because that part of the river is so mellow that many people would pack ice chests (these are big rafts) full of beer, before it became illegal a few years ago. Not that we ever did that, of course. And if we ever did, at least we kept all of the cans and bottles in the ice chest to dispose of properly. We had a few beers in our day. And Mike's Hard Lemonades (Anastasia's choice).

The boyfriends and husbands made sure of that. And when you get three sisters together over a period of that many years, there will be several significant others along the way. A few times, we've invited friends. We've included my two sons (my niece and nephew aren't old enough yet) and their friends, and once, we went with our mom and aunt, neither of whom had been on the Rogue and were quite wary.

We have experienced a few injuries on the Sisters Rafting Trip, none of them as a result of alcohol. A few years ago, it rained on the designated day of the trip, which can't easily be changed because it involves reservations and travel time for two of us. We had a husband (Macrina's) and at least one boyfriend on that trip, and we all thought we'd spent enough of our lives in Oregon to be able to tough out a little rain. Rafting in the rain – yeah! So we got out there, all gung-ho, and within twenty minutes, decided the idea was ill-conceived. Even though it was raining, the river was low that year, and as we rounded a bend and hit a big rock, I, seated on the edge of the raft with my back to the water, didn't brace myself, and flew out of the raft. Like a falling cat, I quickly righted myself just as I hit the water and saw a huge boulder racing toward my head. I stuck my hand out to cushion the blow and smashed it between my forehead and the boulder. Momentarily dazed, I felt myself being pulled back into the raft. Completely soaked with no way to dry off in the rain, I sat there shivering for two more hours. Later, I noticed I had broken two blood vessels in my hand. We all vowed we would never go rafting in the rain again.

But typically, Macrina's the first one in the water, and spends the most time in it. Anastasia, in her aviator sunglasses, works on her tan in the raft, and I occasionally dangle my legs over the side (even on a hot, sunny day, the Rogue is cold). The part we raft takes three hours to get to the pull out point because we make a couple of stops along the way. There's a suspension footbridge that we used to walk across, but that is now prohibited. There was a small fork of the river that had a slow-moving area with a rope swing that we stopped at years ago. And there's a huge rock, sort of like an island, where we used to pull over and jump off. But our favorite place to stop is a country store/burger joint where we often eat lunch. It's right on the river! And the best part: it has an old wooden outhouse right next to the chemical toilets that is rigged to make a dummy dressed in long red underwear move inside when someone opens the door. Whenever we have a newbie along, we always make that person open the door. And we always laugh.

We always. That's the phrase that surrounds traditions, makes us feel connected and part of a group. It means there were shared experiences in the past, and there will be more in the future. It means that we laughed together, drank beer, got squirted, jumped off rocks, and shared all of it with others. It means that, no matter where we live or how different we are, we're always sisters. Many people have gone on our annual rafting trip with us, faces and circumstances have changed, a lot of water under the proverbial bridge. But one thing has remained the same, one constant: the sisters were always there, like the river itself, flowing endlessly to the sea. Here's to sisters and traditions and all the good that comes with them.

. . . . .

Tanya Savko is a writer, blogger, and mother of two sons, one with autism, epilepsy, and bipolar disorder. She founded TeenAutism.com in 2008 and is the author of Slip, *a novel about a single parent raising an autistic child. She blogs at TanyaSavko.com and lives in southern Oregon, where she tries to find time to work on her next novel when she's not out hiking, rafting, or wine tasting. Connect with her: www.facebook.com/tanyasavkoauthor, https://www.goodreads. com/author/show/4026952.Tanya_Savko, and Twitter @TanyaSavko.*

After

Nina Tepedino

Elder sister needs to speak
after years of neurotic encounters,
stricken by stroke,
taken by scourge of cancer,
the familial feminine counterpart of my life
has come to an end,
to be lived only in my memories.
I now watch from my place on Earth.
I sleep to dream of our celestial reunion.
I am the lone survivor,
who carries the regret
of unrealized sisterly love.

. . . . .

Sebastopol, California, resident Nina Tepedino has been writing poetry since 1975. Her poems have been published in several collections, including Pacific Northwest Ferry Tales, And the Beat Goes On, *and the Redwood Writers* Vintage Voices 2013 *and* 2014 *anthologies. Her poem "Beach Mural" will appear in a forthcoming Green Wind Press anthology dedicated to Fukushima. In 2012, her first children's book,* If You Lived in Sam's Neck, *was published. Besides writing, Nina enjoys photography, Tai Chi, walking/hiking, gardening, music, drumming, and activist pursuits for peace and justice.*

Set Seven

. . . .

The Face of the Following Eyes – memoir, John Boe

Her Sister's Keeper – short story, Jennie Marima

Cranes for Judy – memoir, Ruth Friesen

Somewhere Near Jordan – poem, Carson Pynes

Idealizing Sisterhood – memoir, Wendy Kennar

Pink Ribbons – poem, Monica Nawrocki

Barbed Wire – short story, Conda V. Douglas

A Unique Gift – memoir, Bernadette Pabon

Segovian Riff – poem, Dianalee Velie

You Women! You're Such Bitches! – essay, Cath Bore

Safe To Dream – memoir, Laura McHale Holland

Before I Forget – poem, Ana Manwaring

The Face of the Following Eyes

John Boe

I was the youngest of three children, with sisters Margaret (three years older) and Karen (a year and a half older). No wonder my favorite fairy tale was *Hansel and Gretel*. It seemed to describe reality to me, for the sister, Gretel, rather than the seemingly younger Hansel, has both intelligence (she tricks the witch into the oven) and magic (at the end of the story she understands the language of ducks).

We moved frequently because my father was an encyclopedia salesman, working his way up. So I would regularly find myself in a new town (suburbs of Chicago, Los Angeles, San Francisco, New York), with no friends. So my sisters and I would play together, usually fantasy games of one kind or another. I remember how when we would visit my mother's parents in St Louis, we would bring no toys, and there would be no toys in the house (except for an old dominoes set, a game we never learned to play). Instead we would go down to their cavernous basement and convene a meeting of the Goggle Stamp Company, planning our new stamp designs, worrying about our rival the Acme Stamp Company. Margaret was the leading imaginer in all these games.

The only vacation my family ever had, we took by accident. My father had gone back to work for his old company, Collier's Encyclopedia. So when the school year ended, we moved from San Francisco to Chicago (our second move to Chicago). Because we didn't yet have a place to live in the Chicago area, we spent July at Lake Okowchie, just outside of Milwaukee. My father only spent weekends with us—he worked in Chicago during the week.

For me, age nine, it was an ideal vacation. I learned to swim between the piers, first with water wings, then without. My mom never went in the water, but one Saturday, when my sisters and I were swimming, we complained to our parents standing on the pier that Mom never went in the lake. My father immediately picked up my mother (who was wearing a housedress) and threw her in the lake. Splash! We were delighted. Mom swam to the pier and climbed out, smiling in spite of herself. The manager of the Milwaukee Braves, Charlie Grimm, lived next door, and he used to take his rowboat out on the lake at night after a tough loss. And, sometimes, he had loud parties with the players. I learned to fish that July, catching sunfish off the pier, which Mom would fry up. I enjoyed casting large plugs for pike, even though I didn't know what pike were and never did see, much less catch, one.

At night, Margaret, Karen and I would play in the attic. One of our fantasy games (attics are as good as basements for fantasy games) was called "College," which we played even though our parents had each only gone to one year of college. I think we had intuited that college was in our future. The only detail of the game I remember is that Karen would always be going to the Junior Prom with a boy named Don or Dave (whom I got to act). Amazingly, when she really did go to college, she went to the Junior Prom with a boy named Don and subsequently married him. Our game had scripted her life.

One of the great things about that lake house was that it had an ice-box. Not a refrigerator—an icebox. I had never seen one before, so I found it incredibly exotic. I especially liked using the ice pick to chip off pieces of ice from the big block. Every Saturday morning, my father would drive to town and pick up a big block for us. By the middle of the week, the ice would be gone, but so would my father and his car. And so, every Wednesday, my mother, my sisters and I would walk down the hill, a mile or so, into town. At the soda fountain, we'd get the best sundaes I'd ever had, chocolate ice cream with melted marshmallow sauce. We'd each get to buy a comic book—usually *Little Lulu* or *Archie*. Then we'd get the block of ice, in a box, and we'd take turns pulling it behind us up the hill.

One day, when Mom was buying the ice and we were selecting our comic books, Margaret noticed new items on the rack. This was 1953, just after *Mad Magazine* had debuted, and I don't think comic books were regulated. At least they weren't well regulated, for the comic books in front of us were not suitable for children. We saw titles like *Tales of Terror, Horror,* and *Sick Stories*; garish covers strewn with blood, body parts, and disgusting dripping monsters; promises of stories about dead babies who come back to life then eat their mothers' eyes—evil, horrible, vile, loath-some stories of perverted violence. This was '50s pornography for kids, and we wanted it.

We quickly picked out three. Margaret, being the eldest, went to the counter and bought them. No questions asked! And the goods were safely tucked in a plain brown bag. When we joined our mother to begin pulling the ice up hill, she asked us what comic books we had gotten. I was frozen silent, but my sisters lied in unison: "A *Little Lulu* and two *Archies*."

That evening, in the attic, we devoured our comic books. Then, instead of playing College, we drew pictures on the back of those pieces of cardboard that were in shirts when they came back from the cleaners. Margaret, who always drew really well, sketched a scary face and sat it on a chair.

As I was working on my picture, I looked up at the chair and realized the face was watching me. "Margaret! The face! It's staring at me!"

Karen, who was drawing on the other side of the attic, looked up and shouted, "No, it's staring at me!"

"You're both wrong," Margaret said, trying to sound calm. "It's staring at me."

We all screamed, then madly scrambled around the attic, checking out every corner, every hiding place. But wherever we went, whenever we peeked out, the face was looking at us—at each of us. It was the face of the following eyes!

We worked ourselves into some serious terror. Soon we were cowering close together in a corner, gaping at the eyes that stared back at us. "Dobby," Margaret said, using the family nickname that I'm still known by. "Dobby, go and get the ice pick."

This was my first conscious experience of sexual stereotyping. Here we were, three kids, two girls and a boy, the girls twelve and ten, the boy nine. There's a murder to be done, so who do you think is called on to do it? Like many before me, I bravely accepted the social role thrust upon me by my sisters. I was called to be a man. I would be ready.

I left the attic and walked down the stairs to the kitchen, to the ice box. My mom was there, drinking coffee and smoking a cigarette. "Hi, Mom. Just getting a Coke," I lied coolly. I grabbed a soda, but I also grabbed the ice pick, carefully keeping it hidden from Mom as I opened the Coke and left the kitchen. At the top of the stairs, I paused and downed the drink. I could hear occasional wails from inside the attic, but I was ready.

When I opened the door, I discovered my sisters had been transformed into screaming maenads. They were rolling on the floor; their eyes were bulging; inarticulate screams and moans were erupting from deep inside them. I looked on them with pity and disdain. I had the ice pick. I had a mission. I was cool.

I pressed my body flat against the wall and edged toward the wooden chair on which the face sat staring its horrible stare. I blotted out my sister's senseless sounds. As I moved closer, I avoided looking directly into its eyes, but I felt its gaze drawing me in. In a final burst of courage, I leapt, plunging the ice pick into its left eye, pinning it to the chair. Behind me, my sisters' screams intensified; I pulled the pick out; the face fell to the floor; I stuck it again and again, pulling and tearing until it was in little pieces. When my flurry slowed, I saw most of one eye still looking up at me from the floor. I stabbed the ice pick hard through it, into the wood floor. I was done.

Behind me, my sisters' cries came into focus.

"Dobby! Dobby! Stop it, stop it!"

I turned around, unbelieving.

"You ruined it!" Margaret yelled at me. "I can never draw that good a face again!"

After a long pause, I responded, "But you told me to get the ice pick."

"We were plaaaying!"

I looked blankly back.

"You just can't play with boys," Karen said to Margaret as they went to the other side of the attic to play without me.

This was the first time in my life, but not the last, when I did something a female encouraged me to do, but then after I did it, she denied having encouraged me.

My sisters, I realized later in life, had been right. As is usually the case, I guess, the male hears what he wants to hear. They had been playing, but I had been possessed. We were all feeling guilty from reading those comic books. The following eyes, I discovered much later, are a traditional symbol for a guilty conscience—but I, more than they, being younger or just more immature, had been unable to handle the combination of guilt and terror that had formed itself into our fantasy of the following eyes.

The market for horror films and books is, of course, mostly young adults and older children. Before age ten or so, you want to stay naive, don't want to face the horrors of life. After age twenty-five or so, life has probably brought you enough horrors that you don't need to seek them out in fantasy. Once you've dealt with a few real dead bodies, imaginary ones may not hold the same fascination. But when we played that game in the attic, I'd been the youngest. I hadn't yet reached that age where kids not only tolerate horror, but crave it.

Still, I did regret having destroyed the face with the following eyes, having ended the game. I'd felt so alive during the confrontation, so caught up in the fantasy. One of the reasons I write and tell stories is to recapture the power of that image, to experience the reality of a fantasy, a fantasy world I was first led into by my sisters. For much of my writing life, when I was stuck as to what to write, I would imagine writing a letter to Margaret, and then the words would flow. My sisters were (and I hope still are) like muses to me, leading me into the world of imagination.

* * * * *

John Boe recently retired from UC Davis, where he taught Shakespeare, Fairy Tales, Storytelling, Children's Literature, and various writing courses. He has won teaching prizes from UC Davis and Phi Beta Kappa and first prize in the H. R. Roberts Literary Awards, Informal Essay Category. He has published widely, including Life Itself: Messiness is Next to Goddessness and Other Essays. *He is also a professional storyteller.* The Face of the Following Eyes *first existed as a performance piece.*

Her Sister's Keeper

Jennie Marima

December 1998, Nairobi

Kami remembers how the missionary boy, Ed, came unexpectedly into their lives. Dreams about Ed and her elder sister, Wendo, are frequent now. They're no longer just dreams, but visions, too—Kami's eyes are wide open when they happen. She is haunted by flashing images: Wendo's chocolate brown and Ed's pinkish-white fingers intertwined like piano keys, and their remarkable height difference—Ed was nearly a foot taller than Wendo.

Today is Wendo's wedding day. Although a bridesmaid herself, Kami feels like a fly on the wall watching their house buzz with activity. Camera operators squeeze into narrow corridors to get the best shots of the bride; beauticians dust and paint the bridal party's faces, fingers, and toes; hairdressers weave participants' hair into spectacular styles they'll probably never wear again. Women gather outside the gate in their elaborate vitenges and towering headgear as they sing themselves hoarse to be let in. Kami strains to see Wendo's face and finds the bride's expression is unreadable, neither unhappy nor elated, yet far away. Kami feels a familiar, guilty choke in her throat, and wonders if her actions were the deal breaker. If she had, intentionally yet unintentionally, determined her sister's fate.

December 1992

Kami and Wendo, both in their late teens, scampered out of the living room whenever Father came home from work. Father's terror was so constant it seemed almost normal. Kami believed that hers was a typical Nairobi home; she wouldn't know better because her family didn't socialize much. Although Mother didn't rush away like the girls did when father arrived, she was often scolded and punished like a child and, sometimes, when Father was really upset, she would be locked out of the house altogether.

And then Ed happened.

Wendo came home one day looking flushed. "There's a guy at church fellowship," she said.

"And you like him?" Kami posed.

"Well, I mean, he's nice, and tall, and he's the one that said hi first, and he usually wants to sit by me at fellowship."

"Name?"

"It's Ed. And...we didn't just meet, he's always been there, well, not always...I mean...oh, anyway, never mind." Wendo floated around the room like a bird. "He is Ed—Ed, Edd and Eddy," she sang, referring to the cartoon she and Kami sometimes watched when their father was away. Then she whistled the cartoon program's signature tune.

Kami was a little surprised by this performance. In all the years they had grown up together in the city, Wendo had never shown interest in boys. But strange things had happened to Wendo lately. For instance, she'd been "saved" in her fourth year of high school. Kami was sure her sister's salvation was a passing phase. But when Kami threw away her secular music tapes that she'd worked so hard to dub from the radio station, destroyed the exercise books where she wrote lyrics to her favorite songs, burnt the novels that she had scraped together her pocket money to buy, Kami knew her elder sister had been converted.

Wendo now went to a Pentecostal Church. This was kept top secret because, if Father ever found out, it would be World War III. Mother knew, but she also knew better than to mention this to the girls' father.

Kami had often rebuked Wendo about her conversion. "What's wrong with our church?"

"I prefer my new one," Wendo would say politely.

"You should thank God that Father doesn't go to church. If he ever found out, you know all of us would be in trouble, especially Mother." Kami would shake her head at her sister's selfishness.

"Then we'll make sure he doesn't—for now," Wendo said.

And now there was Ed.

"Ed is American. Yes, a mzungu one," Wendo unleashed the bombshell.

"Are you deliberately trying to get us killed?" They both knew how Father felt about white people. This would be like spitting in his face.

"He's a missionary's grandson, and he wants to meet my family. You have to come meet him," Wendo pleaded.

"I'll meet this missionary boy of yours, but that's it."

Ed was far taller than Kami had expected. She and Wendo had always been tall girls, towering higher than the rest of their age mates, but Ed was long.

He hugged them both outside the church building. "It's great to meet you, Kami. Wendo talks a lot about you," Ed said.

Kami got the sense that he spoke a little slower, pronouncing every word, perhaps for her sake. "Likewise," she said and found herself staring at the freckles on Ed's face, his large, green, cat-like eyes and mop of curly blond hair.

"I'm Ed — Ed Long, but Wendo has probably already told you."

Kami almost laughed. Ed Long, no kidding.

Ed slipped his fingers into Wendo's. Kami could tell Wendo was a little uncomfortable, but she didn't wiggle them out.

Kami found out that Wendo and Ed had been "together" for more than a month. She learnt Wendo didn't like holding hands in public. Ed revealed he found it cute the way she pronounced "cut" and "cat" the same way, the way she made that African sound "NKT" when she was irritated. He was now practicing it. Ed told Kami details of his relationship with Wendo that she would never ever have known. Ed also told her he was bummed because his parents were getting divorced; that's why he came rushing to his granddaddy in Kenya, away from all the grief. And who knew he'd meet Wendo, the love of his life? This was way more information than Kami cared to know.

Many years later, Kami asked herself why she did it. Soon after meeting Wendo's dashing new American beau, she was at home with Mother. And the words just floated out of her mouth. Everything that Ed had said, everything she'd seen them do.

And Mother had a betrayed look in her eyes. "They can never really truly love people like us," she said to Kami. "We are like playthings to them. They despise us. And we, them. They don't value family, that's why they get divorced like it's a sport."

That night, when Father came home and the girls scampered out as they usually did, there was murmuring in their living room. Kami wondered if it was about Wendo; if Mother was telling Father. The girls heard the unmistakable sound of a slap, and the door opening and banging shut.

They knew their mother would be spending the night in the cold and dark. Then their bedroom door flew open. There was a depth of rage in Father's eyes they'd never seen before.

"Wendo, you are not to leave this house, for any reason. Is that clear?" He banged the door shut before any response came.

The sadness was almost tangible. Wendo stopped speaking altogether. It would be a long time before she would crack into a smile again.

Weeks later, Kami walked by Wendo's church and spotted Ed looking restless.

"Where is she?" he asked. "Nobody around here knows where you live."

Kami felt her eyes getting misty. "She went to Narok, my grandmother's place."

"She could have at least told me." Ed looked like he was going to cry.

Kami could tell there was much about Wendo that Ed would never know.

"I don't have much time," he said urgently. "Give this to her." He handed her an envelope he'd been carrying around for days, hoping he'd have found Wendo by now. "There have been intelligence reports of possible unrest in Kenya, especially Nairobi and all American citizens are being asked to leave. Could you please make sure she gets it?" Ed took her hands. "She's the love of my life, tell her that." Then he disappeared out of the church compound.

Kami thought of how selfish Wendo had been getting them all in trouble with her choices. First the new church, then the missionary boy. Didn't she see what this was doing to their family? To Mother, especially, for she was always on the receiving end of Father's wrath. Why couldn't Wendo see this? Angrily, Kami tore the letter into little bits and tossed it away.

December 1998

It's like an out-of-body experience. Kami watches Mother—today, mother-of-the-bride, in her brand new kitenge, posing next to Wendo for a "goodbye" photo. Father is waiting outside the house in a new suit, flanked by uncles who never visit. Kami studies Wendo—her shimmering white gown that cost an arm and a leg, her hair, her face all dolled up to the point that she is unrecognizable. A tear trickles down Kami's face.

"Hey," says the lady doing Kami's makeup. "No crying allowed. You'll spoil all the work we've done." And then she whispers in her ear. "Don't worry, yours will come, too. Just trust God, and you'll be as happy as your sister is today."

With that, Kami begins to shake and snuffle, then sob. She tries to stop, but quickly grows louder. All wedding preparations stop; everyone stares at Kami.

"I kept the truth from you, Wendo," Kami says tearfully. "I didn't mean to. I did it because it was so hard to see what your secrets were doing to us, to Mother. It's Ed I'm thinking of. He told me you're the love of his life!"

Mother looks stricken. "How dare you!" Her hand flies across Kami's face. "How dare you try to destroy your sister's day!"

Thereafter, Kami remembers the deadness in Wendo's eyes when she learned of Ed's love—six years-too late. The same look she had when Father slammed their bedroom door and forbade her to leave the house.

Kami is haunted by memories of Wendo drifting down the aisle to a man their parents had approved. She breaks into tears every time she recalls the strain in her sister's voice as she said her vows.

And when Wendo vanishes off the face of the earth barely a month into her marriage, Kami asks herself over and over if she had inadvertently sealed her sister's fate.

* * * * *

Jennie Marima (a.k.a Shi) is a Kenyan author. Her first picture book Rundo the Elephant *was published in 2008 by East African Educational Publishers. Her story* The Runaways *made it to the top 20 in the 2012 Golden Baobab Prize for the most captivating unpublished manuscript for children. Her short story* Almost Family *won the Storymoja May 2013 Photo Contest. She is currently working on a collection of short stories and a novella for teens.*

Cranes for Judy

Ruth Friesen

I recognized the white paper bird perched in my mail slot. It had been floating around the SouthWest Writers office for several months, but this was the first time it was designated especially for me. Or so it seemed. During a board meeting, I placed the bird in front of me and admired its tightly woven body and multi-"feathered" tail. Sometime between the treasurer's report and the discussion of upcoming classes, inspiration hit: I should fold cranes for my sister!

My eldest sister, Judy, was on my mind a lot lately. Since her diagnosis of inflammatory breast cancer five months ago, she'd withstood procedures as aggressive as the cancer itself. After three months of weekly chemo sessions and a double mastectomy, she had no strength or energy. I saw her enveloped in the isolation that major illness brings, and I worried about depression sliding her into a huddle of darkness.

In my subconscious, absorbed with myriad other tidbits of information, was the knowledge that origami cranes were often folded as gestures of hope and wishes for good health. And not just one crane, but one thousand, were needed to make the wish come true. Judy could use hope and good health.

Would she appreciate one thousand cranes? She propped every get-well card on her mantel, overflowing to other tabletops in her living room. Reading them over and over, she was warmed by their messages and the concern of the senders. I thought an abundance of cranes made just for her would feather the nest of her soul with love and courage to endure the storm.

I could hardly wait to get home and research the project. My fingers flew over the keyboard as I googled "one thousand origami cranes." I found instructions and a video on how to fold them. One site mentioned that, often, friends fold forty cranes each for a loved one. So I'd need to contact twenty-five people to help me fold. I was ready to fold all of them myself, but that would take a long time, and Judy needed encouragement now. Twenty-five friends seemed the way to go.

How hard would it be to fold origami cranes? Could I ask twenty-five people to learn? I'd never done origami, but the websites told the story of nine-year-old Sadako Sasaki, diagnosed with leukemia after being exposed to radiation after the bombing of Hiroshima, who folded 644 cranes and whose friends completed the count to one thousand after Sadako died. Surely, if she could do it, so could I.

Just to be on the safe side, I enlisted the help of my nine-year-old niece, Rachel. If the two of us could master the technique, then I could ask Judy's friends to learn, too. One Saturday morning, we laid the sheet of instructions in front of our pile of origami papers bought from a local hobby store and creased the first folds. During the time I fumbled through the first five folds, Rachel finished two cranes.

"Rachel, what am I doing wrong?" I asked.

She unfolded my crane. "Here, Aunt Ruth. Do it this way. You had the paper upside-down." When I finally succeeded in completing one crane, after tossing several, her words of encouragement, "That's right, Aunt Ruth. Good job," were music to my ears. Maybe I wasn't old fumble-fingers after all. Now I could, in good conscience, ask other people to try it.

I emailed a couple of cousins, Judy's daughter, my other sister, and I contacted two or three of Judy's friends. The project took off. Most people wanted to help, and they talked to others in Judy's circle of friends. After only a week, I had commitments from twenty-five new origami aficionados.

The stories started coming in. Two groups held coffees to socialize while they learned to fold. Aficionados isn't an accurate description of their devotion to origami. None of them had done any before and, as one of the gals told her group, "I'm glad you asked me to help, and happy to do it for Judy, but don't ever ask me again." After a four-hour coffee klatsch, each person had folded one crane. But they promised to continue folding at home.

My daughter, Christie, and her husband, Dave, folded cranes, accompanied by a bottle of wine, and she sent me photos via her cell phone as they progressed. I wasn't sure those were actually cranes. When she mailed me her forty cranes, she included the first efforts, and they most definitely did not resemble cranes. But everyone eventually learned the technique.

I set a date for the presentation of the cranes to Judy. Getting them to her posed another challenge. Six of the strands of forty cranes were traveling from Albuquerque to Kansas, where Judy lives. Would they pack without crushing? I folded the flights of brightly colored birds into my suitcase. I wondered if the TSA would ask me to open my apparently empty luggage—I assumed the cranes wouldn't show up on their X-ray machine. "Careful," I'd say. "They'll fly away!"

Two strands of cranes were overnighted from Judy's granddaughter in the Philippines. I picked up another strand from Heidi, who lived in London and had brought her cranes to a conference in Albuquerque. Christie mailed hers to my sister Debbie in Kansas, where I strung them with a bead on the end of a length of fishing line.

After all one thousand cranes were collected, I arrived at Judy's. and said, "I brought a surprise for you." Debbie and Pat were there, having "just dropped in," and knew what was going on. As I opened my luggage and pulled out the first strand, Judy looked puzzled, uncertain what she was seeing. I handed her a parchment page with the story of the cranes.

"Twenty-five of your friends have folded cranes for you, to send you hope and good health," I said.

"But...this isn't one thousand," Judy said.

Debbie and Pat then went to their cars and brought in the boxes and bags of cranes they had gathered. That's when Judy's tears started.

"All these cranes … just for me?" Judy's voice caught in her throat. "All these people … so much thought and effort … for me?"

We continued to pull cranes from their nesting places and laid them over the couch and chair in Judy's living room. No more dark days for her: she was now surrounded by color and love.

Judy hung the cranes throughout her house, as reminders that she wasn't going through this difficult time alone. Our encouragement gave her a cradle of support that she hadn't felt before the flock of cranes settled into her life. Four years later, they continue to perch on the railings and walls of her home.

"When will you take them down?" her husband asked.

"When I don't need them anymore," she replied.

* * * * *

Ruth Friesen's fingers don't remember the crane folds after four years. She lives in Albuquerque, New Mexico, where she edits the quarterly journals of two historic trail associations: the Santa Fe Trail Association and the Old Spanish Trail Association. Her essays have appeared in several anthologies, including Voices of New Mexico 1 *and* 2, *and* Going Green: True Tales from Gleaners, Scavengers, and Dumpster Divers.

Somewhere Near Jordan

Carson Pynes

In the back room of a tiny shop,
a girl is on her own, arranging
long-stemmed flowers in a vase.

The weight of her bird-like bones
just heavier than soft wings tucked
sharp between blades of shoulder.

Flight? you might ask,
but she knows better; the danger of unfurled pinions
in this space (close walls, razor crystal, mirrors)

would leave her bleeding and bewildered.
Instead, she places flowers inside translucent vessels,
firmly names each (Amaryllis, Strelitzia, Jonquil)

in a glinting, armored voice, my winged sister de-thorns
fanged roses, never the type to paint them red, while
close a radio plays a song about a river while

(Snapdragon) she names another flower,
she never lifts her head to sing.

* * * * *

Carson Pynes grew up in a small town high in the mountains of northern Arizona. Her previous work has appeared in Menacing Hedge *magazine. Her debut collection of poetry,* Secret Toast, *is available from Blurb Books. She lives and writes in Galway, Ireland.*

Idealizing Sisterhood

Wendy Kennar

I once thought sisterhood would be a lifelong experience. Having a younger sister was supposed to guarantee having an abiding confidante, best friend, and supporter. Ideally, it does. But real life isn't always ideal.

My sister, Julie, is three years younger than I am. Growing up, we were close. In hindsight, I realize our closeness was somewhat coerced. We had to be close: We shared a bedroom. We looked a lot alike. We attended the same small schools. We had to get along because there was no alternative.

But even in our youth, our differences stood out. My sister has always been more assertive and more opinionated. She never hesitated to tell me she didn't like my hairstyle or that long skirts made me look fat. I was, and continue to be, the diplomat—refusing to give a straight answer for fear I may hurt someone's feelings.

Moving out of our parents' home and choosing different paths after high school magnified our differences and created a wedge between us. My sister began working full time upon her high school graduation, enabling her to rent an apartment and buy a car. I began my college education at the local community college, then transferred to a four-year university, all the while commuting on public buses. Our daily lives and responsibilities were vastly different.

We both married young (me just shy of my twenty-third birthday, Julie at the age of twenty-one). The next year, she was a mother. I delayed motherhood for nine years. My husband and I continued to live in the city, renting an apartment. My sister and her husband purchased a home in the suburbs and bought a minivan.

I'd hoped that when I became a mother, the divide between us would be bridged. I expected the lines of communication to be reopened. We'd both be raising little boys. In my new role as mother, I hoped to regain my prior role, as close sister.

Things didn't work out as I'd planned. We parented differently. My sister was a stay-at-home mom; I returned to my teaching career. Our different lifestyle choices carried over to our parenting choices, and instead of becoming closer, we continued to drift apart.

Quietly, I've come to realize that, while we share a history, we don't necessarily share a future. It's been a painful lesson to acknowledge that someone I readily said "I love you" to isn't someone I can readily say "I like you" to.

· · · · ·

Wendy Kennar is the mother of a six-year-old son and was a public school teacher for twelve years. A prolific writer, she has had work published in the Los Angeles Times, Christian Science Monitor, L. A. Parent, United Teacher, Lessons From My Parents, Beyond the Diaper Bag, *and* Write for Light. *She is a weekly contributor at MomsLA.com and writes a weekly blog at wendykennar.blogspot. com.*

Pink Ribbons

Monica Nawrocki

she wears the uniform
— the kerchief and waxy skin colour —
she pulls up in a BMW
(a Toyota)
(a Ford Escort)
she is accompanied by her daughter and son-in-law
(her partner)
(her friend from the support group)
in her approach, visible confidence
(anxiety)
(exhaustion)
through the doors she walks
to the waiting room
eager
(anxious)
(dreading)
to see —
doctor
lab technician
pharmacist
nurse
doctor
lab technician
pharmacist
nurse
she leaves, hours later,
exhausted
(exhausted)
(exhausted)
she sees another uniform descending the steps beside her
on the way to her BMW
(Toyota)
(Escort)
the look they exchange is small and big

encompassing and guarded
generous and protective
they stare at one another
— sisters —
and wonder who will claim the survivor statistic.

* * * * *

Monica Nawrocki lives with her partner and dog on a small island off the west coast of Canada. She earns her living as a substitute teacher—often reading "under-construction" manuscripts to captive classroom audiences and happily impersonating someone different every day. She is the author of one book, and her fiction and nonfiction pieces have appeared in various journals and anthologies in Canada and the United States. Visit her at http://monica-nawrocki.blogspot.ca/.

Barbed Wire

Conda V. Douglas

"What are you doing with Aunt Joan's box?" I stepped into the living room, where it was scorching hot from a fire roaring in the fireplace— despite the eighty-degree temperature outside. Mom didn't look up from the paper she held, a note written on a page of my aunt's old prescription pad. She tossed the note into the fire.

"Don't do that." I snatched Joan's shoebox off the table.

Mom grabbed the corner of the box and tugged.

Rage flamed into my face. "It's not yours, it's Aunt Joan's, it's—"

The box corner Mom held gave way, spilling the contents around us. Letters, old photos and tiny origami tumbled around Mom's chair.

I stooped to pick up the pieces.

"Don't," Mom said.

The habitual fury in my mom's voice stayed my hand. I sighed deep into my chest, forcing my anger down. It bit, pin prickles of pain I ignored. Despair roiled up.

Mom was destroying a woman's memories, a woman who'd always been another mother to me, sometimes better than my own. Mom never saw gray in her life, only the white of the few joys or the black of her many real griefs.

I eased down to sit cross-legged on the floor. I reached out my fingers and tried to snag a delicate origami crane. I figured to secrete the lovely bit of history behind me. Save a piece of history.

"Leave it," Mom said.

She flapped her hand, a threat. Before she could smack my hand, I dropped the crane. I searched every shadow of my mind for a way to stop my mother's annihilation. I rubbed the aching spot between my eyes. Once decided, once determined, my indomitable mom carried out her plans.

With a grunt, Mom leaned over and grabbed a photo. She frowned, then picked up a pair of scissors and cut it in half. She threw one half into the fireplace.

"Mom, please," I whispered. She ignored my plea.

The flames grabbed the old paper and tore into the image of an American Japanese internee at Minidoka. His arm was flung around a waist and ended at the elbow, an abrupt amputation. A woman's ghost hand lay on the man's shoulder, relaxed, friendly.

Mom placed the surviving half of the photo next to her on a small pile. Truncated, my Aunt Joan smiled up at me, her pleasure at being the doctor for the Minidoka Internment Camp evident in her grin. When Aunt Joan died, my mom received the letters, photos and handcrafted thank you gifts from her days there.

Once filled to bursting at the corners and now, half-empty, torn corner sagging, the box hollowed of soon-to-be-lost history.

My mother's fingers, twisted with arthritis, pulled her hands into claws. Her calloused fingers tore at the paper, like beasts feeding. She plucked a letter from the shoebox. I curled my own fingers into claws, to resist the urge to slap the letter out of her grasp.

"Why now?" I asked. I touched her age-spotted hand. She crumpled the letter in her fist.

With firelight marking her face as if anger flamed her skin, Mom lifted her chin to point where a letter sat propped upon the coffee table. "They want to create a memorial to the internment camp," she said. "They want your aunt's materials for the museum."

Warmth comforted my heart at the honor for my aunt.

Mom frowned. "How dare they even ask?"

"But Mom, it's a great honor—" Why did I even try? I squeezed my eyes tight for a few seconds. I tried because it mattered. To me and to the memory of Aunt Joan and what happened so long ago, and to Mom as well. I forced my eyes open.

"Honor?" Mom stared at me, her eyebrows so high they created a washboard of her forehead.

"For Aunt Joan to be recognized for her work," I said. I tried because I loved my mother, a woman who carried fury around as a shield.

"Why would she want to be recognized—" Mom spat the word "recognized" with venomous spittle "—for that?" She licked her lips. "Joan always said it was the only opportunity she had, in those days, to be a doctor, but she should have turned them down." Her litany, repeated by rote, over decades. "Now everybody says it was an injustice to put people in a camp. But it was for their own protection."

She looked up at the wall. There, in pride of place, a shrine where my mother entombed her grief, hung a large portrait of a young woman and her toddler son.

I'd never known my Aunt Sarah, my mother's oldest sister, or her child. I'd been born after their deaths. I'd studied the portrait and wondered who these people, my family who lived before me, were. When I'd asked Mom the first time, she'd told me one story. I'd asked for another, different, happy story once, twice, and a third time. Each time my mother had responded with a rebuke.

Aunt Sarah sat in a cobra-backed cane chair, her son in her arms, his wide grin shining with baby teeth. One fist waved in a baby's greeting. Aunt Sarah's only child, Jimmy died with her. He woke early that December morning and insisted on playing on the beach at dawn. His last morning light. They played on one of the Hawaiian beaches the Japanese planes strafed.

"In that camp, those people were safe. They survived. Some wanted them dead." Mom tossed the letter into the fire.

I wanted to snatch the letter from the flames, but feared my mom would toss all of the memorabilia into the fire at once. I feared she wouldn't even save the photos of Aunt Joan, that her anger would turn her love to ashes.

I watched my mom's tight face, her eyebrows drawn down, the years of grief and struggle sliced in her forehead and around her mouth. How could I reach her scarred and battered heart and help it heal?

I slipped a photo from the old shoebox. The light from the fireplace, still bright with the fuel of an old war, made the images appear to move. Another Japanese American internee, a boy of about twelve, stood dressed in a tattered baseball uniform, a baseball bat in his hands. He held the bat high in a proud batter's stance.

The crackle of the letter burning brought me back to the living room. Mom plucked an origami crane.

I grabbed her wrist. "No, wait."

Mom winced. "Let go," she said.

I realized I held her fragile bones too tight. I opened my fingers and looked at the crane in my mom's palm; a bird nestled within a nest of wrinkled skin. I remembered Aunt Joan telling me how the internees, especially the old women, crafted crane after crane, symbols of long life, from the silver foil of gum wrappers. How arthritic fingers created instead of destroyed.

"Once," I began, "Aunt Joan told me she asked one elderly woman at the camp why she didn't come see her, the doctor, when the woman knew she was ill."

"I don't want to hear," Mom said. But she didn't return to her destruction.

I continued as if she hadn't spoken, "'That's what I'm here for, to help you,' Aunt Joan told the woman. The tiny old woman had curled her arms around her middle, huddling around her pain, and she said to Joan, 'Today you are here, but tomorrow … best not to make trouble.'

"'It's no trouble,' Joan replied.

"'Not today. What if tomorrow the war goes badly? Best not to be noticed.'

"'But you're an American, like me.'

"The old woman stared out at the locked, barbed wire fence that surrounded Minidoka. 'No, not like you,' she said. Then she left, without letting Aunt Joan help."

"That old woman understood." Mom lifted her chin high.

I knew Mom was daring me to contradict her words. She wanted to return to the safety of the old, familiar arguments. I settled further down on my sitting bones. I could be as stubborn as my mother; she'd taught me how.

Mom placed the crane onto the save pile. Then she picked up another photo, this one of a tiny clapboard building with Aunt Joan's precise lettering beneath: "Infirmary." She tossed it into the fire. It crisped black as if the long ago building burned.

"Does destroying Aunt Joan's mementos make it better?" I asked.

My mother hunched her shoulders as if Japanese warplanes were roaring overhead. "No. No. No."

The pain in her face brought another memory to mind. "One time

Aunt Joan took me out to where the internment camp stood," I said. I reached my hand toward the fire, and the heat burned, intense like the sunshine on that August day, long ago. Out on the high desert plain we had stood; the sagebrush rustled like internees whispering. "Aunt Joan said, 'It's all gone.' Then she kicked at a piece of rusted barbed wire. 'Save for this, tough stuff to get rid of, once it's there.'"

"There's barbed wire everywhere," Mom said. She lifted the crane from the save pile.

I reached for the tiny bird then stilled my hand. "Yes, Aunt Joan said the same," I continued, "and then she said, 'Your mom, she's barb wired around her heart.'"

Mom placed her other hand on her chest. She pressed down as if razor wire cut deep and said, "What nonsense. Joan was—"

"She said, 'Trouble with barbed wire, it cuts no matter how it's touched,'" I interrupted.

Mom dropped the crane. It fluttered to the floor; for a second it seemed alive. She looked down at the shoebox, all that remained of a hard life lived well. Her shoulders raised once, twice, and then fell still.

Wings of hope fluttered in my chest. I handed her the photograph of the boy in the baseball uniform. "Was this young boy the one who strafed the beach at Pearl Harbor?"

Mom flinched. "No. Of course not."

"Did he kill your baby sister and her baby?"

"That doesn't matter …" Mom's voice dropped and faltered.

"He was just a boy. Why should he be punished? Forgotten?" I asked.

She peered at me, eyes narrowed.

"Look at him. Please," I asked.

She brought the photo closer to her wizened eyes. "I know this uniform." She touched the boy's face. "Joan set up teams so the boys could play, found them uniforms, and equipment." Tears rolled down her face. "I helped her find the stuff, going from store to store for donations. Until they had their first game, and I found out who played." Mom raised her hands and scrubbed at her tears. "Joan begged me to come to their first game. But all I could think about was Sarah and her baby. The one casket. They lay together, mother and child, it couldn't be open—" Mom's chin dropped to her chest. She sobbed.

I hugged Mom tight, stroked her hair and said nothing until her cries subsided.

She pulled away and wiped her face. "So many years ... so long ago ... all gone."

"Not all gone," I insisted.

Mom raised her eyebrows, surprised, questioning.

"Tell me a story about Aunt Sarah, about Aunt Joan, about the three of you when you were little." The old, aching pain of loss beat at the base of my throat.

"I can't—" Mom folded her hands in her lap, over the photo of the boy, as if she no longer trusted her appendages.

I clasped her hands in mine. Her tensed hands seemed about to crumble. "Don't keep Aunt Sarah and Jimmy locked up secret in an old photo."

Mom shook her head.

"Your words will make Aunt Sarah and her baby alive again."

My mother sighed long and soft. I believed I heard barbed wire releasing from around her heart. She freed one hand from mine and brushed her fingertips across my forehead.

"Sarah told me how your little cousin Jimmy loved to toss fistfuls of sand in the air," she began. "Sand everywhere." My mother smiled as if she smelled the sea, could feel the cool, soothing sand beneath her twisted fingers. "He loved to see the dawn colors through the falling sand." She picked up the origami crane and cradled it as if she held a living bird. "I believe Jimmy laughed as the planes flew in, as he saw them through a veil of sand. That he thought they were great seabirds."

"I can see him, playing, laughing, alive," I said.

Mom placed the crane back in the shoebox and moved the box farther from the consuming flames. "I'll send the box off tomorrow to the museum."

"Thank you," I said, warmth swelling in my chest. I hadn't known how much barbed wire had crept around my heart too.

"Did I ever tell you," Mom said, "about when Sarah—who always led us straight into trouble—and Joan and I ..." She laughed, a high, strong laugh of a much younger woman. A woman whose heart was open and free.

Together we sat and spoke of Aunt Sarah, of Aunt Joan, of others gone, with the honored dead crowding close around, until the fire went out.

* * * * *

Conda Douglas grew up in the ski resort of Sun Valley, Idaho. Her childhood was filled with authors and artists and other creative types. She grew up with goats in the kitchen, buffalo bones in the living room and rocks in the bathtub. Now her life is filled with her cat and dog and permanent boyfriend and writing, with the setting always her beloved Idaho. Find more about Conda and her writing at https://www.amazon.com/author/condadouglas.

A Unique Gift

Bernadette Pabon

We were a happy family of seven until our mother died giving birth. Unfortunately the baby also died, leaving behind a grieving husband, three girls and two boys. At five years of age, I was the second oldest of the girls. My little sister, Hedda, was only three. Wherever I went she followed. I dressed, fed and otherwise took care of her. At the time, this didn't seem unusual.

Seeking better opportunities, our father moved us from Puerto Rico to Chicago, but he turned to the bottle for strength, which made him do things that no father should do. Soon, he remarried and had three more children. Our stepmother was young and just wanted to be with people her age. When our father was not home she made us handle every chore around the house, including looking after the younger siblings.

When I was seven and my little sister five, we attended catechism classes taught by the Cordi-Marian Sisters, who prepared us for our First Holy Communion. I vividly remember Hedda and me holding hands, our brothers not far behind, as we walked the long blocks to St. Francis of Assisi church in Chicago. The Sisters embraced us with love and attention, and even fed us. My ten-year-old sister Norma, who had been cooking for us, had left home. (I didn't know until I was grown that she had been placed in foster care.)

During this time, food was scarce. Our stepmom and dad squandered grocery money on baubles for her and alcohol for him. We children roamed the streets searching for food. My father often sent us inside a tavern for cigarettes. While one of my brothers bought the tobacco, Hedda and I would hide under the bar stools and gather every nut and chip we could find on the floor and counters. After we collected all we could hold, we would dash outside. For us, these treats were delicious. The fact that most of them came from the filthy floor did not bother us. We would also lift already chewed wads of gum from the pavement and chew them. Then we'd put them on sticks and fish for lost coins that had rolled into the sidewalk's metal drainage grates. With a nickel or dime we were able to buy candy. Other times we trooped hand in hand over two miles to the restaurant where our father worked. There we hid under the tables and ate leftovers.

It wasn't long before we became wards of the state, placed in different facilities by Catholic Charities. My little sister and I remained together, but this was the beginning of a horrific journey. Our broken hearts yearned for our family; everywhere we turned, we thought we saw our brothers and sister. We were transferred from one foster home to another, each one more frightful than the last. I tried to take care of Hedda. She was small and delicate, and it was more dreadful to watch her suffer than to accept punishment myself. We suffered beating after beating, hunger, pain, and mental and sexual abuse—with no one to turn to but God. We had learned from the Sisters at school that God was all knowing and all powerful, and as children, we counted on him to rescue us with his super powers.

When Hedda cried for Mom, I told her the only thing I knew, "Pray, and she will come and take us with her." Not yet understanding this was impossible, we knelt in prayer by our bed and begged for her and the rest of our family, and after we crawled under the covers, we'd pray ourselves to sleep night after night. At the time, believing that our mother could come back gave us the strength we needed each time we were abused. In one home, we were locked in our room at night; we could not get out even to use the bathroom. When we wet the bed, our foster mother would tell the social worker that we were lazy. Later, she would beat us. Thinking that maybe the problem was that God could not hear our prayers, we opened the windows to our room so maybe it would be easier for God to come in and rescue us.

In the worst of times, I would tell Hedda, "Let's pray some more. God will hear us soon. Perhaps He is a busy God." We prayed day in and day out. Sometimes, though, my sister would not stop sobbing, and when I could not comfort her, I hit her to shut her up, for if the foster parents heard us making noise, we would be severely beaten. We grew up with such a considerable amount of fear that even to this day, fear consumes many areas of our daily lives.

In another home, the foster father would enter our room at night and prey upon us. Many times I remained awake all night, fearing he would sneak in to assault us yet again. When a social worker took us to be examined by a doctor, our foster parents threatened my sister. They told her I would die if she didn't say we were abused by Blacks living in projects we passed on the way to school. At yet another home, we were sent out to steal meat and clothes. When we got caught, the foster mother told the authorities, "They are foster kids that have bad habits." Believing that we had sinned, Hedda and I attended daily confession. We also confided in the Sisters at school about our situation and told the priest. Nothing changed. It seemed no one cared or listened. We felt lonelier than we ever had.

One summer, however, we attended summer camp for two weeks. We learned table manners, games and songs. We got to bathe daily and enjoy the company of other children. This was the happiest we had been since our mother's death. We treasured our experience at camp; it was a life of joy, peace, and love. We never imagined the suffering yet to come, because we told our camp counselors of our situation at our foster home, and we thought surely they would do something on our behalf. Still, the memory of those days lifted our spirits. One of the songs we learned at camp still brings us joy when we sing it today: "You are my sunshine, my only sunshine. You make me happy when skies are gray. You'll never know, dear, how much I love you. Please don't take my sunshine away."

In the following years, Hedda and I remained very close. We thought alike and felt each other's pain. Though I felt overwhelmed by taking care of her, at times exhausted and trapped, her dependence on me kept me sane and energized me to continue the fight. Her weakness gave me strength. Sometimes I wanted to die, but I could not give up, because I realized if I died, who would take care of my little sister? When we were placed in different homes, I missed her so much, because we were two people, but we had become one. I believe God stretched out his hands at this time and empowered us to continue the journey of life despite our separation. Prayer continued to be a dynamic part of our lives, and when we were reunited years later, we understood that it really was God who held us together, and God who was and remains our sunshine.

My sister is a blessing to me, as I am to her, and the faith we cherished as children was our salvation. The solution we were seeking from God was already given: to stand together and encourage and protect each other. My

SISTERS BORN, SISTERS FOUND

little sister and I learned that united we prevailed against all odds, and what we faced made us stronger. A sister is a unique gift, and love is the essence of this gift. The experiences we encountered secured our sisterhood with a seal that can never be broken. Hedda is an integral part of me; the heart that beats within her is the same heart that beats within me. Though we are different in so many ways, in essence we are one in spirit.

* * * * *

Bernadette Pabon was born in Caguas, Puerto Rico. She is married and has four children and seven grandchildren. After graduating from Holy Family Academy in Beaverville, Illinois, she studied religious education at Loyola University in Chicago. She taught religious education at schools throughout the Chicago area and facilitated youth retreats. She also published The Garden of Life is the Garden of the World, *a memoir likening people she's known to plants in terms of the impact their distinct characteristics have had on her life.*

Segovian Riff
Dianalee Velie

Soul, /turn orange-colored. Soul, /turn the color of love.
– Federico Garcia Lorca

Con passione
A Segovian riff drifts through the latticed windows
of their waterfront cottage, settling in the garden
where my sister plants golden fall mums. Dressed
in short overalls and a yellow, long-sleeved shirt,
muddy gardening debris scatters around her, a Spanish
sunflower to her husband, strumming his favorite guitar.

I float through fields of Andalusian sunflowers,
plucking at this domestic passion like a scavenger bird
masticating a simple seed into poetic sustenance.
What would I trade for a moment like this?
My journey through solitude so punctuated
by pain even the stones in my garden weep.

Lamenting like Lorca, I let this poem settle around
me like a blanket of fallen needles, smelling of pine
but not the living thing. Thousands of reasons exist
to love this life I lead, each one sufficient, each one
a recorded rhapsody of longing. Plaintively, I
pencil the perfect fret, gathering sympathetic strings

of words to resonate into a sonata, yearning someday
to strum a duet, before tomorrow's orange sun sets.

* * * * *

Dianalee Velie is a graduate of Sarah Lawrence College and has a Master of Arts in Writing from Manhattanville College. She has taught poetry, memoir, and short story at a number of East Coast universities and colleges, as well as in private workshops throughout the United States, Canada, and Europe. Her award-winning poetry and short stories have been published in hundreds of literary journals. She is the author of four books of poetry and the short story collection Soul Proprietorship: Women in Search of Their Souls.

You Women! You're Such Bitches!

Cath Bore

We're frequently told, aren't we, that women don't like other women: we hasten to criticize, we're eager to pounce on any alleged flaw; we're blood in the water attracting sharks. Such statements are often followed by the rolling of eyes, like an echo, and the exclamation: You women! You're such bitches!

The term "bitch" is thrown about with abandon. Any comment by a woman is bitching. A conversation between two women, that's bitching. Two bitches bitching. A woman expressing an opinion? That means she's a bitch, yeah? Another bitch bitching again. Bitch is part of our discourse. Bitch is a woman, bitch is talk, bitching is women talking. "Bitch" used this way is misogynistic. We've totally fallen for it.

Men talking or a man commenting on another man? Unremarkable, of course. No eye rolling there, no bitching. Silence everyone. Nod your head and furrow your bitching brow. Keep on walking; there's nothing to see here. Don't question, bitches. We've fallen for that, too. It's crept up on us, bitches.

I am the compère at an open mic night. I introduce singers, poets and storytellers who come along to entertain and be heard each month. Open mics provide a forum and a microphone in pubs and cafes, for anyone wanting to perform. Sounds nice, doesn't it? Those who don't go to open mics might imagine them romantic affairs: strumming minstrels and acoustic loveliness, Bob Dylan thoughtfulness and earnest songwriters. In the real world, though, open mic events are notoriously curious and sometimes hostile affairs—competitive and sneery, my guitar's bigger and better than yours, male dominated.

Me, though, I run a comfortably tight ship. Just call me Captain Bitch. No one talks when the acts are on, or dares leave after they've performed. Applause is mandatory. We have a full house right until the end.

Last month, one of the women putting her name forward to sing was a service user at our local hospital's mental health unit. She wanted to sing the song *Valerie* by Liverpool indie band The Zutons, not only solo but acapella, too. A brave decision. Even if I could sing, I wouldn't do it on my own with no accompaniment. The whole premise to me feels vulnerable, naked. I don't have the backbone. The woman's performance started well, but she forgot the words of the second verse.

That could've been the end of it, but no. Instead of sniggering and being "bitchy" as eye rollers would love, three young women from a youth group got up, walked across the floor and stood with this visibly upset and distressed woman, and sang the song with her. Sisters, truly.

It was beautiful, and not just the singing. A simple gesture, unremarkable on the surface, was powerful, true sisterhood in action, nudging its way in like the lemon light of early morning warms, nourishes. There's nothing to eye roll at, here. No bitching, bitches. It's sisterhood, sisters, and it goes on all the time. We just need to choose to see it.

* * * * *

Cath Bore lives in Liverpool, UK. She writes crime fiction and short stories about the things keeping her awake at night. Cath's work has earned success in competitions and at festivals, including Harrogate Crime Writing Festival, Bloody Scotland, the Festival of Writing in York, and the North West Short Story Festival. She has an MA in creative writing from Liverpool John Moores University. Her website is www.cathbore.com.

SISTERS BORN, SISTERS FOUND

Safe To Dream

Laura McHale Holland

Gliding through freshly fallen snow on my way to visit Kathy at Hinsdale Sanitarium and Hospital, I imagine I'm an Olympic contender. I get a running start and then slide down the sidewalk, leaving marks like ski tracks in my wake. Roy Orbison's *Pretty Woman* blasts through the transistor radio in my hand. Whenever I hear it, I imagine some cute guy admiring me as I walk by, even though I'm not a woman yet. Well, in the physical sense, I guess I am.

My first period leaked out just two weeks before I started high school and three weeks before my fourteenth birthday. I welcomed it with about as much enthusiasm as I would a quart of Penzoil poured into my underpants. I was one of the last girls from our neighborhood to menstruate. That's what Jillie said anyway. She finds out stuff like that from her mom, who actually has friends in town, unlike my stopmom, Wanda the Wicked Witch of the Western Suburbs.

Wanda acts as though everyone in Hinsdale thinks she's a leper. There's some truth in that. She's different than other parents, and not just in the way she treats Kathy, Mary Ruth and me. Take her clothes. She wears only floral patterned, synthetic house dresses that zip up the front. Even when the temperature plunges below zero. That's all she'll wear under a ratty car coat my sisters and I outgrew ages ago. The dresses were cartoonish when new; they get worse with wear. Threads stick out at the seams like legs on a centipede. The only footwear she puts on her tiny feet are sandals with wedged heels and black canvas straps crisscrossed over her toes and behind her ankles. She calls them "wedgies." In winter, she wears white bobby socks with her wedgies, making them look even more bizarre.

A couple of years ago, I accompanied Wanda to Ben Franklin, which is not far from the junior high. The store was having a half-price sale on wedgies. While I was helping her search a bin of shoes for size 4-1/2, two girls from school sauntered in. I slinked to another aisle. Head down, I pretended to be absorbed by a jewelry display. But then Wanda yelled, "Laura!" The girls approached me, their faces aglow with a devilish mirth.

"Is that your mother?" one of them asked. The other snickered.

"Uh, no, she's just somebody I know." I backed away and returned to the wedgie aisle.

"Where were you?" Wanda snapped as we walked to the cashier.

"Just over looking at some circle pins."

"Liar. You wanted to get away from me, didn't you. You're just like everybody else in this town. You think you're too good for me."

I kept quiet, feeling guilty as Peter when he denied knowing Jesus. I also feared Wanda might raise her voice and make a scene before we were safely inside her Chevy Bel Air, where nobody else would be able to hear her rant.

Classmates used to taunt me about Kathy and Mary Ruth, too. "She's not your sister, is she?" they'd say when one of my sisters passed by. When I'd answer in the affirmative, their laughter would hit like a basketball aimed at my gut. That was in junior high, when, despite everything our teachers said to the contrary, the only thing that seemed to matter was how you looked, not who you were on the inside. As the eldest, Kathy had to face this scrutiny first, wearing second-hand outfits that looked like they'd been swiped from the set of *Oklahoma*.

These days, we babysit, clean houses and do other odd jobs, and we buy our own clothes. The ribbing has subsided. It seems, overall, things are going well this year for all three of us, that is, if you don't include Kathy's fall, which broke her back. I visit her at the hospital every day. Just a few more glides on the icy sidewalk, and I'll be dashing to the elevator, headed for her room.

A ball of yarn rolls on the floor while I concentrate, perched on the edge of Kathy's hospital bed. Under, over, under, over—I finish a row and pass the half-completed scarf to her.

"That's very good, Laur, nice and even." She runs her nimble fingers along my stitches. "See, you can do it." I'm not used to Kathy encouraging me. I wonder if she might be setting me up for some kind of ridicule like when we were younger and I was the butt of all the family jokes.

Kathy hands the project back to me. "Do another row. You'll be knitting a sweater soon."

I doubt that. I tried knitting once before back in Brownie Scouts. Each girl was supposed to make a scarf to give to her mother for Christmas. I stuffed my twisted disaster in the back of my closet, where it sat like contraband for months, until Wanda did one of her routine purges of all possessions she deems useless or unnecessary.

I start on the next row. Under over, under over. How I envy Kathy's fortitude. She's been here for two months and has kept up with all of her schoolwork, and she's teaching me how to knit to boot. She's always up to something productive, like theater, where she works magic backstage. That's what led to her broken back, though. She was painting scenery for a play when she fell fourteen feet from a scaffold.

Friends on the scene helped her up and asked if she was okay. She said she was fine and even walked around for several minutes. Then the stabbing pain hit. She asked Lainie, her closest friend on the crew, to take her to the emergency room.

"Should we call your mom?" Lainie asked.

"No. Take me to the hospital first, otherwise I'll never make it there." Kathy knew too well that, without intervention, Wanda would give her an aspirin, send her off to bed and tell her to be in school the next day.

Lainie drove Kathy to the emergency room, where Wanda was notified after Lainie made sure the doctor on duty saw Kathy and knew she was badly hurt.

I'm finishing another row when Mary Ruth tromps in, the lenses of her brown tortoise-shell glasses still a little steamed up at the edges, her cheeks rosy from the cold outside air. She's just finished a study session with her calculus buddies.

"Ready for a ride?" Mary Ruth asks. She unbuttons her coat and lays it across an upholstered chair by the window.

"Sure thing," Kathy says. Earlier today, her doctor gave her the okay to use a wheel chair, and we intend to take full advantage of that development. The three of us giggle as we ease Kathy out of the bed and into the chair. And we're off. Mary Ruth and I walk her down the hallway to a window. Then we spin her around and push her to the other end of the hall. Up and down we go, one end to the other. Mary Ruth and I take turns pushing the chair, and with each switch at the helm, we increase our speed until we're running so fast, we can barely stop at the windows on either end of the hall. All three of us find this hilarious.

"Watch it, girls," a nurse calls. "You know you're not supposed to run in the halls." We slow down, stop at the elevators and move our frivolity to another floor, until a nurse there tells us to slow down too. "Think of the other patients here," she scolds.

Feeling guilty, we return to Kathy's floor, where aides are bringing dinner trays to all the patients. It's time for Mary Ruth and me to go.

Mary Ruth hugs Kathy. Then it's my turn. "See ya tomorrow," I say. Mary Ruth and I back out the door and then shuffle, arm in arm, toward the elevators. I'm sorry Kathy got busted up, but I enjoy seeing my sisters every day at the hospital, a place where Wanda never visits, a place where we are safe from her rage, safe to let our armor down, safe to dream of love washing bitterness from our home like showers flushing away decay and awakening the earth in spring.

✦ ✦ ✦ ✦ ✦

Laura McHale Holland is the editor of Sisters Born, Sisters Found: A Diversity of Voices on Sisterhood. *Her prior publications include the flash fiction collection,* The Ice Cream Vendor's Song, *and the award winning memoir,* Reversible Skirt. *Her writing has appeared in print and online in community newspapers, business periodicals and literary anthologies. Her play* Are You Ready? *was produced by Sixth Street Playhouse and Redwood Writers in 2014 and shortlisted for the Short+Sweet Sydney 2015 international festival. For more info, please subscribe to her newsletter at lauramchaleholland.com.*

Before I Forget

Ana Manwaring

I need to write it down:
to-do lists of everything
that can't be done
undone
calls not made
to people now gone:
  Hello how are you?
  How'd your chemo go?

Say things
that should have been said—
forgive things that shouldn't.

I want to remember times we laughed,
danced under ever-shifting lights,
shared secrets;
times we found something in common—
See's candy
books
gossip about family.
The times we were sisters.

Before I forget, I confess—
I borrowed your silk bandana,
I still have it;
too late to give back—
too precious to let go.

. . . . .

Petaluma Post *columnist Ana Manwaring teaches creative writing and memoir through Napa Valley College—Upper Valley Campus and privately in Sonoma County. In addition to writing poetry, Ana crafts fiction, both literary and thriller genres, and performs her work in bookstores, coffee houses, on public radio, at book festivals, in senior centers, community centers, libraries and classrooms. To learn more about Ana, please visit www.anamanwaring.com.*

Acknowledgements

I want to thank my family: Kathy and Mary Ruth, who, in addition to being my sisters, have been my life-long co-conspirators and companions—Kathy also designed this book's magnificent cover and interior; my husband, Jim, who has put up with all the evenings I've spent paying only partial attention to him as I've pecked away on my laptop, setting in motion the various phases of this project; my daughter, Moira, and stepsons, Ryan and Jackson, for always being so encouraging to me; and my dear uncle John, Unc, who is proud of me, no matter what.

I also want to appreciate the talented editors and proofreaders who helped me shape and polish this anthology: Skye Blaine, Claire Blotter, Patrice Garrett, Marie Judson-Rosier, Ana Manwaring, Denise O'Hare, Julie Fadda Powers, Harry Reid, Maxine Reyes Tyler, and Daniel Watkins; Ruth Stotter, whose enthusiasm, support and terrific ideas have helped me bring this project to people I couldn't have reached otherwise; and Chris Johnson, who continues to welcome sister-themed readings at her chic boutique.

And, of course, here's a big shout out to the superb writers whose voices fills these pages. Thank you for trusting me to do justice to your work; I will forever be grateful for your faith in me.

Pubslush Supporters

I'd also like to thank the generous individuals and businesses that donated $15 or more to this project via Pubslush, a crowdfunding platform dedicated to literary projects.

Laurelai Barton and Tam Nguyen, The Mac Advantage

Brenda Bellinger

Elspeth Benton

Skye Blaine and Boudewijn Boom

Olivia Boler

Claire Blotter

Michelle Busey

Ruth Kessler Dallas

Patty Purpur de Vries

Cathryn Fairlee

Kate Farrell

Bridgitt Fleming

Martha Folger

Sher Gamard

P. H. Garrett

Mary Ruth Gross

Moira Holland

Mary Knight

Jerry Kohut

Dale Laszig

Ana Manwaring, JAM Manuscript Consulting

Karen McAuliffe

Michael McCullaugh and Mustaph Jamal, the Redwood Café

Kathy McHale

Lynda McIntyre

Mona Mechling

Jeanne Miller, JAM Manuscript Consulting

Linda Morganstein

Elizabeth Musch

Robin Nielsen

Bernadette Pabon

Ann Philipp

Rita Marie Powell

Julie Fadda Powers

Linda and Harry Reid

Lilith Rogers

Sal Rosselli

Helen Sedwick

Jeane Slone

Sally Smith, the Noe Valley Voice

Pamela Taueffer

Marc Velez, Cotati Community Acupuncture

Courtney Wagle, Damia Salon

Michelle Walford

Dan Watkins, Verbworks

Bonnie Bedford White

J.J. Wilson

Jean Wong

Several other contributors wish to remain anonymous.

Author Index

Lindsay Ahl 68

Nadia Ali 172

Diana M. Amadeo 163

Sara Catalina Dorame Bard 58

Vicki Batman 40

Gloria Beanblossom 203

Brenda Bellinger 98

Karen Benke 10, 133

Elspeth Benton 100

Skye Blaine 69

Claire Blotter 84

Jan Boddie. 158

John Boe 238

Olivia Boler 36, 64

Cath Bore 269

Catharine Bramkamp 104

Debra Ayers Brown 166

Erica Brown 189

Mara Buck 96

Karen DeGroot Carter 199

Delphine Cingal 78

Nancy Cook 62

Conda Douglas 257

Janie Emaus 114

Susan Ford 141

Ruth Friesen 248

P. H. Garrett 179, 217

D. A. (Daisy) Hickman 181, 232

Laura McHale Holland 271

Patricia Jackson 182

Mercilee Jenkins 125

Joanna Jones 20

Marie Judson-Rosier 225

Nardia Kelly 56

Eva Kende 143

Wendy Kennar 253

Jesse Kimmel-Freeman 93

Dipika Kohli 33

Mary J. Kohut 44

Erica Lann-Clark 74

Nancy Pogue LaTurner 50, 148

Karen Levy 30

Lisa Marie Lopez 134

David Lucero 138

Ana Manwaring 17, 275

Jennie Marima 243

Lynn Millar 212

Marie Millard 8

Wilda Morris 92, 208

Monica Nawrocki 255

Gwynn O'Gara 146, 162

Fabia Oliveira 116

Bernadette Pabon 264

Ella Preuss 106

Carson Pynes 252

C. R. Resetarits 52

Sue Rumbaugh 192

Tanya Savko 233

Laura Simms 21

Diane Sismour 122

Elspeth Slayter 221

Jordan Steele 28

Ruth Stotter 111

Paige Adams Strickland 54

Lisa A. Sturm 85

Pamela Taeuffer 174

Anne Tammel 120

Nina Tepedino 236

Barbara Toboni 209

Dianalee Velie 16, 268

Gaurav Verma 194

Maria de Lourdes Victoria 11

Elaine Webster 154

Mark Wisniewski 187

Jean Wong 4

Nellie Wong 170, 219

Other Books by Laura McHale Holland

Reversible Skirt, a Memoir

When the mother of three little girls commits suicide, their father wants more than anything to keep his family together. He remarries in haste and tells his daughters his new wife is their mother. The youngest, Laura, believes her mother must have gone through an eerie transformation.

Reversible Skirt is written from Laura's perspective as a child sifting through remnants of her mother's existence and struggling to fit into a community where her family's strict rules are not the norm. When Laura's father dies, her stepmother grows increasingly abusive, which propels Laura and her sisters into a lasting alliance. Their father's wish that they stay together comes true, although not in the way he'd imagined.

The Ice Cream Vendor's Song

Arresting and original, *The Ice Cream Vendor's Song* introduces a new side of Laura McHale Holland, whose memoir, *Reversible Skirt*, won a silver medal in the 2011 Readers Favorite book awards. In this richly nuanced collection of very short fiction, the author tilts the everyday and spins characters in unexpected directions. From an online purchase that takes over a woman's life to a plain box that brings a tired clerk a magical gift, from a spurned woman hiding in her ex-husband's closet to a doting wife coaxing her ailing husband to eat, *The Ice Cream Vendor's Song* reveals worlds familiar yet strange, haunting yet tender, all rendered with emotional clarity and exquisite prose.

For more details about these titles, as well as news of projects in development and reflections on being creative in today's always-on world, you are welcome to subscribe to Laura's newsletter, *Letters From Laura,* at lauramchaleholland.com.

CPSIA information can be obtained
at www.ICGtesting.com
Printed in the USA
FSOW02n1033141114
3481FS